THE FOOLISHNESS
OF PREACHING

AND OTHER SERMONS

•

ERNEST FREMONT TITTLE

NEW YORK

HENRY HOLT AND COMPANY

To My Daughter

ELIZABETH ANN TITTLE

CONTENTS

Introduction

CHAPTER   PAGE

I. THE FIELD OF THE PULPIT—LIFE . . . 4

Religion and the Individual

II. WHAT IS WORTH WHILE? 18

III. SPIRITUAL ADVENTURE 34

IV. SEEING THE INVISIBLE 49

V. AS A LITTLE CHILD 63

VI. THE LOVE OF GOD 77

VII. THE GOOD OF PRAYER 91

VIII. CHRISTIANITY AND RESPECTABILITY . . . 105

IX. REFORMER, REFORM YOURSELF 123

Religion and Society

X. CHRISTIANITY IN A MACHINE AGE . . . 139

XI. RELIGION AND ART 155

XII. THE PROHIBITION PROBLEM 169

XIII. THE MODERN JONAH 187

XIV. PATRIOTISM 200

XV. AN ADEQUATE NATIONAL DEFENSE . . . 214

v

CHAPTER   PAGE

XVI. THE UNFINISHED TASK 227

Jesus' Experience of Life and Ours

XVII. IN THE WILDERNESS 241

XVIII. ON THE MOUNTAIN 256

XIX. IN THE GARDEN 271

XX. ON THE CROSS 286

In Conclusion

XXI. THE FOOLISHNESS OF PREACHING 301

THE FOOLISHNESS
OF PREACHING
AND OTHER SERMONS

I

THE FIELD OF THE PULPIT—LIFE

NOW and then the "World's Greatest Newspaper" undertakes to tell preachers what they should talk about and especially what they should not talk about in the pulpit. This newspaper believes that it is altogether right and proper for the Christian pulpit to discuss personal piety and domestic morality, but altogether wrong and improper for it to discuss business or industry or politics.

It is interesting to note that the "World's Greatest Newspaper" has a very different conception of its own proper function. A few years ago its editor and publisher delivered an address before the Chicago Church Federation. He spoke to the question, "What is a newspaper?" and he said, among other things, this: "News is the basis of the modern newspaper, but it cannot live by news alone. It must also amuse and serve. There are strips of comics; there are book and theatre reviews; there are columns of advice on health, investment, radio, law, love, complexion, corsets, cooking, good manners; substantially all subjects that interest the general public." He also said this: "The greatest importance of the newspaper comes from a function that has developed upon it, a function not mentioned in the Constitution and without which the Constitution could not continue to function. This is the exposure and denunciation of corruption in government." And he concluded by saying, "I am now led to give a final definition of the newspaper: The newspaper is an institution developed by modern civilization to present the news of the day, to foster commerce and industry through widely circulated advertisements, and to furnish that check upon government which no constitution has ever been able to provide."

All this is very interesting, to say the least. The Christian pulpit must confine itself to conventional discussions of personal piety and domestic virtue, but must the newspaper confine itself to the publication of news? Not at all. The newspaper may furnish "columns of advice" on "substantially all subjects that interest the general public." It may likewise expose and denounce corruption in government and furnish that check upon government which no constitution has ever been able to provide. Substantially all subjects that interest the general public may properly be discussed from the secular standpoint. It is only from a religious standpoint that nothing about them must be said. Corruption in government may and should be exposed from an editorial chair, but the pulpit must keep its hands off. A check upon government may and should be furnished by an editor, or by an association of editors and political cartoonists, but may a check upon government be furnished by a preacher or a ministerial association? God forbid! Indeed, having in mind the particular newspaper whose position we are now considering, would it not be perfectly fair to conclude that what this position really means is that if you accept in the main the principles which governed the lives of Napoleon Bonaparte, Julius Cæsar, Alexander the Great, not to mention Machiavelli, you may, with perfect propriety, talk about any subject under the sun; but if you happen to accept the principles that governed the life of Jesus Christ, you must stick to personal piety and domestic virtue?

If any newspaper, even the "World's Greatest," were alone in this position, question might be raised as to the propriety of discussing it. But the Chicago *Tribune* is by no means alone in this position. To many persons, unconnected with any newspaper, this position appears to be perfectly reasonable and sound. Many people believe that the Christian pulpit ought to confine itself to somewhat conventional pronouncements on domestic virtue and personal piety, and say nothing at all about business, or industry, or politics. Nor are all such persons to be found outside the Christian church. Many of them are to be found in it. It cannot be denied that a considerable number of laymen are greatly troubled by the manifest disposition of many a modern pulpit to discuss subjects with which they sincerely believe the pulpit has no legitimate concern. There is, therefore, sufficient occasion to call attention to this controvertible position and to raise the question, "What is the primary and essential message of the Christian pulpit?"

It is, I should say, undebatable that the Christian pulpit should not neglect to address itself to the intimate personal needs of individual men and women. Jesus himself never did. Having before him all the time the haunting vision of the Kingdom of God—a great social transformation—he, nevertheless, carried on a ministry to individuals which no modern ambassador of his can afford to neglect. I cannot agree with the author of "Beside the Bonnie Briar Bush" when he says that the chief end of preaching is comfort. The preaching of Jesus did not give a great deal of comfort to the Pharisees who sat in his congregation. It made some of them as mad as hornets. But I can, I think, understand what Joseph Parker meant when he said to a group of young ministers, "Preach to broken hearts"; and what Dr. Robert W. Dale of Birmingham meant when he said, "People need consolation. They really need it, and not merely long for it." People do need consolation, and once and again the man who stands in a Christian pulpit ought to preach very directly to broken hearts. On any given Sunday morning, there is probably no single congregation assembled anywhere in this world in which there are not at least a few persons who are in truly desperate need of personal help. And if from the Christian pulpit there comes to them no single word of comfort or of encouragement, not without reason may they go away feeling disappointed and cheated.

Grant for the moment that a preacher has a perfect right to discuss from the Christian standpoint the ethics of industry or of international relationships. Still it does not follow that it is incumbent on him to discuss such themes as these every Sunday or nearly every Sunday, and almost if not quite to the neglect of themes which are related to the intimate needs of weary and heavy-laden men.

It is also, I should say, incontrovertible that whenever a man stands in a Christian pulpit and delivers a message that message ought to have a religious flavor. The church is like other human institutions in that it is composed of men and women who have a fair share of human frailties. It is unlike other human institutions in that it is composed of men and women who are definitely committed to a religious conception of life. There is, or at least ought to be, something distinctive about a church. When people go to church, they have a right to expect that they will hear from the pulpit something a bit different from what they would hear were they to go to a lecture, or from what they would read were they to turn to the editorial page of most daily newspapers. And when they go away from church, if what they have heard is nothing more than a lecture on political economy, they have a right to feel somewhat indignant. The persistent complaint of many a layman that he does not go to church for the purpose of listening to lectures on sociology is not altogether without justification if what he is compelled to listen to, Sunday after Sunday, when he does go to church, is a discourse that is no more definitely or warmly religious than the speeches of Lenin or the writings of Karl Marx.

Here again, for the moment, let it be granted that a preacher has a right to discuss any subject that is of vital interest to men and women. Still is it not encumbent upon him to discuss that subject, whatever it is, from a definitely religious standpoint, and in such a way that those who listen to him will find themselves looking at it through the eyes of God?

To do this is, among other things, good strategy; for, many appearances to the contrary notwithstanding, it is probably true that even today the vast majority of human individuals on this little planet believe in God and have at least some regard for what they conceive to be the will of God. If, therefore, men can be made to see and believe that what is being advocated from the pulpit has the sanction of God, they will feel under at least some obligation to accept it and act in accordance with it. Once the conviction was established in this country that human slavery was wrong, that God Almighty was opposed to it, slavery was doomed. If ever a day shall come when the conviction is established that international war is wrong, that by a court from which there is no appeal it has been pronounced a criminal and an outlaw, international war will be doomed.

For a preacher to discuss any subject from a definitely religious viewpoint is good strategy. It is also, I am constrained to add, simple fairness; for a preacher is, after all, the responsible spokesman of an institution that is definitely and distinctively committed to the religious conception of life.

I should also suppose that no preacher has a right to offer advice in respect of any matter about which he is unqualified to speak. He himself would be quick enough to resent advice given by persons totally unacquainted with the peculiar problems of his own profession. Having said this, however, I should like to add that there are some preachers in the world today who are qualified to talk about something besides personal piety and domestic virtue.

There are preachers, for instance, who know a great deal about the human side of industry. They have lived for years in industrial communities. They have seen with their own eyes the human effects of long hours, low wages, and seasonal employment. They know from actual first-hand observation why a just judge recently declared that there can be no freedom of contract unless there is equality of bargaining power. There are preachers, too, who know a great deal about war—more, one suspects, than is known by many men who have viewed war from the safe distance of an editor's chair, or the mahogany desk of a manufac-turer of munitions. They have seen war close up. They have seen what it does to the bodies of men. They have seen what it does to the souls of men. They have likewise acquainted themselves with the causes of war. They have read history, more of it than appears to have been read by the average politician.

If such preachers are bound in any way to stick to per-sonal piety and domestic virtue, it is not because they are unqualified to talk about anything else. When it comes to purely technical questions such as industrial processes or military tactics, there is, I should suppose, hardly one preacher in a hundred thousand whose knowledge and experience would entitle him to express an opinion. But when it comes to questions of policy, questions on whose answer hangs the welfare of literally millions of people, there are, I should suppose, many preachers who are at least as well qualified to express an opinion as is, let us say, the editorial board of the "World's Greatest News-paper."

A recent edition of that widely read paper contained one of those political cartoons which are designed, I suppose, to furnish "a check upon government such as no constitution has ever been able to provide." This cartoon presented two pictures, one entitled "Peace Without Security," the other entitled "Peace with Security." In the first picture, a badly frightened and very foolish looking young lady, holding an olive branch and carrying a peace pact, is about to be set upon by two villainous looking creatures who appear to be determined not only to kill her, but to eat her up. In the second picture, a young lady with head thrown back and nose turned up carries a peace pact parasol (which is of course entirely useless on a bright January day) and is accompanied by an enormous bulldog, representing "a rea-sonable naval preparedness." And as *she* strides down the street, she is greeted on all sides by gentlemen with lifted hats and smiling faces, gentlemen who may be villains at heart but who, seeing the bulldog, feel constrained out-wardly at least to be polite.

Notice now the political sagacity displayed in this car-toon. The villainous looking creatures are, of course, the other nations of the world—France, England, Russia, Japan, etc. And the virtuous young lady? She is the United States, in imminent danger of being set upon by British brigands if she goes about with only a peace pact, but nobly protected if she is accompanied by a reasonable bulldog. The cartoon fails to suggest that there may be a little virtue in the other nations of the world and not only in the United States. It also fails to suggest that the other nations of the world might breed a bulldog or two; that, indeed, there might develop among the nations an unreasonable competition in the breeding of reasonable bulldogs; that in a time of crisis these bulldogs might cease to be reasonable and get out of hand; and that the result might be an unintended but disastrous dog-fight in which not only everybody's dog but everybody himself would get unreasonably chewed up.

It is altogether probable that the average High School student would be able to find a few fallacies in this cartoon. I have, however, no objection to its being published as a "check upon government such as no constitution has ever been able to provide." But if such a cartoon may properly be published by a newspaper, surely it cannot be consistently claimed that the Christian pulpit must withhold comment on governmental policies because it is incompetent to express an opinion!

Even so, however, the question remains whether the nature of the Christian pulpit does not preclude the discussion of sociological or political themes. Well, here is a message for the preacher to which I think no exception of any kind will or can be taken. "I am determined," says St. Paul, in the first letter that he sent to the church at Corinth, "not to know anything among you save Jesus Christ and him crucified." A preacher talking continually about Jesus Christ and him crucified—surely nobody could object to that. In Paul's own case, to be sure, it was fiercely objected to; he was beaten, stoned, and finally beheaded. But that, of course, was nineteen hundred years ago when Christianity was first being presented to the world. Now that Christianity has become the professed faith of probably a third of the human race, the whole situation is very different. Almost nobody would refuse to acknowledge that a Christian preacher has an indisputable right to talk about Jesus Christ and him crucified.

But now let us begin to consider whereunto a continuous discussion of Jesus Christ and him crucified might conceivably lead. It will be remembered that according to the testimony of a very distinguished editor and publisher, a modern newspaper has an undoubted right to offer "columns of advice on health, investment, radio, law, love, complexion, corsets, cooking, good manners; substantially all subjects that interest the general public." It is interesting to observe that in the very letter in which Paul announces that he is determined not to know anything among those Corinthian Christians save Jesus Christ and him crucified, he proceeds to offer chapters of advice about litigation, marriage, wedlock, falling in love, personal liberty, the exercise of personal gifts, the length of women's hair, the veiling of women in the churches, and the taking of a collection. When Paul had finished the writing of that letter, he might have reflected, "I have covered substantially all subjects in which our Christian folk at Corinth are vitally interested."

Was he, then, insincere in his announcement that he was determined to know nothing among them save Jesus Christ and him crucified? Who could seriously hold that he was? Of whom was Paul thinking when he wrote to these Corinthians, "Brothers, for the sake of Our Lord, Jesus Christ, I beg of you to drop these party cries"? Or when he wrote, "The foundation is laid, namely Jesus Christ, and no one can lay any other"? Or when he wrote, "You are not your own, you were bought with a price; then glorify God with your body"? Of whom was he thinking when he wrote, "Love is very patient, very kind. Love knows no jealousy; love makes no parade, gives itself no airs, is never rude, never selfish, never irritated, never resentful"? Or when he wrote, "O death, where is thy victory? . . . Thanks be to God who giveth us the victory through our Lord, Jesus Christ"? Or when he wrote, at the close of this letter, "The grace of the Lord Jesus be with you. My love be with you all in Christ Jesus"?

Would it be going too far to say that St. Paul was always thinking of Jesus Christ? His thought began and ended with Christ. He had only one ambition in this world and that was to exalt the Lord Jesus Christ. Not only the matter of his discourses but even the manner of their delivery was dictated by his thought of Christ. And would it be an unwarranted conclusion that *therefore* he felt constrained to talk about any and every matter that was of vital interest to his converts? He would have them look at all matters through the eyes of Christ. He would have them measure everything by the standards of Christ.

He would build up in every one of them the mind of
Christ. In all their relationships to God, to one another,
and to the world at large he would have them express
the faith and the spirit of Christ.

Now, suppose that some modern preacher were as profoundly convinced as was St. Paul that there is but one
true and abiding foundation on which human life may be
built, namely Jesus Christ. About what would such a
preacher feel constrained to talk when he stood in his
pulpit on the Lord's day? Personal piety, domestic morality? Of course! He would be eager to have men think of
God in terms of Christ. When men wonder, as they
sometimes do, what is the meaning of life, or whether
indeed life has any meaning, any purpose, or goal, he
would have them feel able in their heart of hearts to believe that the meaning of life is Christ, that the hidden
source from which life comes and the hidden goal toward
which it is moving are most fully revealed in Christ.
And in all their most intimate relationships to those who
dwell with them under the same roof, he would have them
express the spirit of Christ.

But would this modern preacher with St. Paul's conviction about Jesus Christ be content to stop there? Would
he feel that he had any right to stop there? After all,
men are something more than husbands, or brothers, or
fathers, or sons. Men are brick-layers, or plumbers, or
walking delegates, or contractors, or industrial executives,
or bank directors, or physicians, or teachers, or ambassadors,

or governors. If, therefore, a modern preacher sincerely and even passionately believes that Jesus Christ is life's one true and abiding foundation, is it not only natural and right that he should plead with men to build upon that foundation, not only their personal and domestic life, but their business life, their industrial life, and their political life? Might not such a preacher announce to his congregation that he was determined not to know anything among them save Jesus Christ and him crucified, and then that very morning proceed to preach a sermon on industrial or international relationships viewed through the eyes of Christ?

This determination to build the message of the Christian pulpit about Jesus Christ and him crucified has another implication that is highly significant. To St. Paul, Jesus Christ and especially Jesus Christ, the Crucified, was something more than a human ideal. In the thought of Paul, the cross of Christ was a revelation of the heart of God. It was even more than that, it was the very deed of God. God was in Christ reconciling the world unto himself. In that pathetic, tragic figure of the man of Galilee hanging upon a cross, God was suffering for men—suffering in order that by his suffering men's eyes might be opened, their consciences stabbed, their vision cleared, and their wills enlisted for a noble cause. In this present connection—the essential message of the Christian pulpit—let it never be forgotten that in the thought of St. Paul, and in the thought of Christian preachers through nineteen hundred years, what we have to deal with is a universe that is on the side of Jesus, a God who is supremely revealed in the crucified Christ.

Now if that message be true, is it not altogether the most comforting and heartening declaration that could possibly be made to individual men and women? It ignores nothing, neither human joys nor human sorrows. It takes account of all the facts including "the very worst facts of human existence." But it insists that there is, at the heart of the world, something on which, in life and in death, weary and heavy-laden men may depend. Something that is comprehending and just and kind and merciful and forgiving—in a word, Christ-like. Something, too, that is not weak or powerless to help, but mighty as it is meek. Something that, even when it dies on a cross, placarded before the world as a thing of shame, is nevertheless the master of life, abundantly able to mold life in accordance with its own pattern and purpose. It is Sunday morning. The chimes in the church tower have summoned the people to worship. And when they come, some of them with troubled minds and some of them with aching hearts, what more comforting message could be brought to them than this declaration that what we have ultimately to deal with is a God who is like Christ?

But if that be true, if the universe is on the side of Jesus, if God is like Christ, is there not something which may and should be said from a Christian pulpit about the conduct of business, and the organization of industry, and the acts and policies of government? This assertion that what we all have to do with—men in low position and men in high position—is a universe that is making for Christ-likeness is, if true, nothing less than tremendous. For what it means is that no kind of business can hope permanently to succeed in this world, no kind of industrial organization can hope permanently to prosper in this world, and no nation, no civilization, can hope permanently to endure in this world unless it takes practical account of the principles of Christ. Suppose, then, that the Christian pulpit should confine itself to personal piety and domestic morality. Suppose it should make no demand at all for the enthronement of Jesus Christ in the world of "big business" or in the world of politics. Would not that pulpit be recreant to its own high calling? Would it not be a traitor to the future welfare of mankind, and a weak and timid traitor at that?

Surely it is not only the right but the imperative duty of the Christian pulpit to insist that the grand total of human life should be brought into harmony with a universe that is making for Christ-likeness.

II

WHAT IS WORTH WHILE?

WHO does not recall that dramatic scene in "The Merchant of Venice" in which the Prince of Morocco makes his choice of the three caskets:

> The first of gold, who this inscription bears;—
> Who chooseth me shall gain what many men desire.
> The second, silver, which this promise carries;—
> Who chooseth me shall get as much as he deserves.
> The third, dull lead, with warning all as blunt;—
> Who chooseth me must give and hazard all he hath.

And who does not sympathize with the anxious prince as he asks, "How shall I know if I do choose the right?" We may well sympathize with him because his predicament is not dissimilar to our own. Let the hand of the fair Portia stand for what is worth while in this world, and the three caskets stand for the many goods and seeming goods which life appears to offer, and that dramatic scene in "The Merchant of Venice" becomes a very familiar situation.

Twenty-five hundred years ago Plato portrayed the same situation in the form of a myth in which, under the direction of the three Fates, men were compelled to choose their destinies, and many made choices that were "sad, and laughable, and strange." And one recalls with a start that it was this self-same situation which Jesus had in mind when he said, "The lamp of the body is the eye: if, therefore, thine eye be single, thy whole body shall be full of light. But if thine eye be evil, the whole body shall be full of darkness. If therefore the light that is within thee be darkness, how great is the darkness!" How great indeed is that darkness in which a man goes all the way through life failing to see what is worth while. Is there not, one feels constrained to ask, some way in which so great a darkness may be avoided?

Students of ethics are familiar with the distinction that is commonly made between "intrinsic value" and "instrumental value." In order to have intrinsic value a thing must be good in itself. It must be worth having for its own sake, so much so indeed that a man is justified in paying down a large price in terms of struggle or of toil in order to get it. But in order to have instrumental value, a thing need not be good in itself. It need only be useful as a means of obtaining certain other goods.

Now, it is perfectly obvious that many of the things for which men strive possess both kinds of value. Good health, for instance, enables us to go after other goods and it is also good in itself; as who does not realize once he has lost it. Knowledge, too, enables us to go after other goods. Yet knowledge is good in itself; it broadens one's horizon, enriches one's life. But there are two things for which men strive, and for which many of them chiefly strive, which have no intrinsic value whatsoever; all they have is instrumental value. I am thinking, of course, of wealth and of power.

The instrumental value of wealth is beyond dispute. It is written, "Man shall not live by bread alone," and nothing truer than that has ever been written. But it is also true that men cannot live without bread; and in this case, no less than in the other, the word "live" must be interpreted to mean something more than bare physical existence. What needs to be acknowledged here is not only the obvious fact that a man cannot without money keep body and soul together, but the somewhat hard and bitter fact that a man cannot without money get an education, or acquire culture, or command leisure, or participate in the creative work of the world. It is doubtless true that, as compared with my good name, "he who steals my purse steals trash"; but the fact remains that he who steals my purse compels me to go hungry, not only for bread, but for books and paintings and music and travel. He who steals my purse impoverishes my life.

The instrumental value of power, also, is beyond dispute. I am thinking now, not of the power which goes with knowledge or with character or with personal charm, but of the power which goes with certain positions in human society. Persons who occupy these positions have power thrust upon them. They may have no more of intelligence or of character or of personal charm than is possessed by thousands of people occupying less conspicuous positions, but they exercise an influence that is simply tremendous. An obscure preacher preaches a sermon on prohibition. It is listened to more or less by a few hundreds of people. On the Floor of the United States Senate,

Senator Borah says substantially the same thing and he is listened to by literally millions of people. A relatively obscure college professor delivers before a woman's club an address on International Relationships, and it is a good address, a really significant deliverance. But just suppose, if you can, that Mussolini should deliver that address verbatim; how enormously more effective it would immediately become! The mere occupancy of a certain position may confer upon the occupant an extraordinary degree of power, and that power may be used as an instrument for securing some great benefit for mankind. As President of the United States, Abraham Lincoln could and did issue a proclamation which brought about the emancipation of four million slaves.

It is, therefore, undeniable that both wealth and power have instrumental value. It is also undeniable that they have no intrinsic value. Wealth has not. Money is not a good thing in itself. It is not worth having for its own sake. It may even curse him who does have it. Money may be made in ways that injure men, distributed in ways that embitter men, and spent in ways that degrade men. Whether or no money is a good thing depends entirely on how it is made, how it is distributed, and how it is used. It has no intrinsic value whatsoever. Nor has power, the power that goes with place. Can you imagine anything more pathetic than the spectacle of a small man rattling around in a big position? And can you imagine anything more dangerous than a bad man sitting in one of the seats of power?

Inasmuch as neither wealth nor power has any intrinsic value, it ought never to be sought after for its own sake. To seek after either wealth or power as though it were good in itself is to make one of the most tragic mistakes that a man can possibly make in this world.

Here is a man who is ambitious to be rich. Why? Because he supposes that in the acquirement of riches great happiness may be found. But in his intense, concentrated pursuit of riches, he passes by a number of things that possess inherent and permanent value. He says that he is not in business for his health and evidently he is not, for he is sacrificing his health to his business. He might also say that he is not in business for friendship, for he is sacrificing one friendship after another and certainly the spirit of friendliness to his business. He might even say that he is not in business for God, for many of those supreme values in which the eternal God abides he is sacrificing to his business. Will such a man find happiness? How can he find it when he is blindly passing by or throwing away those intrinsic values in which alone happiness has ever been found?

Here is a man who is ambitious for power. Why? Because he supposes that there is an immense amount of satisfaction to be obtained in the exercise of power. In order to experience that satisfaction many a man has sacrificed the happiness which he might have had in his own home. He has neglected his wife. He has neglected his children. He has applied all the energies of his being to the securing of power. And when he has got it, it has turned out to be what? A burden grievous to be borne, calling for increasing expenditures of time and strength. Many a man, too, has "sold the truth to serve the hour" and "bartered with eternal God for power," only to discover that having, in order to get power, hopelessly compromised and entangled himself, he was no longer free to use it in ways that would have given him any real and lasting satisfaction.

Wealth and power are valuable as instruments but only as instruments. The pursuit of either of them as an end in itself leads always to frustration, disillusionment, defeat. Instrumental values should always be subordinated to intrinsic values.

Another distinction between values appears in the fact that some of them are transient and others permanent. Physical enjoyment is always transient. Mental enjoyments may be permanent. Most of us enjoy a tender, juicy steak, but we do not enjoy it very long; whereas our enjoyment of a good book or a great painting or a beautiful friendship lasts as long as we live. Physical hunger of any kind is soon satiated, and as we grow older our very capacity for sense enjoyment grows less; but intellectual hunger is never satisfied and a man's capacity for spiritual enjoyment may actually increase with the passing of the years. In his old age, a man like Lyman Abbott or Charles W. Eliot, although he is no longer able to obtain very much enjoyment from physical activity, is able to find a delight in intellectual activity which many a younger man knows not of.

At this point, therefore, what is the course of wisdom if a man really wants to get out of life what is worth while? There is a passage in the book of Ecclesiastes which offers some very curious and yet not unfamiliar advice. As translated by Professor Moffatt it reads:

> "Rejoice in your youth, young man,
>   be blithe in the flower of your age;
> follow your heart's desire
>   and all that attracts you;
> banish all worries from your mind,
>   and keep your body free from pain
> (for youth and manhood will not last)
>   ere evil days come on,
> and years approach when you shall say,
>   'I have no joy in them';
> ere the sun grows dark,
>   and the light goes from moon and stars,
> and the clouds gather after rain;
>   when the guards tremble in the house of Life,
> when its upholders bow,
>   when the maids that grind are few and fail,
> and ladies at the lattice lose their lustre,
>   when the doors to the street are shut,
> and the sound of the mill runs low,
>   when the twitter of birds is faint,
> and dull the daughters of song,
>   when old age fears a height,
> and even a walk has its terrors,
>   when his hair is almond white,
> and he drags his limbs along,
>   and the spirit flags and fades."

Stripped of its beautiful poetic imagery, what this passage really says is, "A day is bound to come when all your physical delights will be taken away; your very capacity for them will have been lost. Therefore, young man, eat and drink and enjoy yourself while you can." This advice is not unfamiliar; it has been offered by cynics and sensualists in generation after generation. It is being offered in some quarters today. But would it not be far better to say, "Rejoice in your youth, young man, and see to it that you cultivate those intellectual and spiritual interests which will enable you to rejoice also in your old age"?

On his seventieth birthday, Victor Hugo acknowledged that winter was on his head but declared that eternal spring was in his heart. For fifty years, he said, he had been endeavoring to express himself in poetry and prose, in fiction and drama, but he felt that he had not said a thousandth part of what was in him. In his eighty-third year, Goethe wrote to his friend Zeller: "I am delighted to find that even at my great age ideas come to me, the pursuit and development of which would require another lifetime." It is possible to grow old beautifully. It is possible to "fade as the leaf" which develops richer tints in the autumn of its life. It is possible to mellow with age, to outgrow the asperities and morbidities of middle life, and become wiser, braver, and kindlier. When that does happen, old age is never a tragedy. It is never a burden, nor a bore. There is joy in it, and beauty. The deep dents which thought and emotion, and it may be pain and sorrow, have cut in the physical medium of the soul are infinitely more becoming than the straightened forehead of the fool. Even the stooping shoulders and the faltering gait do but tell how that which is corruptible is putting on incorruption and the soul is building for itself a house not made with hands, eternal in the heavens. It is possible to grow beautiful as you grow old, but only in case you cultivate those intellectual and spiritual interests which provide permanent satisfactions.

Nor is it only sense enjoyment that is fleeting. The enjoyment which a man gets out of the accumulation of material possessions is likewise transient. In another astonishing passage, the unknown author of Ecclesiastes makes this frank and significant confession:

"I went in for great works, built mansions, planted vineyards, laid out gardens and parks in which I planted all kinds of fruit trees, and made pools to water the trees in my plantations; I bought slaves, both men and women, and had slaves born within my household; I had large herds and flocks, larger than any before me in Jerusalem; I amassed silver and gold, right royal treasures; I secured singers, both men and women, and many a mistress, man's delight. Richer and richer I grew, more than any before me in Jerusalem; nor did my wisdom leave me. Nothing I coveted did I deny myself; I refused my heart no joy—for my heart did feel joy in all this toil; so much I did get from all my efforts. But when I turned to look at all I had achieved and at my toil and trouble, then it was all vain and futile."

He had spent a lot of money building a big house and filling it with all sorts of costly furnishings, and while he was building and furnishing it he "got a big kick" out of it; but once it was up and completely furnished, the "kick" was gone.

It is, perhaps, unnecessary to add that many a modern

American has had a very similar experience. He has sunk a quarter of a million dollars, in some cases half a million, in a house far bigger than he and his wife and one or two children really needed. Then he has gone in for oriental rugs, medieval tapestries, modern original paintings, and everything else that is expected to go with that kind of a house. And, undeniably, "his heart did get joy" out of all this collecting, but the enjoyment was in the collecting; *it is not in the possession*. He does, to be sure, derive some satisfaction out of all those beautiful things with which he has surrounded himself, but he is surprised to discover that he does not in the mere possession of them get nearly as much satisfaction as he expected to get. He finds that in order to derive any continuous satisfaction he must go on collecting things; and he begins to wonder where in the world he is going to put them after he gets them.

Contrast such an experience with the experience of a man like President Goucher of Women's College, Baltimore. He was a lover of books and pictures and music, and he never denied himself or his family any tool that was really needed for the development and enrichment of personality. But although he was financially able to do otherwise, he lived simply and plainly, without display. The money which he might have sunk in a big house and elaborate furnishings and a retinue of servants he invested in educational enterprises in India, China, Korea, and Japan. And as long as he lived, he "got a big kick" out of what he was doing.

Like the pursuit of wealth or of power for its own sake, the mere accumulation of material possessions leads to frustration, disillusionment, and defeat. For the enjoyment which one gets out of material possessions is almost if not quite as fleeting as the enjoyment which he gets out of sensuous activity. Activities which yield transient satisfactions ought always to be subordinated to activities which yield great and permanent satisfactions.

There is also another distinction between values which merits attention—the distinction between wealth without and wealth within the human spirit. Jesus once told the story of a fat farmer whose barns bulged but whose soul shrank. One day this farmer patted himself on the back and said, "Now you have great wealth laid up in store for years to come, so take it easy; eat, drink, and enjoy yourself." But that very night he died! Jesus said that he was a fool and that he was typical of all men whose wealth is outside them rather than inside them.

Surely it is foolish for a man to set his heart on wealth without rather than on wealth within his own soul. Any kind of wealth that is external to the human spirit is subject to the vicissitudes of life. It may quite literally be swept away in a night, as it was in California by an earthquake and in Russia by a revolution. A man may lose his money. He may wake up some morning and find himself called upon to face the fact that his economic standard must be scaled down. He can no longer afford to live in the kind of house in which he has been living, nor to maintain three motor cars, nor even two, nor even one. Nor can he afford to retain his membership in half a dozen expensive clubs. But if he has any wealth within his own soul he will be able before long to adjust himself to his new economic status, as has many a Russian refugee who has discovered that great external possessions are not after all essential to happiness. Given the ordinary comforts of life, and the means of making a living, some real zest in one's work, a few staunch and stimulating friends, wide intellectual interests, and a vital religious faith—a man can find an abundance of happiness in circumstances that are greatly different from those to which he was once accustomed. As a matter of fact, the only degrading poverty is poverty of life, the sort of poverty that goes with incapacity to find and enjoy the intrinsic values of life. A man may thoroughly enjoy a symphony concert even though he is obliged to sit in the second balcony. He may enjoy a spring morning or a brilliant winter night even though he is obliged to live on the "third floor back." He may enjoy a great painting even though somebody else owns it. He may enjoy a thousand things which nobody can own—mountains and sunsets and friendships and the spontaneous, contagious laughter of little children at their play. He may enjoy all these things if he has the capacity to enjoy them, if he is not poverty-stricken in soul. But let a man whose wealth is all, or nearly all, outside his own spirit be required to face the necessity of making drastic alterations in his economic status and he will be poor indeed.

Not only wealth but health may be swept away over

night. A man may wake up some morning and discover that he is a paralytic, or that he has contracted tuberculosis, or that he has developed an inoperable cancer. He may go to bed some night with the knowledge that he is growing deaf or blind. And if then he has no wealth within on which to draw his situation is certainly desperate.

But here is Henry Drummond, stricken down in middle life by a strange and baffling disease, a malignant growth of the bones which causes him constant and excruciating pain. What does he do? Give way to despair? Not he. To the very end his sense of humor remains unabated. He keeps up his interest in sport, politics, literature, and religion. He keeps in touch with absent friends, "surprising them with telegrams of congratulation or of sympathy." Those who come to cheer and comfort him are surprised to discover that it is he who has cheered and comforted them. And here is Beethoven, who goes on producing immortal music after he is deaf and cannot hear it. And here is Milton, who goes on writing immortal poetry after he is blind. Surely it is wise for a man to set his heart on those inner riches of which nothing can deprive him, neither the loss of fortune nor the loss of health.

Concerning these inner riches there are two other significant things to be said. One is that they defy all the rules of arithmetic. They actually multiply with division. When it comes to material possessions the more you give the less you have; but when it comes to intellectual or spiritual wealth the more you give the more you have. In that case, to give is to get; to teach is to learn; to love is to have a greater capacity for love, and indeed for all the supreme experiences of life. As Whitman put it in some memorable lines:

> The song is to the singer and comes back most to him.
> The teaching is to the teacher and comes back most to him.
> The love is to the lover and comes back most to him.

It is possible, perhaps, for a man to make a million dollars in ways that will enrich other people. If any man can discover how to make a billion dollars in ways that will enrich other people, and not impoverish anyone, I, for my part, would feel disposed to say to him, "God help you, but go to it." But it can hardly be denied that it is also possible for a man to make a million dollars in ways that impoverish other people. As a matter of fact, it has happened once and again that in the mad scramble for material possessions one man's gain has been another man's loss. Such a calamity never occurs in the struggle for intellectual or spiritual possessions. Once the thirteenth chapter of First Corinthians has been written, or "Hamlet," or "In Memoriam," or "The Forsyte Saga," everybody who reads it is enriched by it. Once the life of St. Francis of Assisi has been lived, or of Abraham Lincoln, everybody who knows anything about it is inspired by it. In this case the one man's gain becomes the gain of a multitude. The individual who thus gains intellectual or spiritual wealth for himself, and then spends it, suffers no lack; the more he spends the more he has to spend. And the world as a whole benefits by what he has gained and given.

Now, I think it may be said without dispute that the greatest of all the values which human beings have ever experienced is God. What would represent the very greatest loss that any man could possibly sustain? Would it not be the discovery that there is no God? That discovery would bring along with it the knowledge that all that mankind has most nobly cared for and striven to attain has no abiding place in the constitution of the world; that it is therefore impermanent, at the mercy of cosmic weathers and destined in the end to perish in some wild cosmic storm. A way back in the dim distance of pre-historic times, human beings somehow lighted a torch which illumined their darkness and cheered their hearts, and in generation after generation that torch has been kept lighted by gifted and devoted spirits. But suppose one certainly knew that a time was coming when that torch would go out and all who bore it would be annihilated by blind and furious cosmic forces which noted neither their coming nor their going. Would not that represent the very greatest loss that anyone could possibly sustain?

The greatest of all values, because the sum of them all and the guarantee of their imperishableness, is God; as has been suggested in those two lines which George Bernard Shaw once declared he would rather have written than the whole of Karl Marx:

> O God, our help in ages past,
> Our hope for years to come.

And where is God, the greatest of all values, to be found? Not in sense experience, nor in the scramble for power, nor in the accumulation of material possessions, but rather in that wealth within the human spirit which increases when shared, and which neither the loss of fortune nor the loss of health can take away.

The conclusion, therefore, of the whole matter appears to be that what is worth while may be secured only by subordinating instrumental values to intrinsic values, transient values to permanent values, and the values without to the values within the human spirit.

III

SPIRITUAL ADVENTURE

WHEN Tennyson's "In Memoriam" was first published, Professor Sidgwick declared that it impressed upon him, as it did upon others, the ineradicable conviction that humanity will not and indeed cannot acquiesce in a godless world. In a recent article, Professor Harry Elmer Barnes declares that there is absolutely no reason to doubt that man is capable of going on happily and sanely without any sense of dependence upon God and without any apprehension of cosmic support. He does not, to be sure, rule out the possibility that a conception of God acceptable to modern science may some day be formed, but he believes that such a conception would have no value at all for personal religion, and with a good deal of confidence he looks forward to a day when men generally will feel no need of divine support.

Which of these two convictions is probably true? Was Professor Sidgwick right in his belief that humanity will not and cannot acquiesce in a godless world, or is Professor Barnes right in his belief that humanity can and will learn to get along without any God who may be personally apprehended? When one is dealing with the future, and especially with the far future, and considering what may or may not happen, say, one hundred thousand

34

years hence, it is probably well for him not to be too dogmatic. But certainly it may be said that the experience of the race hitherto would seem to support the contention of Professor Sidgwick and refute the contention of Professor Barnes. During the hundreds of thousands of years which the race has already spent upon this little planet, humanity has not acquiesced in a godless world. Up until now men have never reached a point where they felt no need of God, or of any kind of cosmic support. And it may, I think, be further said that humanity has not reached that point today.

If St. Paul could stand in the heart of Chicago, I suppose it would not immediately occur to him to say, as he did say to first century Athenians, "I observe at every turn that you are a most religious people." What he would immediately observe at every turn would be a mad rush to get across the street before a green light became red. But if only he could stay long enough to become acquainted with the deeper concerns of that hurrying crowd, would he not discover that twentieth century Chicagoans are as deeply interested in religion as were first century Athenians, and this notwithstanding the fact that modern churches are not always packed to the doors?

My own personal conviction is that certainly not in the near future will humanity feel able to get along without God. Human faith in a God who may be personally apprehended is not dependent, as Professor Barnes appears to think, upon the validity of certain beliefs that have been shown to be unscientific, anthropomorphic, and indeed childish. It is rather dependent upon the reality of certain values which represent the supreme concerns of the greatest and best men the race has ever produced. In order to believe in God today it is not necessary to believe in the Hebrew Jehovah, the God of battles, the God of a chosen people; nor is it necessary to believe in a venerable and gigantic person who dwells somewhere above the sky. In order to believe in God today it is only necessary to believe that the truth and love which men find in themselves are not only in themselves but in the very constitution of the world; that truth and love are, in a word, not merely transient, historic facts, but eternal, cosmic facts. The Barnes article simply does not touch the place where intelligent Christians live. From beginning to end, it moves in a realm where modern scientific discovery has revealed the childishness of ancient world views and medieval theologies. It never enters that realm where truth and beauty and goodness are as real today as they ever were, and where, notwithstanding any and every fact which has been brought to light by modern science, intelligent faith may dare to suppose that truth and beauty and goodness have cosmic significance.

But it is one thing to have a vague sort of religious belief and quite another thing to have an inspiring kind of religious faith. A vague sort of religious belief is undoubtedly, as the psychologists would tell us, conditioned by our environment. We absorb it from our surroundings. We grow up among people most of whom have few if any doubts concerning immortality, and no doubt at all concerning God. And this vague sort of religious belief which we absorb from our surroundings serves us fairly well so long as life does not make any demands upon us which are hard to meet. But the moment life hits us and hurts us, or strikes down someone who is dear to us, it is worth to us just next to nothing. Those religious beliefs which seem to be so sure so long as life never challenges them begin now to fail us and forsake us. We begin to wonder whether there is any truth in them at all. What we now need is a kind of religious faith which is born of a man's own personal experience of the great realities in the world of the spirit. And that of course is what we have always needed. That is the kind of faith which we ought through all the years to have been cultivating.

I am convinced that a really vital religious faith can never be secured except through moral and spiritual adventure. Indeed, I am beginning to suspect that it never has been. We speak often of the ages of faith, by which we mean those historic periods in which the great affirmations of religion were almost universally accepted. And yet, as Principal Jacks has suggested, the difficulties of faith have always been up to the limit of human endurance. A broken heart, as he reminds us, is very much the same in one age as in another, and wherever it exists the soul of man has all that it can bear. Even in those generations for whom the great questions of religion were supposed to have been settled by sheer ecclesiastical authority, one suspects that there were many persons for whom they were not so easily settled—men and women who had to struggle for all the faith on which they lived, and whose eventual certainty as regards God and immortality was something which they won as the result of a long and heroic spiritual adventure.

But before I undertake to elaborate on this thesis that a vital religious faith comes only out of spiritual adventure, let me say a preliminary word concerning authority in religion. In our present revolt against authority we are, I think, in no little danger of going too far. We have come to the conclusion that there is no such thing as infallibility in any church or book or creed, and in that conclusion we are certainly right. There is no infallible church, no infallible book, and no infallible creed. But are we justified in leaping to the further conclusion that there is in religion no kind of authority to which appeal may be made, that there is nothing beyond our own limited personal experience which has for us any significance at all?

William James once said, and revealed no trace of shame in saying it, "Our faith is faith in someone else's faith and in the greatest matters this is most the case." It is certainly the case with most of us in respect of the great affirmations of science. I frankly confess that my own faith in the theory of relativity is not only largely but entirely faith in Einstein's faith, and in the faith of such men as Professor Michelson who believe that they have discovered evidence in support of this theory. Professor Barnes declares it to be a fact that improved astronomical instruments have revealed to us a cosmic universe of universes of staggering dimensions. Well, most intelligent people today believe that this is a fact, yet the vast majority of them have never used the instruments which have revealed it. One cannot help wondering just how much personal acquaintance Professor Barnes himself has had with spectroscopes and interferometers. I should not be at all surprised to learn that his personal acquaintance with improved astronomical instruments is exceedingly slight, and that his own faith in this cosmic universe of universes of staggering dimensions is largely faith in somebody else's faith.

We say of a man like Professor Milliken that he is a distinguished authority in the field of physics; and of a man like Dr. Rosenow, of the Mayo Clinic, that he is a great authority in the field of focal infection; and of such men as Charles Evans Hughes and Elihu Root that they are great authorities in the field of international law. And when they speak concerning any matter which falls within their particular field we all listen. We listen attentively and with profound respect. We feel inclined to believe what they say and do believe it partly because they say it. We are not at all ashamed to acknowledge that in respect of such matters our faith is largely faith in their faith. A stubborn refusal to believe anything on authority would compel us to live in a world of mental darkness.

But if it is perfectly legitimate in respect of the great affirmations of science that our faith should, at times, be faith in somebody else's faith, why should it be deemed illegitimate that in respect to the great affirmations of religion our faith should be influenced to some extent by somebody else's faith? If Professor Milliken may be re-

garded as a great authority in the field of physics, may
not a man like Rufus Jones be regarded as a great authority in the field of religion? And would there be any
shame in some college student's confession that he himself
has not yet lived long enough to accumulate very much
experimental knowledge of God, but that nevertheless he
believes in God, and that his present faith in God is faith
in the faith of men like Rufus Jones?

Galileo, Darwin, Homer, Shakespeare, Michael Angelo,
Rembrandt, Beethoven, Wagner—we pronounce such
names as these with profound respect. We believe that
they represent certain great achievements in science and
poetry and art and music. Isaiah, St. Paul, Augustine,
Francis of Assisi, Thomas à Kempis, David Livingstone,
Phillips Brooks—these names, also, ought we not to pronounce with profound respect and to believe that they represent certain revelations of ultimate reality?

Not without reason are many people today suspicious of
authority in religion. Religious authority, represented in
some preacher or Sunday School teacher or mayhap in parents, has taken an unfair advantage of them. It has tried
to impose upon them beliefs that were intellectually disreputable. It has sought to saddle and bridle them with
beliefs that were unscientific, uninspiring, and untrue. It
is not, I suppose, to be wondered at that a college student
has recently announced, "I have come to the conclusion
that the thing for me to do is to clear the universe of God
and start in at the beginning to see what I can find."

But what a dreary business it would be to start in at

the point where the cavemen began and see what one could find. What a dreary business it would be to live one's life as though the saints and seers of the centuries had never been born; as though a man of the name of Wesley, as he closed his eyes in death, had never said, "The best of all is, God is with us"; as though a man of the name of Paul, as he proceeded upon a great adventure, had never said, "I am persuaded that neither death nor life can ever separate us from the love of God"; and as though a man of the name of Jesus had never died saying, "Father, into thy hands I commit my spirit." What a dreary business it would be to go all the way through life in utter disregard of the most significant things ever discovered by the most significant people. Nobody would think of disregarding all the discoveries of scientific men and starting in at the beginning to see what he could find. Why should it be considered desirable or necessary to disregard all the discoveries of religious men and start in at the beginning to see what one may find?

There is a kind of authority in religion which commands profound respect, namely, the spiritual experience of the race, and especially of its noblest representatives. It is not easy to believe that life has spoken truly to sceptics and cynics, that only to men like Wesley and Paul and Jesus has it lied. It is not easy to believe that ideas which in generation after generation have enriched the souls of men, given them strength and courage to go on, and enabled them in not a few cases to lift the level of life for the race— it is not easy to believe that such ideas are sheer delusions.

It does not follow that every specific doctrine to which some saint has subscribed is true, but is there not abundant reason to believe that the essential faith of the saints in the existence and glory of God is something that is rooted in the soil of reality?

In religion, also, there is a legitimate place for authority. But even the sort of authority which I have been describing, although it is a legitimate aid to religious faith, is a very poor substitute for religious experience. I have not hesitated at times to advise hard-working students to borrow a little money, especially in their senior year, in order to get through college without a physical smash, and in order also to enjoy some of those extra-curricular activities which are an important part of a college education. Nor would I hesitate to advise a sorely perplexed and hard-beset student to borrow a little religious faith until such time as he could accumulate a faith that would be his very own.

But what should be thought of a student, or anybody else, who undertook to go all the way through life on borrowed capital? Economically speaking, we do not try to do that for plainly it cannot be done. But, religiously speaking, many of us do try to go all the way through life on borrowed capital. Instead of developing, through moral and spiritual adventure, religious beliefs that we might call our own, we attempt to live on the religious beliefs of the community. We, who would be ashamed to ask for a "hand-out" of food or of clothing, apparently feel no shame at all in asking for a "hand-out" of religious beliefs. Nor do we hesitate to use religious words and phrases which other generations have coined out of their own most vital experiences but which stand for nothing which we ourselves have ever personally experienced.

Borrowed religious capital—we try to use it and manage to get along fairly well on it until life hits us between the eyes. Then we discover that we are religiously bankrupt. Those borrowed beliefs which we have never in any sense made our own no longer support us. Those borrowed phrases which stand for nothing we have ever personally experienced stick in our throats. We try to assure ourselves that "underneath are the everlasting arms"; we try to say, "Earth hath no sorrow which heaven cannot heal"; we try to ask, "O death, where is thy sting?" But the words won't come, or if they do, it is only from the lips, not from the heart. Sometimes we find ourselves crying out in utter bitterness of spirit that these soothing religious phrases are, after all, only a kind of opiate which people take to relieve their pain. And that, of course, is the inevitable, eventual result of any prolonged attempt to live on borrowed religious capital.

At an age which most of us have reached, and many of us have passed, we ought to be getting some first-hand experience of those great realities in the world of spirit which inspire and support religious faith. Consider the question of God. How enormously important it is! There are many things in this world which we could get along fairly well without, but faith in God is not one of them. The belief that a man is not alone in a universe which is blind to his need and deaf to his prayer—that is not one of the things which we can get along fairly well without. But is there a God and the sort of God that human need appears to require? How are we ever going to find out?

A question of this sort can never be settled by argument. If the fact of God could be established by argument, would it be too much to suppose that it would have been established long before this? But it cannot be, and for the very best of reasons, namely, it should not be. It ought not to be possible to prove by formal logic that there is a God. If that were possible the greatest of all discoveries would be too easily made. It would be made on conditions that would leave the human soul undeveloped. "Blessed," said Jesus, "are the pure in heart; for they shall see God." Suppose it were not necessary for a man to become pure in heart in order to see God! Suppose this greatest of all visions could be had by any scoundrel who was able to pass an examination in formal logic! In that event, where would be life's challenge to the heroic in the human spirit? What, in that event, would call forth the latent nobility in human hearts? It is precisely because the fact of God cannot be established by intellectual processes alone that religion appeals to and develops all that is greatest and best in the human soul.

One recalls that the Pharisees demanded of Jesus some sign of the authenticity of his message. They wanted him to prove that what he was saying was true. It was as though some authority on art should say concerning the frescos in the Sistine Chapel in Rome, "These frescos represent the supreme achievement of human art"; and as though some tired and bored American tourist should say, "Now, prove that." Or as though some student of Shakespeare should say concerning Hamlet, as indeed William Hazlitt does say: "Hamlet is a name. His speeches are but the creations of a poet's brain. What then, are they not real? They are as real as our own thoughts"; and as though some habitual reader of *Snappy Stories* should say, "Well, now, prove that." Or as though some lover of music should say concerning the Ninth Symphony, with its Chorus on an Ode to Joy, "This is the most marvelous concourse of sounds that ever burst from a human soul"; and as though some devotee of jazz, some moron who prefers a saxophone to a violin, should say, "Prove it."

There are some things that simply cannot be proved. Some things? The greatest of all things! By no process known to any mathematician or logician can it ever be proved that it is better to be chaste than licentious, or that it is better to be generous than selfish, or that it is better to be brave than to be a coward, or that there is a God and the sort of God that human need appears to require. By a wise provision of nature, these greatest of all things must be discovered. They reveal themselves only to people who take the initiative and make the great adventure. To that first century demand for a sign, Jesus could only reply, "If you will travel the road that I am going, you will presently discover for yourself that what I am saying is true."

In college fraternities, today, sessions are occasionally

held in which all sorts of subjects, including religion, are freely and frankly discussed; and far be it from me or anyone else to discourage the holding of such sessions. That they possess some value, I have not the shadow of a doubt; but the fact remains that the great affirmations of religion can neither be proved nor disproved in a "bull session." If college students really want to know whether there is a God, a far better thing for them to do would be to try to eliminate prejudice and cruelty from race relationships on their own campus, and try to achieve in their own hearts purity and courage and kindness. If any man out of college really wants to know whether there is a God, instead of waiting for some kind of intellectual demonstration that he will never get in a million years, it would be better for him to devote himself to some such cause as the securing of peace for a long-suffering world. Only in moral and spiritual adventure can the greatest of all discoveries be made!

Here also is man's hope of immortality; and how very much it involves. Not merely, as many people appear to think, an instinctive shrinking from the thought of annihilation; nor merely, although this is unquestionably involved in it, a pathetic longing for reunion with those whom one has loved and lost. A demand for justice—in this world justice is not always done. A recognition of the supreme worth of human personality—a great human soul is too beautiful and costly a thing to be tossed as rubbish to the void. A realization of the fact that unless human individuals are preserved a day will come when the race itself will have vanished from a planet no longer capable of supporting life, and all the travail of the ages will have been for naught. That also is involved in man's hope of immortality.

But does life go on after death? How can we ever find out? Here again is a question that cannot be settled by argument, and for the best of reasons, namely, that it ought not to be. We sometimes wonder why it is that immortality, if it be a fact, has not been inescapably revealed to the hungry hearts of men. But may it not be that in this very absence of a kind of evidence that would compel belief lies life's challenge to all that is most heroic in the human soul? Should we deplore the fact that it is necessary for a man to climb to a considerable height before he can really see that death is just an incident in the on-going of life? Should we not rather rejoice that such is the fact, for therein lies that spur to heroic adventure which we all need. If any man wants to know whether life goes on after death, there is laid upon him the glorious necessity of developing the best in himself. Let him devote himself for a period of years, as Goethe did, to the discovery and expression of significant truth, and he will be able with Goethe to say, "The thought of death leaves me in perfect peace, for I am convinced that the human spirit is indestructible."

Instead of waiting for some kind of intellectual demonstration of God and of immortality, a kind of demonstration which, if we had it, would probably do us far more harm than good, how much better it would be for us to make those brave adventures of faith and love out of which alone religious certainty has ever come.

IV

SEEING THE INVISIBLE

"TO be carnally minded is death, but to be spiritually minded is life and peace." As you read that statement you have the feeling that something very important has been said. If Saint Paul had written, "To be heterodox is death, but to be orthodox is life and peace," you would perhaps have thought of some noble heretic like John Haynes Holmes and felt called upon to protest. And if Paul had written, "To be out of the church is death, but to be in the church is life and peace," you would certainly have thought of some splendid non-churchman like Abraham Lincoln and felt called upon to do something more than protest. But when he writes, "To be carnally minded is death, but to be spiritually minded is life and peace," he says something that captures and holds the attention. That statement points to a distinction that goes deeper than men's intellectual opinions and far deeper than their ecclesiastical affiliations. And yet, strangely enough, it is not easy to say precisely what this distinction is. Just what is a carnal mind or a spiritual mind?

Without any thought that I am about to say everything that may or should be said in this connection, I shall offer the suggestion that at least one important distinction between the carnal man and the spiritual man lies in the fact that the carnal man sees for the most part only what is visible, whereas the spiritual man sees also the invisible. And I shall present and undertake to defend this thesis: to see only what is visible is death, but to see also what is invisible is life and peace.

But when a man begins to talk about seeing the invisible, what does he mean? When you turn to your dictionary and open it at the word "invisible," you discover that the invisible is the "not visible"; it is that which cannot be seen. Well, if the invisible is the not visible, to talk about seeing it is sheer nonsense. When you ask a man to see something that cannot be seen you expose yourself to the question, "How do you get that way?" or even to the question, "Who is your bootlegger?" But suppose the invisible is not that which cannot be seen but only that which cannot be seen with the naked eye, or through a microscope, or through a telescope, or by means of any other instrument which the wit of man has devised. There are in this world a great many things which no human eye has ever seen, or ever will see, but of whose existence intelligent people have no doubt.

Even in the physical world that appears to be true. No scientist today has any lingering doubt as to the existence of atoms. A scientist will tell you that there are many kinds of atoms and that some of them represent structures which are exceedingly complex. He will even describe for you these complicated atomic structures. Yet nobody has ever seen an atom, much less an electron or a proton. The assertion that there are such things as atoms is purely an inference drawn from their behavior under certain controlled conditions. The mind has seen something which to the eye is invisible. There are likewise certain filterable viruses which nobody has ever seen, even when using the most powerful of microscopes, and yet of whose existence no reputable physician has any doubt. He knows that, although they are invisible, they are nevertheless potent enough to cause measles and scarlatina. The fact of the matter seems to be that a large part even of the physical world is absolutely invisible to any eye save the eye of the mind.

Intelligent people, when they are dealing with the physical world, no longer suppose that because something is invisible it is therefore non-existent. Why, then, should anybody feel disposed to question the existence of a world of spirit because it is invisible? If the reality of atoms may be inferred from their behavior, may not the reality of ideas and ideals be inferred from their behavior?

David Livingstone once undertook a long and hazardous journey from the interior of Africa to the Western Coast in the hope of opening up a highway for legitimate commerce and thus striking a blow at the illegitimate slave trade. After months of incredible toil and hardship he managed to reach the Western Coast, but when he arrived he was more dead than alive. He lay for weeks in the home of the British Commissioner in Loanda, unable to move hand or foot. The moment, however, he was physically able to do so, he set about the preparation of his report to the London Missionary Society under whose auspices he had gone out; and when at last he had finished his report, he was offered a passage home by the captain of an English ship.

He had seen neither his wife nor his children for more than two years. He was still far from being a well man; and over against Africa, with its swamps and fevers, its torrid heat and torrential rains, was England with security, comfort, loved ones, fame. But Livingstone had given his word to his twenty-seven black attendants that if they would accompany him to the coast he would lead them back to their homes in the interior. And so, on the day appointed for the sailing of that English ship, he sent on board his invaluable maps, charts and observations. He stood on the shore and watched her sail away until she became a mere speck on the horizon. Then he announced to his black people that he was ready to start and back he went into the interior.

If the reality of an atom may be inferred from its behavior, may not the reality of honor be inferred from its behavior? What Livingstone saw when he made that decision not to go home but to go back into the African jungle was something no human eye has ever seen, or ever will see; but it was real enough to constrain him to do what he did.

During recent months, no less than nine men have given up their lives in an heroic quest of the still hidden causes of certain terrible diseases. One was a North American, one a South American, one a Russian, one a Japanese, one an Irishman; two were English, and two were French. Dr. Alvin, the Brazilian, lost both hands as the result of X-ray experimentation. Dr. Williams, an

Englishman, underwent no less than forty operations made necessary by similar experiments. When Dr. Stokes, a brilliant young Irish physician, died on the African Gold Coast in quest of the cause of the African yellow fever, his fellow workers sent out a cable which read: "Morale here excellent; the work goes on." So it does; and why? For what do men such as these risk their lives? For something which is quite incapable of sense perception, and yet so utterly real and compelling that men can be found to die for it.

It is a great day in any man's life when he makes for himself the discovery that visible reality is not the whole of reality, that certain things unseen are quite as real as anything that can be seen.

Concerning these invisible realities in the world of spirit there are several things which may and should be said. One is that they and they alone abide. In his illuminating discussion of poetry, Alfred Noyes calls attention to the fact that the song of Homer still lives, whereas the world in which it was created has vanished; that passages of Virgil still move us like a living voice whereas Imperial Rome has crumbled into dust; that the song of Dante is sung today where medieval potentates have long since been forgotten; and that from the Elizabethan Age all that still lives is that supreme voice which said concerning a king, "After life's fitful fever he sleeps well."

> Say never more
> That dreams are fragile things. What else endures
> Of all this broken world save only dreams?

And strange as it may seem to carnal minds, the invisible is not only more permanent than the visible but far more powerful. The things that are seen are no match at all for certain things that are unseen. It has been cynically observed that providence always seems to be on the side of the heaviest battalions, but how very different is the testimony of history. Pontius Pilate had the battalions, not only the heaviest battalions but all the battalions there were; yet his name has barely escaped oblivion. He is recalled today solely because of his momentary association with a man who had no battalions except those invisible ones called truth and right; and the name of that man is now above every name in the history of mankind.

Marion Crawford tells a story of Carlyle that is worthy of much repetition. On a certain evening Carlyle was sitting at a dinner table where lesser men were doing most of the talking, as lesser men are prone to do. They were discussing current political and economic questions, and with all the assurance of economic success and social prestige they were insisting that mere theories don't count. Carlyle stood it as long as he could. Then he said, "Gentlemen, once upon a time there was a Frenchman named Rousseau, who wrote a book called 'The Social Contract.' From beginning to end it was mere theory, and the nobles of France thought that they could afford to laugh at that theory. But, gentlemen, their skins went to bind the second edition of the book."

On the first day of January, of the year 1831, there

appeared the first edition of a little typographically insignificant sheet called *The Liberator*. Its editor and publisher and printer was a young fellow just entering upon
his twenty-sixth year. He was not like Emerson, his great
contemporary, college bred; nor did he have back of him,
as Emerson had, seven generations of college-bred ancestors.
He was poor, self-taught, obscure; and when he began his
journalistic career he did not have a dollar of capital or a
single subscriber. He slept in his printing office "with a
table for a bed and a book for a pillow." He prepared
his own meals which consisted chiefly of "bread and milk,
a few cakes and a little fruit." He had no battalions. All
he had was a few ideas that happened to be true and right
and some paper and some printer's ink. He was despised,
threatened, mobbed. But today, in the City of Boston,
there is a monument to William Lloyd Garrison. It was
erected by public subscription, and its inscriptions are two
quotations from that little typographically insignificant
sheet which appeared on the first day of January, 1831.
One reads: "My country is the world. My countrymen
are mankind." The other reads: "I will not equivocate,
I will not excuse, I will not retreat a single inch, and I will
be heard."

The mightiest things in this world are things which nobody has ever seen through eyes of flesh. And if the
invisible is more permanent than the visible and more
powerful, must it not further be conceded that it is more
important? It is very important that people should have

something to eat, something to drink, and something to put on. But, as a distinguished Englishman has recently reminded us, "After everybody has been adequately housed, clothed and fed, the problem still remains, what to do with life—a problem for which they have no solution to whom philanthropy is the whole of life."

Many a social worker has made the discovery that what the people to whom he was ministering needed most was not something visible but something invisible; not a new suit of clothes but a new attitude toward life. Many a physician, also, has made the discovery that the chief trouble with many of his patients lies not in their bodies but rather in their minds. There are human ills which can never be removed by pills or powders or surgeons' knives. They can be removed only by faith and hope and love and a right attitude toward life. And how are you going to remove the ills of civilization? Merely by lifting the economic level? Nobody can believe that who has any personal acquaintance with the bitter unhappiness that is the daily and nightly companion of many a man, and particularly many a woman, who has no economic worries whatsoever. After you have met all life's visible requirements there is still the problem, what to do with life—a problem which many rich people have never solved and never will solve until they learn how to meet life's invisible requirements. The ills of civilization can be removed only by the right kind of ideas and ideals—those things unseen which, because they are unseen, seem to some people to be unimportant, but which are as a matter of fact so profoundly important that their presence makes all the difference between a healthy civilization and a sick civilization and between human hope and human despair.

Here, by the way, is something that is worth thinking about by any young man who is facing one of the most crucial questions that any young man can face, namely, what to do in this world. There are many places in which you may do it. You may do it in a pulpit, or a class room, or an editor's office. You may do it on a Board of Trade or in a meeting of stockholders. There are many places in which you may do it, but the very most important thing that you could possibly do in this world would be to change the minds of men and open the eyes of men to what is true and right and of greatest value.

Herein lies the justification of the church. When people go to church they do not get anything that is visible. They do not receive anything which they may carry home in their hands or their pockets. That statement probably needs some qualification, for I happen to recall one clergyman who sometimes advertises that he will give to every man, woman and child who comes to his church on a stated Sunday evening a fine big orange! In most cases however the church offers no such inducement. In most cases, when you go home from church, you go with no more of visible, tangible possessions than you had when you came; and you may go with ten cents less! But if a church is doing what a Christian church ought to do, you never leave it unrewarded. You go home with something that is invisible, intangible, imponderable, but so real and so worthful that the whole of the following week is easier for you to live through.

In America, in recent years, there has been erected an astonishing number of churches costing upwards of a million dollars apiece. That question which was raised nineteen hundred years ago, when a certain woman who had an alabaster cruse of ointment, very precious, impulsively broke it and poured its contents on the head and feet of Jesus, might be raised today concerning these million dollar churches: Why was not all this money spent for food and clothing and given to the poor? The answer is that, even from the point of view of the poor, far more essential than food and clothing are faith and hope and love. A man may manage to get through the day with but a single meal; but take away from him all faith and hope and he is likely to jump into the lake. If only the church will do what a Christian church ought to do, if only it will keep on trying to change the minds of men and open the eyes of men to things which really matter, not only will the poor have enough to eat and drink and put on, but by and by the conditions that breed poverty will be done away.

How very significant the fact that Jesus himself defended the breaking of that alabaster cruse of precious ointment. And how very significant the further fact that today the human race numbers its years from the birth of a man to whom the most important of all things were things unseen.

To see only what is visible is death. A man may wake up in the morning and still be dead. A man may go down

to his office and transact business and still be dead. A
student may go into a class room and be as dead as a door
nail; and a long-suffering instructor may sigh and say,
"Why, oh why, doesn't the faculty bury him?" Concerning eighteenth century England, Carlyle wrote, "Soul
extinct, body well alive." Those were the days when
Englishmen were invited to get drunk for a penny and
dead drunk for a twopence; when cock-fighting went on in
the very shadow of Westminster Abbey; when the announcement that a wild bull would be released with its
body covered all over with burning fireworks brought a
huge crowd of calloused spectators; and when, on Sunday
afternoons, the most popular form of diversion was to
go with your wife and children to some asylum and stand
and stare at insane persons chained naked to their cells.
"Soul extinct, body well alive."

Well, even though a man's body may be well alive, if
his soul is extinct he is dead. And a man's soul is extinct
if he cannot see anything except what is visible; if such
invisible things as honor and chivalry make no appeal to
him at all. May it not further be suggested that a man
is dead if he has not anything to live for; if he drags himself through one day after another without any incentive
for so doing; as is apt to be the case of any man who sees
only what is visible. When you do get down to those
metaphorical brass tacks on which matter-of-fact minds
are so insistent, there just isn't anything visible in this
world that is worth living for. The only things that are
worth living for are such unseen things as truth and honor

and love. With no vision of the invisible a man hasn't anything to live for, and when he hasn't anything to live for, even though his body continues to function, he himself is dead.

To see only the visible is death, but to see the invisible is life and peace. It would, I think, be a serious mistake to advise any young man to sacrifice the present on the altar of the future, to deny himself any and every immediate satisfaction and postpone indefinitely the enjoyment of life. I do not think that I know any young man who would consent to listen to such advice, and if one such can be found I devoutly hope that I shall not be called upon to meet him. I should expect to discover in him an insufferable ass. But it would not be a mistake to advise any young fellow to take the future into account. The greatest lives that have ever been lived in our world were lived by men who took account not only of the visible present but of the invisible future. They wrote books which would never have been written had they considered merely the opinions of their contemporaries. They painted pictures that never would have been painted, they produced music that would never have been produced, had they considered only existing standards and tastes. And these creations which not the visible present but only the invisible future could be expected to approve are now regarded as the supreme creations of the world. Think also of men who stood for causes which had no chance whatever of immediate success but which future generations were destined to applaud and advance.

To create something which only in years to come will people praise and prize; to stand for something which only in years to come will the crowd endorse and cheer; to live in the visible present but with your eyes on the standards and judgments of the invisible future—that requires more courage than most of us appear to possess; but it is undoubtedly the way to life and peace. It enables a man to say more and do more and be more than fate would allow were he content to live only in and for the visible present.

"Moses," we are told, "endured as seeing him who is invisible." Just for the moment strike out the word "him" and read simply, Moses endured as seeing the invisible. We may well suppose that this man who chose to be the burdened leader of an oppressed people rather than the idle darling of an Egyptian court did endure as seeing something as yet invisible, namely, the emancipation of a race. And I have no doubt that Senator Borah today is enduring much as seeing something as yet invisible—the actual outlawry of war.

But in his statement concerning Moses, the author of the Epistle to the Hebrews does include the word "him." Moses endured, he writes, as seeing *him* who is invisible. Recall now what was said about that invisible something which constrained David Livingstone to refuse a passage home in order to keep faith with twenty-seven black men, and led Dr. Stokes to lay down his life in quest of the cause of an African fever. Invisible? Yes, but real, more real and more compelling than anything that is visible. What then? Shall we say of God that because he is invisible he is not real? Shall we say of God that because he cannot be seen through a microscope or a telescope he does not exist? If truth and honor and love are real, invisible though they are, may we not venture to believe that God is real, and may not we too manage to endure as seeing him who is invisible?

The vision of a God invisible but real and dependable has sustained men and women in generation after generation. It has fortified the souls of prophets, steadied the feet of pioneers, and comforted the hearts of those who mourned. It has enabled men to face life gallantly and death without fear. Men have endured pain, loneliness, misunderstanding, bitter disappointments and prolonged delays, as seeing him who is invisible. And this, of course, is the secret of those who have suffered a shattering bereavement and managed to remain sane. They have endured as seeing him who is invisible—not only God but the one who has died. They have said with Emerson:

> What is excellent
> As God lives is permanent.
> Hearts are dust,
> But hearts' loves remain.

The individual passes from the scene of his earthly activity. Innumerable generations come and go. Civilizations rise and fall. Even the stars finally fade. Is there nothing that abides? Yes, the mighty "invisibles" abide. The things which are seen are temporal, but the things which are unseen are eternal. Is it not, then, a fact that to see the invisible is life and peace—that peace of Christ which passes all understanding?

V

AS A LITTLE CHILD

Except ye turn and become as little children, ye shall in no wise enter into the kingdom of heaven. Matthew 18:3.

IN this saying of Jesus there is something strangely appealing—and strangely disturbing. What appeals to us is, no doubt, just the reference to a little child; for a little child, of whatever nation or race, is always appealing. What disturbs us is, probably, our half-conscious recognition of the fact that in us a good deal of the child is dead, or very nearly so. Some of us have become old and childish, but not child-like. Some of us who have attained middle age are still pretty much babies; but of certain child-like qualities we cannot boast. But, although for some such reasons as these most of us find this saying of Jesus at once appealing and disturbing, how many of us have ever attempted to think our way through it and come to any conclusion as to what it probably means?

"Except ye turn and become as little children." There is no suggestion here that we ought to *remain* as little children. Fathers and mothers, especially mothers, sometimes look at their little two-year-old, so lovely and lovable, and say with a pang, "Why can't she remain like this forever?" But it would, of course, be truly terrible for her to remain like that forever. To remain physically as a little child is to be a dwarf. To remain mentally as a little child is to be an imbecile. To remain morally as a little child is to be a moron. Not, "except ye remain," but "except ye turn and become." Between remaining and becoming there is all the difference between a simpleton and a saint. What Jesus must have meant was that there are certain qualities in a little child which most of us lose as we grow older, but which, somehow, we must recapture if we are ever to enter into the kingdom of God. As to just what these qualities are there is room, no doubt, for difference of opinion, but we shall, I venture to think, be on a fairly safe side if we name these three: wonder, spontaneity, and trust.

There is in every normal child a notable capacity for wonder. Gilbert Chesterton has remarked that "when we are very young children, we do not need fairy tales; we need only tales. Mere life is interesting enough. A child of seven is excited by being told that Tommy opened a door and saw a dragon. But a child of three is excited by being told that Tommy opened a door. Boys like romantic tales; but babies like realistic tales—because they find them romantic." There is, also, in every normal child a glorious spontaneity, a frank, free expression of self in which there is no apparent effort, no hampering self-consciousness, no inhibiting fear of what other people may think. And in every child who has not been mistreated there is an undoubting trust, not only in parents, but in all men and women and, indeed, in the whole world of life. Here, then, are three qualities possessed by normal children, and

if it can be shown that they are in some way essential to
the development of heaven on earth, may one not venture
to think that they were among the qualities considered by
Jesus when he said, "Except ye turn and become as little
children, ye shall in no wise enter into the kingdom of
God"?

Now it can, I think, be shown that every one of these
qualities is in some way essential to the achievement of a
better world. Consider for a moment the meaning of
wonder. A man ceases to wonder when he begins to take
everything for granted; or, rather, to take everything as
though it had not been granted, as though it just naturally
belonged to him and had not been given to him by the
hand of God or the sweat of men. He wonders at nothing
because he is grateful for nothing. He takes everything as
a matter of course because he fails to appreciate the fact
that everything is a matter of effort—somebody's effort.
Wonder, that is to say, is born of gratitude. Is gratitude
essential to the development of heaven on earth? Try to
build a better world—or even a better garage—with work-
men who are ungrateful!

Nor is wonder born only of gratitude. A man ceases
to wonder when he begins to settle down in a nice comfortable philosophy and a nice comfortable world, and
considers that there is no longer any chance of a big surprise. He no longer wonders whether there is any new
aspect of truth to be discovered. All the truth there is,
all, at any rate, that really matters, may be found in his own
well-tested religious or political or economic creed. He no

longer wonders whether there is any new kind of social order to be one day worked out; the only social order that any sane person could imagine or any reputable person could desire is the one which now exists—that well-ordered society in which he and his wife and his children are so comfortably fixed. Wonder, that is to say, is born also of the expectation that life is full of surprises, that it is, in fact, just one big surprise after another, that there are more things in heaven and earth than are yet included in anybody's philosophy, and always more worlds to conquer. Is that expectation essential to the development of heaven on earth? Try to do anything different with people who do not have it!

Consider, also, the meaning of spontaneity. A child ceases to be spontaneous the moment he becomes self-conscious. So long as he remains unconscious of self, how effortless and graceful his actions are! We self-conscious adults look at him in a kind of amazed delight and almost hold our breath lest something should happen to divert his attention from the thing being done to the little person who is doing it. We know only too well that the moment he becomes aware of himself and, therefore, of his audience, the spell will be broken, the charm lost. Instead of that beautiful, effortless grace there will be an ugly, awkward striving for effect. Spontaneity is born of forgetfulness of self. Is self-forgetfulness essential to the building of a better world? Just to put that question is to answer it.

And what about that third quality of which we have spoken? What about trust? A man ceases to trust when

he begins to doubt. (This statement will need to be qualified later, but for the present let it stand.) A man ceases
to trust when skepticism moves in, and faith moves out;
when he becomes suspicious of the motives of men and
doubtful of the reality of God. Trust is born of faith and
hope. Are faith and hope necessary if men are to pray,
not with their lips only, but with all the energies of their
life, "Thy kingdom come, thy will be done on earth as it
is in heaven"? That, likewise, is a purely rhetorical question.

May we not venture, therefore, to say, "Except ye shall in
some way recapture the spirit of wonder, the spirit of spontaneity, and the spirit of trust, ye shall in no wise enter
into the kingdom of God"?

If ever we are to have any part in the kingdom of God,
some of us will need to recapture the spirit of wonder.
When we were three, we were excited by the statement that
Tommy opened a door. When we were seven, we were
excited by the announcement that Tommy opened a door
and saw a dragon. But now that we are twenty, if someone should inform us that Tommy opened a door and saw
an aeroplane, most of us would merely drawl out, "Oh,
did he?" If we happened to be very busy, we might even
reply, "Well, what if he did?" If someone should come
running with the news that Tommy opened a door and
saw an aeroplane as big as a Pullman coach, then, to be
sure, we would feel excited—until aeroplanes as large as
Pullman coaches had become a common sight in the sky.

Emerson pointed out a significant fact when he observed

that there is ever this difference between the wise and the unwise; the latter wonders at what is unusual, the wise man wonders at the usual. In the wise man the child never dies—the child who sees something wonderful just in the fact that Tommy opened a door. A Charles Lamb feels disposed to return thanks, not merely when he sits down to a well-cooked dinner, but on twenty different occasions in the course of a day. He would like "a form of grace for setting out upon a pleasant walk, for a moonlight ramble, a friendly meeting, a solved problem." And why not, he asks, a form of grace for books—a grace before Milton, a grace before Shakespeare, a devotional exercise proper to be said before reading "The Faërie Queene"?

The wise man, that is to say, takes nothing for granted, accepts nothing as though it had not been granted. Being wise, he understands that nothing comes as a matter of course, that everything comes as a matter of effort. The vegetables on his table represent the sweat and anxiety of men and women who toil on their knees in truck gardens. His fresh, clean linen represents the labor of folk who stand all day in steaming laundries. His daily paper is brought to his door because thousands of human beings have worked industriously to gather and publish news. Into the books which he reads, someone has poured the costly drippings of his brain. Into the music which he hears, someone has poured the joy and agony of his soul. And when he lifts up his eyes on high and beholds the multitude of the starry host, he recognizes the presence of a divine faithful-ness whose vigilance is never relaxed. The wise man wonders at the usual, for he is not unmindful of the fact that even so usual an occurrence as a breakfast or a sunrise represents a creativity and a fidelity which are, in the very most literal sense, "wonder-full."

In the interest of clear thinking, it ought to be said that between the wonder of a child and the wonder of a wise man there is a certain significant difference. In the case of a little child, wonder is the effect of the unknown upon ignorance. In the case of the wise man, it is the effect of the known upon knowledge. The child wonders because he does not understand; the wise man wonders because he does understand. The suggestion of Jesus is not that a grown man should wonder as a child wonders, but that he should wonder as much as a child wonders. At twenty, at forty, at sixty, to the very end, he should be as full of wonder as a child is, not because he does not understand, but precisely because he does understand. Knowing how things are done, having at least some knowledge of the cost at which they are done, a man should be full of wonder and, therefore, of gratitude and, therefore, of desire to make some return for that which has been granted to him.

The spirit of wonder involves not only gratitude, but expectancy, and that, too, some of us will need to recapture if we are to have any part in the kingdom of God. A little child lives in a world in which anything may happen. Do apple trees grow apples? Yes, but they might grow ginger snaps or gay balloons. Does Christmas come on the twenty-fifth of December? Yes, but it might come on the fourth of July. Does some little girl have on a gingham dress and worn-out shoes? Yes, but who knows, this very night a fairy godmother may clothe her like a princess and present her at court to the Prince of Wales. Do grown-up people live in a world in which anything may happen? No, many of them live in a world in which nothing may happen—a world, I mean, in which nothing is expected to happen that has not happened before, with the single exception of new inventions. Even the most unimaginative adult has learned to expect that after the telephone may come the wireless, after the wireless the radio, after the radio an instrument that will transmit sights as well as sounds. But, excepting only new inventions, many adults live in a world in which nothing new is expected.

Both children and grown-up people say, "Do it again," but with what a difference! An excited child cries, "Do it again" because "it" appears entitled to an encore. A complacent adult says, "Do it again" for no other reason than that "it" has been done for hundreds, or at least, scores of years. Industry operated primarily for the benefit of stockholders, and only incidentally for the benefit of the community, has been productive of social maladjustments of the very most serious sort; but, ever since the beginning of the industrial era, industry has been so operated, so "Do it again." Preparation for war leads to war. In our time, European preparation for war very nearly caused the downfall of European civilization; but frightened or ambitious nations always have prepared for war, so "Do it again."

"Do it again" on the lips of a child means the presence

of wonder at what is being done. "Do it again" on the lips
of an adult means the absence of wonder whether anything
better might be done. If, when a child cries, "Do it again,"
you should venture to suggest that something more interesting might be done, he would almost certainly say, "Do
that then." But if, when an adult says, "Do it again," you
should venture to offer a similar suggestion, he would almost certainly say, "Oh, don't try that." In this difference
between the child and the man there is something other
than a needed conservatism born of a sense of responsibility; there is an unneeded reactionism born of fear of personal loss. Men who are seeking first, not the kingdom of
heaven, but their own advancement and aggrandizement,
insist that what has been done shall be done again, because
they hope that if it is done again, they at least may get
what they are after. Lest they themselves should not get
what they are after, they do not permit themselves to wonder whether something better might be done.

"There's no sense in going further—it's the edge of culti-
vation." So says the unadventurous adult. But sometimes
another voice,

". . . as bad as Conscience, rings interminable changes
    On one everlasting Whisper day and night repeated—so:
'Something hidden. Go and find it. Go and look behind the
        Ranges—
    Something lost behind the ranges. Lost and waiting for
        you. Go!' "

That is the voice of the re-awakened child in us, the ex-
pectant, exploring, wonder-loving child in us; and to that
voice, suggests Jesus, we would do well to give heed.

And if, from the wonder of a child, we must pass through a blasé, non-expectant period to the wonder of the wise, must we not also, from the spontaneity of a child, pass through an awkward age to the spontaneity of a completely dedicated life?

Who does not recall those painful days when he first made the discovery that he had hands and feet; when, wherever he stood, he did not know what in the world to do with his hands, or what in the world to do with his feet wherever he sat. Booth Tarkington's novel, "Seventeen" has been both dramatized and pictured, and his royalties from the book, the drama, and the motion picture, amount now, it is said, to a million dollars. People have paid a round million dollars to enjoy a good laugh at themselves as they were during the awkward age. But if awkwardness comes from self-consciousness, are not many of us still in an awkward age? We are able, no doubt, to stand well and to sit well, but are we even yet able to give well, to serve well? Our hands and our feet no longer bother us, but what about our money, our opinions, and indeed, the fundamental purposes of our lives? Are not some of us even yet so overwhelmingly conscious of self that we cannot give away money without inward pain; or express an opinion without considering how it will be received; or, in fact, do anything without very carefully counting the cost? There is, that is to say, no spontaneity in us, none of that effortless grace which constitutes the charm of a little child. We are still in a spiritually awkward age. Is there any way of growing out of it?

Well, the secret of spontaneity is forgetfulness of self, and the secret of self-forgetfulness is a sense of responsibility; a sense, if you please, of mission, born of a religious conception of life. When a man conceives the idea that he is, after all, but an instrument in the hands of God, that he has a mission to perform and woe be unto him if he does not perform it, then does he begin to lose sight of self, and so, to achieve spontaneity.

Here is a man who is beginning to make money. When a man begins to make money, he would do well to look out; yes, and would he not do well also to look up? By looking up, he will be looking out; he will be wondering whether he is making money honestly and justly, in ways that help and do not hurt other people; he will be looking at his money-making through the eyes of God. Furthermore, that upward look will take his eyes off himself. It will reveal to him the fact that a man does not own his money, he owes it. Instead, therefore, of asking such preliminary questions as, Ought I to give? Shall I give? How much will it be necessary for me to give in order to come to any terms with my conscience? he will have only to ask: To what shall I give? Where may I place my money to the best advantage? Where will it accomplish the most good? His giving itself will be spontaneous. It will be one of those things which he does with as little effort as is required for the lacing of his shoes. The only thing which will give him any pause or anxiety will be the selection of agencies through which his giving may be made to do good.

Here, too, is a man who is beginning to make speeches—something which everybody does these days, if not in pulpits or on platforms, at least in drawing rooms and the rear end of Pullman coaches. And when a man begins to make speeches, he does well to look out and up. The awful danger is that he will consider, not what ought to be said, but only what it is politic to say; not what will advance the kingdom of God, but only what will contribute to his own advancement. How little real spontaneity there is in most public and private speaking! But if only the speaker would look up, there would be more. In that case he would forget himself and consider his mission.

What all this means in relation to a better world is evident enough. So long as people must be pled with before they will consent to give a dollar or two; so long as they must plead with themselves before they can secure their own consent to give anything; so long as, when they do give something, they give in a somewhat niggardly and grudging fashion, every movement toward the kingdom of God will be retarded. So long as people do not consider what ought to be said and done, but only what it is expedient to say and do; so long as they are not frank, open, spontaneous, in word and deed, but cautious, cunning, self-regarding, the prospect of building any better world is surely small. But introduce into the lives of adults that glorious spontaneity of a little child. Let them give spontaneously and joyously, let them speak and act without concern for self, and the prayer, "Thy kingdom come," will begin to mean something. It will also begin to accomplish something.

From wonder through satiety and non-expectancy to a more intelligent wonder; from spontaneity through awkward self-consciousness to a more responsible spontaneity; yes, and from trust through doubt and a touch, it may be, of cynicism to a more thoughtful, more courageous trust, a man must pass if he is to have any part or place in the kingdom of heaven.

It is not necessary, indeed it is not possible, for a man to retain just the trustfulness of a little child. May you hope to go all the way through life with no more doubt as to the unfailing goodness of people than is possessed by your little daughter, who supposes that everybody is as kind as you are, and that you are as kind to everybody as you are to her? Hardly! The trustfulness of a little child is born in part of ignorance, and after a man becomes better acquainted with life and the world, he simply cannot recapture the kind of trustfulness which characterizes a little child. Nor should he if he could. A child believes everything he is told. A man ought not to believe everything he is told, for not everything that he is told is true. A child, unless he has been mistreated, trusts everybody. A man ought not to trust everybody, for not everybody is worthy of trust. There comes a day in the life of every growing child when he really ought to question some of the things he is told and some of the people who tell him things.

Unless he does, not only will his own mind remain unenlightened, but there will be no chance of "de-bunking" the mind of the world.

What, then, might one mean by suggesting that an open-eyed man should endeavor to recapture the trustfulness of a little child? Well, here is a man who has no illusions. He knows that some of the things which he was told as a boy he cannot, as a man, believe, for the simple reason that they are not true. He knows that a good deal of what passes as orthodoxy in theology, politics, and economics, is but the hang-over of an uncritical age, or the deposit of a calculating selfishness. He knows that a good deal of written history is precisely what Mr. Henry Ford said it was—bunk; that even historians do not always write history, that some of them write highly colored propaganda. He knows that not everybody is honest, or disinterested, or kind. He is, that is to say, pretty thoroughly disillusioned. But is he soured? No. Has he lost all faith in men, all hope of progress? No. He has come through his experience of disillusionment a little wiser and, perhaps, a little sadder; but he still believes in honor, and that many men are honorable. He still believes in love, and that many people are kind. He still believes that there is in humanity enough of divinity to justify the hope of high and heroic achievements. And so, with a man's knowledge of life and the world, he moves into the future with a child's spirit of trust. To such an one belongeth the kingdom of God.

VI

THE LOVE OF GOD

IN all literature there is, I suppose, no more detestable character than Count Guido in Browning's "The Ring and the Book." As you read this long poem you keep hoping that you will find in this man some one redeeming quality; but you hope in vain. He is mean all the way through. Having murdered his wife—and where in all literature is there so completely beautiful a wife as Pompillia?—Guido is condemned to die. Is he subdued by the sentence which has been imposed upon him? Not in the least. To the very last he remains hard, cold, unfeeling—to the very last moment, almost. But when at the bars of his prison window a light appears, and when on the stairs which descend to his prison door steps are heard, and he realizes that the end has come, even Guido cries out for mercy. He appeals to the highest court on earth. He appeals to the supreme court in heaven. And then, as if in fear of justice, human or divine, he appeals to something that is beyond justice, something that is greater and more redeeming; he appeals to the love which he has known and flouted in his wife:

> Abate, Cardinal, Christ, Maria, God,
> Pompillia, will you let them murder me?

Love very often is despised and rejected of men, but soon or late love comes into its own. We all feel the need of it at last. And who among us would not like to believe that there is love at the heart of everything? When someone asked Frederick Meyers what question he would put to the sphinx if he were permitted to put only one, he replied that of all the questions he could think of putting he would prefer an answer to this one, "Is the universe friendly?" That, I venture to think, is the question we would all want to have put if we could put but one and be assured of an answer. Is the universe friendly? Is there a God who cares for human individuals and whose nature is such that in the direst kind of human need a man may turn to him in confident expectation of understanding and compassion and help?

It is hard sometimes to believe in a God who is love— and equally hard to disbelieve. You try to believe and find yourself thinking of the pain and injustice of life and the apparent indifference of nature to the welfare of mankind. Then you try to disbelieve and find yourself haunted by a sunset, or the laughter of a little child, or the face of a saint, or some deed of heroism which suggests divinity in humanity. You try to believe and have the problem of evil on your hands. You try to disbelieve and have the problem of good on your hands. When you consider that despairing cry from a cross, "My God, my God, why hast Thou forsaken me?" you find it difficult to believe. But when you consider that amazing prayer from a cross, "Father, forgive them for they know not what they do," you find it even more difficult not to believe. Opposed to your faith is all the tragedy of history. Opposed to your doubt is all the moral splendor of history.

My own conviction is that for anybody who believes in God the problem of evil, difficult though it is, is nevertheless not so difficult as is the problem of good for anybody who disbelieves in God. On the whole, is it not easier to account for pain and injustice on a theistic hypothesis than it is to account for beauty and love on an atheistic hypothesis?

It is doubtless true that many a so-called explanation of evil leaves a great deal unexplained. Nevertheless, you can see at least a little way into the meaning of pain. You can see that pain is needed as a warning of danger. How handicapped our physicians would be were it not for the kindly warning that is furnished by pain. It also appears to be true that pain may be, and often is, an illuminating, spiritualizing agent that produces in us clearer insights, finer emotions, quicker and more comprehending sympathies. Might not one venture to believe that a world in which there was no pain would be not nearly so good a world as one in which pain has a chance to educate and refine the spirits of men?

You can see at least a part of the way into the meaning of injustice. That injustice exists in our human world is beyond dispute; but there are many indications that the world is becoming less unjust. There appears to be an increasing number of people who are not only applauding but endeavoring to practice "the square deal" and even the Golden Rule. Injustice is due in part to human selfishness, and in part also to human ignorance; but these awful weaknesses in the human spirit are not unconquerable. They are being conquered. Injustice, that is to say, is no inevitable part of human life. There is some reason now to hope that more and more it will be weeded out of human life. And if the question be asked, But why are men permitted to be unjust? the answer would seem to be that deprived of any real freedom it would be impossible for men to achieve any real virtue.

It is even possible to see at least a part of the way into the meaning of the apparent indifference of nature to human weal and human woe. Under certain conditions natural forces will freeze to death a Captain Scott, notwithstanding the fine idealism that has inspired his quest. Under certain conditions they will produce a drought or precipitate a flood that will leave thousands of human beings hungry and homeless. But there is one thing that nature will never do. Under no circumstances will nature act lawlessly. And so, for all her apparent indifference to many things that we human beings care about, nature renders us an inestimable service. She gives to us a law-abiding world and so makes possible all the glory of human experiment and human achievement.

Venture to believe in God and you can at least partly account for pain and injustice and nature's apparent indifference; but venture to disbelieve in God and what account can you then give of beauty and of love?

However love came to be, it is here. The fact of it is beyond dispute. In one of Victor Hugo's tales, a lost boy, groping his way in the darkness across a cold and windswept waste, stumbles upon a human form which proves to be the body of a mother, frozen to death, with her babe in her arms. The babe, however, is alive and warm, for the mother has stripped herself of her clothing and wrapped it around her sleeping child. In this case fiction is no stranger nor more wonderful than fact. It sometimes happens that a man's actions are such that society considers it necessary for its own protection to take away from him his life. Perhaps it is not necessary for society to do this. The present warden of Sing Sing Prison maintains that the death penalty is neither necessary nor right nor even expedient. Nevertheless, it is still being inflicted. And how many a man among us might confidently say:

> If I were hanged on the highest hill,
>   Mother o' mine, O Mother o' mine,
> I know whose love would follow me still,
>   Mother o' mine, O Mother o' mine.

Love, then, is a fact. Even though you choose to call it a bio-chemical phenomenon it remains a fact, and a mighty comforting fact in any kind of trouble. To some of us it does not appear to be at all likely that love will ever be reduced to a chemical formula; but even though it should be, it would remain the greatest and most beautiful thing in the world, and its power to comfort us, to heal us and redeem us would remain unchanged. If anybody should stand up and insist that love is, after all, nothing more than a chemical compound, I for my part would not feel inclined to argue with him, though I would not agree with him. I would, however, feel inclined to suggest that in that event his respect for that particular chemical compound ought to be commensurate with the respect that humanity has historically accorded to the idea of God.

But now, having conceded that love is a fact, we have next to inquire into its significance. Has human love any cosmic significance? Does it tell us anything about the nature of the world in which we live? May we venture to argue from human love at its best to the character of the process that has produced it? May we venture to believe that the love which we find in mothers, for example, is a revelation of something akin to it at the heart of the world?

It is noteworthy that what we are now asking whether we may do Jesus repeatedly did do. From love in man he argued love in God. He once put the question: Which of you if your son should ask for a loaf of bread would give him a stone, or if he should ask for a fish would give him a serpent? And his inference was: If men with all the evil that is in them are concerned to give good gifts to their children, how much more so must God be. He also put this question: Which one of you, having a hundred sheep, if he loses one of them does not leave the ninety and nine in the desert and go after the one that is lost until he find it? And his inference was: If men are thus eager to recover anything of value which they have lost, how much more eager must God be to recover everything of value in human life. In this connection he told a story of which men have never grown weary, a story which has moved the human heart as few stories ever told have been able to move it. Ours is an ultra-sophisticated generation. There are some among us who feel inclined to boast of the fact that nothing surprises us, nothing shocks us. And how we do hate what we call "sob stuff"! But when it comes to that story told by Jesus of a certain man who had two sons, both of whom though in different ways broke his heart, and both of whom he forgave and sought to redeem, even the most sophisticated among us find that we are strangely moved. That story is so true to life that we almost catch our breath as we read it. And when Jesus suggests that love in parents is an authentic revelation of something at the heart of the world, even the most cynical among us finds himself questioning the grounds of his cynicism.

A drop of water is not the ocean, but being of the same constitution as the ocean it has something to say to us about the ocean. A great human soul is not God; but suppose that it is, so to speak, of the same constitution as God. Does it not in that event have something to say to us about God? That, let it be remembered, is precisely the point which Christianity has been concerned to make in respect of Jesus. The real intention of historic creeds has not always been understood. It has not been to say that Jesus is God, but rather to say that Jesus was so much like God that he could with perfect propriety and profound truth declare, "He that hath seen me hath seen the Father."

"God of God, Light of Light, very-God of very God, being of the same substance with the Father by whom all things were made"—so runs one of our great historic creeds; and, no doubt, the metaphor which it uses is somewhat unfortunate. The word "substance," suggesting as it does something visible, tangible, ponderable, is hardly a suitable word to apply to God. But when the creed-makers used that word what were they trying to say? They were declaring their own faith that in Jesus of Nazareth we have a perfect revelation of the deepest and most significant thing in God.

But does human love, even at its best, have any cosmic significance? Shall we say with Matthew Arnold:

> Ah, love, let us be true
> To one another! for the world, which seems
> To lie before us like a land of dreams,
> So various, so beautiful, so new,
> Hath really neither joy, nor love, nor light,
> Nor certitude, nor peace, nor help for pain;
> And we are here as on a darkling plain
> Swept with confused alarms of struggle and flight,
> Where ignorant armies clash by night.

Or shall we say with St. John, "Beloved, let us love one another, for love is of God." Is human love merely a human phenomenon, telling us nothing at all about the nature of the world in which we live; or is it a revelation of the love of God? The answer to that question every man must make for himself; for, in the final analysis, what it involves is a deliberate personal choice. After all the discussion about it and about, all the argument pro and con, we must each one of us make up his mind either to believe that human love is human love and nothing more, a mere bubble on the surface of life, or to believe that love in man is a revelation of love in God.

Let us suppose for the moment that it is a revelation of love in God and then ask, What follows concerning God? It is well for us to remind ourselves that human love even at its best is by no means incapable of anger. Men recalled concerning Jesus that when he was reviled, he reviled not again; when he was struck he did not strike back. They also recalled concerning him that there were some occasions when his anger flashed like lightning on a stormy night. When widows and orphans were being robbed; when the weak, the poor, the ignorant were being exploited by pious people under the cloak of religion; when one of God's little ones was being caused to stumble by the very people who ought to have protected him, the anger of Jesus revealed itself in words that still flash and burn.

A friend of Dr. James Hope Moulton recalls three occasions when that great and gentle scholar's anger suggested the fury of a tempest. Once Moulton spoke of men unworthy of the name of England, men who called black folk "niggers." Once also, when recalling some vile horse play practiced by under-graduates, he declared that on that occasion he was ashamed of his university. And once, when somebody related to him the pitiful, tragic story of a girl who had been betrayed, he gave forth "a cry of agony like the wailing of a lost child on a lonely moor." And what American does not recall that the hand which penned the words, "With malice toward none, with charity for all," was once clenched in the determined resolution concerning negro slavery, "If ever I have an opportunity to hit this thing I will hit it hard."

That kind of selfless, self-forgetting anger seems to be characteristic of human love at its best when it is confronted with evils that are cursing or hurting the lives of men. And if love in God be essentially the same as love in men, must we not venture to assume that there is in the nature of God a similar capacity for anger?

If the fear of God is the beginning of wisdom, there are some of us who have hardly begun to be wise. We are afraid, we moderns, of poverty. Some of us are afraid of pain. Most of us are afraid of unpopularity. We are afraid of men and of the judgments of men; but when it comes to God, how little fear we have! In respect of God and his judgments many persons belonging to our generation appear to have taken the optimistic view expressed by one of Omar Khayyám's philosophical pots concerning the potter:

> They talk of some strict testing of us—pish!
> He's a good fellow and 'twill all be well.

But if only a man were wise, he would fear the judgments of love as he fears no other judgment ever rendered in this world. True love is not blind. It is not blinded by passion nor by prejudice nor by selfishness nor by fear. It has no selfish ends to serve. It is very kind, very patient, always eager to believe the best. Woe therefore unto any man whom that kind of love feels obliged to condemn. Woe unto him because he is deserving of condemnation. There is something in him that is radically wrong, something of which he has every reason in the world to feel ashamed.

We appeal sometimes from the judgments of today to the judgments of tomorrow, and from the judgments of earth to the judgments of heaven; but from the judgments of love there is no appeal. There is no higher court to which a man may carry his case. You may read condemnation in the eyes of hate or of prejudice or of selfish fear and remain undisturbed by it; but what if you read condemnation in the eyes of love? What if somebody whose love for you and whose eagerness to believe the best about you you simply cannot question is found condemning you? The jolly good fellow conception of God is just about the most sentimental and superficial idea that has been set afloat in modern thinking. If God is love it will not all be well with anybody whom He condemns.

To say this, however, is not to say that God is going to punish anybody whom He finds it necessary to condemn. Love, for one thing, has no desire to punish. What sort of satisfaction does love get out of punishing anybody or seeing him punished? Suppose a man were hanged on the highest hill, what sort of satisfaction would his mother get out of that? When some boy runs amuck, and falls into the clutches of the police, and is brought into court and sentenced to spend from one to twenty years in the penitentiary, what sort of satisfaction do his parents get out of that? The satisfaction which some pious people appear to feel in the expectation that their godless neighbors will be compelled to suffer forever in a mediæval hell is surely a proper subject for psycho-analysis. It probably reveals a "suppressed desire" for revenge.

Love, certainly, has no desire to punish. If only it could, love would save men from the consequences of their own folly. It is heartbroken over the fact that there are some consequences from which it is powerless to save them. We talk about men breaking laws; but, strictly speaking, it is not men that break laws. It is laws that break men when they are disregarded. As Gilbert Chesterton has characteristically put it, "The man who leaps over a precipice does not violate the law of gravitation, he merely illustrates it." We talk about repealing laws. A number of people, it appears, would like to repeal the Eighteenth Amendment. Well, they may some day be able to repeal it, but never the law which decrees that if you get drunk on Saturday night you will have a fierce headache on Sunday morning. Love is tormented by the fact that from the worst of all punishments—those which sin itself inflicts—it is powerless to save those whom it loves.

What love desires is not to see the prodigal punished but rather to see him "come to himself." That is what every father desires whose son has made a misstep, and every mother whose daughter has played the fool. Parents do not want to see their children punished; they want to see them "come to themselves." And if love in God is essentially the same as love in men, must we not venture to believe that that is what God wants and is seeking to bring to pass; that, indeed, the divine shepherd takes the initiative and goes after that which is lost until he finds it?

"Until he finds it." It is always perilous to hang a great hope on any text and I have no intention of doing so now.

But, looking in the direction of those last words of Jesus' parable of the shepherd and the sheep, I shall make bold to state my own conviction that the divine shepherd will seek that which is lost until he finds it, if it takes a thousand, thousand years! Personally I do not see what else love could do.

Let us also remind ourselves that love is very patient. It must be. The methods which love employs to secure its great results require patience. When Mr. Sinclair Lewis stands in a Kansas City pulpit and gives God three minutes to strike him dead, Mr. William A. Sunday announces that if he were God he would "soak him so hard that there would be nothing left for him to stand on." Such action would, no doubt, relieve the feelings of Mr. Sunday—and some of the rest of us—but hardly contribute to the spiritual development of Mr. Lewis.

The knock-down, drag-out method appeals to us. It appeals to the vindictiveness in us and the impatience and the laziness. If you have enough physical strength to do so, it is always easier to knock a man down than it is to reason with him and appeal to the best in him. The only trouble with the knock-down, drag-out method is that it is seldom if ever effective. For thousands of years we have been knocking people down, boxing the ears of our children, hanging our criminals, and, on one pretext or another, shooting our neighbors across the frontier. And during the thousands of years which our human race has been on this little planet, how much good has come from all that boxing and hanging and shooting?

God did not strike Sinclair Lewis down. He permitted him to live. He even permitted him to write *Elmer Gantry!* Love *is* very patient, *and very effective!* In the end it gets results—radical, far-reaching, permanent results. It changes the human heart. It creates in men a right spirit. Slowly but surely it builds a better world.

When, some time ago, I read that in one of our American cities several hundred people stood one day on a street corner and watched some representatives of a humane society climb the sloping roof of a tall building in order to rescue a sparrow whose claw had been caught in a bit of cord, my first thought was, "Sentimentality of the stickiest sort!" But presently I recalled a saying whose full significance up until that moment I had never grasped: "Are not two sparrows sold for a penny? and not one of them shall fall on the ground without your Father." And my second thought was that the love which notes the predicament of a sparrow is the greatest power in the world.

VII

THE GOOD OF PRAYER

WHEN we were children, most of us prayed. Possibly it would not be going too far to say that we all prayed. We prayed to a big and powerful man-like God who lived somewhere in the skies, a kind of idealized Santa Claus. And we prayed for anything that we wanted. If it was raining and we wanted to play out of doors, we asked God to make the rain stop falling; and when, as occasionally happened, it actually did stop, we had no doubt at all that it was our prayer that had stopped it. If we lost a pen-knife, we asked God to help us to find it; and when, as occasionally happened, we did find it our faith in the power of prayer became boundless. Sometimes, to be sure, the rain kept on falling and the penknife remained unfound. Then, indeed, for a day or two we reflected somewhat upon the mystery of life and began to wonder whether prayer was, after all, as dependable a means of getting anything one wanted as we had thought it was. But before long we usually succeeded in persuading ourselves that the fault lay not in prayer but in ourselves. We had failed to employ the right technic; we had used the wrong formula, prayed in the wrong name or for the wrong sake. In any event, prayer was altogether too valuable an instrument to be laid aside, so we kept on praying in hopes that if we did not get what we wanted today we might do so tomorrow.

By and by, as human beings are wont to do, we grew up, and although we no longer indulged in the practice of prayer to the extent that we had once done, we still entertained no serious doubts as to its efficacy. We went for days on end without praying, but whenever we felt the need of a more than human help, we prayed. And sometimes, more often than not in fact, we felt that it had done us good to pray. Not always did we get what we prayed for, but we got something. The mere fact that we had given expression to some pent-up emotion appeared to relieve the tension from which we had suffered. The mere fact that we had become conscious of a real and dependable world of spirit within us and around us appeared to supply us with new resources of courage and strength.

But presently something happened which greatly disturbed us and made it increasingly difficult for us to go on praying. It did not happen to all of us, but it did happen to so many of us that reference to it is surely called for in any such discussion as this.

It cost us but little to give up all attempt through prayer to regulate the weather or to locate lost penknives. We began to suspect that the weather belongs to a world in which prayer can hardly be expected to operate, and that lost penknives represent problems of too trivial a nature to bring to the attention of the Almighty. We did, however, begin to ask how, in a world where, so far as we can see, everything is governed by law, prayer can be of any avail. Yet even to that question we found, after a time, a satisfying answer. We realized that human personality, far from being limited by law, is actually liberated by it.

Does any writer ever complain that the laws of syntax cramp his style? Yes, a few modern writers are making such a complaint, and they are seriously advocating the repeal of all laws that have until now governed the expression of human thought and emotion. They themselves are, indeed, actually nullifying the laws of syntax. And the result? Well, here is something from the pen of Gertrude Stein. She calls it "A Portrait of Constance Fletcher," of whom we read with growing wonderment: "When she was quite a young one she knew she had been living in a family living and that that family living was one that anyone could be one not have been having if they were to be one seeing one thinking about being one having been having family living."

Now writing such as this has certain obvious advantages. You need not be sane in order to accomplish it. And when you undertake to read it, you need not begin, as in the case of law-abiding composition you are required to do, at the beginning of a sentence and read forward. You may, if you choose, begin at the end of a sentence and read backward. You may even begin at the middle of a sentence and read in either direction. In fact, you may dispense with reading altogether and know fully as much as you would have known if you had read. For this sort of writing has also certain disadvantages, of which one is that nobody can make any sense out of it. In writing which is not governed by the laws of sentence structure personality cannot express itself. Far from being limited by law, human personality is liberated by it. Given the laws of syntax, a great human soul may express itself in a Gettysburg Address, a play called "Hamlet," and a parable called "The Prodigal Son." And if this be true of human personality, why should it be deemed not true of God? Why should it be considered impossible or even difficult for God to express himself in a world of law-abiding forces?

Many of us, therefore, are no longer bothered by the fact that everything, so far as we can see, is governed by law. And yet we are bothered, and to such an extent that we sometimes wonder whether we can go on praying. What bothers us now is just the awful question whether there is any superhuman intelligence to which prayer may be addressed. It appears to be true that human beings have always prayed. They have not always prayed to a personal God. In uncorrupted Buddhism, for example, God has never been thought of in personal terms. Yet Buddhists for centuries have practiced prayer. But it is to my mind far from certain that human beings would or could go on praying if ever they should definitely surrender their belief in any kind of cosmic intelligence; except, of course, in times of crisis when fear and anxiety might wring from the heart an irrational plea for help.

I am not unaware of the fact that a man may commune with his own higher self or with his idealized self. I can even see the value of such communion. There is, no doubt, a good deal of value in the contemplation of an ideal. But to call such contemplation prayer is, it seems to me, a misuse of language, and I am bound to confess that for me mere self-communion is ofttimes a rather lonely and unsatisfying experience. If that "other" which I am invited to contemplate is, after all, just my own other self or possible self, if there is no "other" beyond myself and other human selves, I may, to be sure, and certainly should go on aspiring and striving for that which might be and is not yet. But please do not try to tell me that in so doing I would find an equivalent of communion with God. Commune with ourselves and with other human selves? Yes, we can certainly go on doing that. But can we go on communing with God if there is not, when all is said, any universal spirit with which we may commune? That is a question by which many people today are greatly disturbed. A revival of faith in God would, I suspect, do more than anything else to revive the practice of prayer.

It may and should be said that from one point of view the fact of God is not at this present moment in question. Almost anybody will readily admit that there is something back of the visible world—something which has produced it and which even now is maintaining it. What is in question is the character of that something. Is it a something akin to the human spirit and with which, therefore, the human spirit may hold communion; or is it a something so different from the human spirit that the practice of prayer should be regarded as a somewhat pathetic superstition?

It will not and, indeed, cannot be doubted that the "something" behind the visible world has expressed itself not only in inert crystals but in living cells; not only in the unconsciousness of stars and seas but in the consciousness of men and women; not only in the mental deadness of rivers and rocks but in the marvelous intelligence of a Plato and an Einstein; not only in the amorality of trees and flowers but in the conscience and moral idealism of the human race. Why, then, should we not dare to believe that life and consciousness and intelligence and moral concern are attributes of that invisible something which is behind the visible world?

The fact is now accepted by all intelligent persons that man belongs to the world of nature. He is not apart from it; he is the most significant part of it. Lay aside, then, the old distinction between the natural and the supernatural and frankly admit that there is only that which is natural— nothing which is supernatural. But ask yourself this question: What is the character of that natural order which has manifested itself not only in crystals but in Christ and in many another human spirit who, not content with that which was, has striven valiantly in sweat and blood for something which ought to be? What is the character of that natural order out of which have come the intellectual geniuses and moral heroes of the race? Surely it is not impossible or even intellectually dishonorable for a man to venture out upon the belief that all that is highest and best in himself is a revelation of something beyond himself, that invisible something which one may dare to say must be behind the visible world. When, therefore, some man in dire need feels an impulse to pray, he need not be deterred by the thought that there really is not any "other" save his own better self with whom he may possibly commune. He may venture to obey an impulse which is itself a very significant expression of that invisible something which lies behind what the eye can see of the world.

Here is a statement which may at the moment provoke dissent but which upon reflection will almost surely be acknowledged to be true: The right kind of prayer not only gets results but gets the very most important kind of results obtainable in this world.

Many of us, as has been said, have abandoned all attempt through prayer to regulate the weather. The weather belongs to a world in which prayer not only does not get results but in which it ought not to be permitted to do so. Just imagine a small boy with a gift for prayer being granted the desire of his heart, namely, that it will stop raining in order that he may go on a picnic, when for miles around fields of developing grain are badly in need of water. Dependent as we are upon the forces of nature and not a little afraid of them at times, it is not to be wondered at that we should desire to control them; and control them we actually do to a very wonderful degree, but not directly by offering up petitions to the throne of grace. It would be well for us once and for all frankly and contentedly to accept the fact that the place where prayer may properly be expected to get results is not in what we commonly speak of as the world of nature but rather in the world of men.

The first place in which to expect results from prayer is in the heart of the man who prays. And there results are obtained times without number.

Here is a man who is afraid. Of whom? Himself. And not without reason, for his present self is painfully and perilously divided. One part of him wants to do right; another part exhibits a strange and troublesome tendency to do wrong. One part of him earnestly desires to be a hero; another part of him occasionally insists upon playing the coward. One part of him is kind; another part cruel. And he can never be sure which part of him is going to prevail. Not without reason is he afraid of himself. And added to his fear of moral failure is the fear also of professional failure, the fear, I mean, that in his chosen field of endeavor he will fail to accomplish all that he aspires to do. So much of his energy must now be spent in keeping that intractable part of himself in line that he has only a fraction of the power which he ought to have to apply to his task. If only he could find something great and noble enough to command him, all of him, so that with one undivided self he might undertake to do his work in the world!

Let us suppose that such an one begins to pray: "O God, in my great need I cry unto thee for help. My life is tragically divided. Help me to put an end to this wasteful conflict within my own soul. Help me to achieve within myself a degree of unity that will bring me peace and give me power." I have ventured to put certain words upon his lips; but, of course, it is not the words that matter most. A man's real prayer is in the attitude of his heart, not in the words on his lips. When it comes to prayer, the sole function of words is to express and by expressing strengthen a desirable attitude. But let it be supposed that this man's attitude is one of sincere and earnest desire for moral harmony within his own soul. Will not that attitude expressed in appropriate words begin, by and by, to get certain results?

Here, too, is a man who is afraid of his fellows—as who among us is not, more or less?—afraid not only of what they may do, but of what they may say or think. Some men go all the way through life in abject fear of public opinion. They are concerned above all else to be on the side of the majority, notwithstanding the indisputable fact that majorities have nearly always been on the wrong side at the start. Human progress has been how often delayed simply because man after man lacked the courage to stand by his own conviction of truth and right. And for those who do fear the face of man there is, so far as history shows, but one sure way to develop courage, and that is to look more steadfastly into the face of God. Let some man who does feel afraid of his fellows, if not of their actual opposition at least of their ridicule and cold-shouldering, turn away sometimes from the hasty, passionate judgments of today and contemplate the calmer, clearer judgments of tomorrow. Let him pray for courage to live his own life in the light of judgments which the coming years will approve, and discover for himself whether that kind of prayer does not bring results.

Here, again, is a man whose fear is that he will run out of ideas. Writers, preachers, artists, musicians—all persons engaged in creative work—experience most dreadfully at times that kind of fear. Richard Curle tells us that again and again Joseph Conrad would say to his friends, "I can't think of a subject." The famous author of "Lord Jim," "The Nigger of the Narcissus," "The Mirror of the Sea," and a dozen other novels that seem destined to live, found it difficult at times to think of a subject! "He was forever tormented by the fear that he would be deserted altogether by ideas and by the very power to create." Nor was he able by conscious thought to get ideas. He was obliged to wait for them to come. But come they eventually did; that is evident. And whence did they come? Conrad himself, so far as I know, never expressed an opinion upon this point. He was an unusually reserved man and concerning some of his convictions even his closest friends appear to be in doubt. But many another man of genius has not hesitated to commit himself to the assertion that his inspiration came from God. Haydn, listening to one of his own compositions, cried out, "It is not from me, it is from above!" Goethe maintained that he himself was merely a vessel found worthy to receive the divine influence. Jesus declared, "The words that I speak unto you I speak not of myself."

Venture, then, to suppose that great ideas do come from God. In that event, might it not be contended that what men of prayer have described as "waiting upon God" constitutes a very real and essential part of all human creativity of the highest order? Might it not be contended that prayer is or at least may be an invaluable means of preparing the mind for the reception of significant truth? Certain it is that under the influence of prayer the mind becomes more alert and elastic, as anyone may discover for himself by making the experiment. Something happens when a man opens up the channels of his life to the inflowing of the divine spirit. He becomes, as we rightly say, inspired.

One thing which we all need is a proper perspective. How often do we permit mole hills to look like mountains! How often do we allow ourselves to be swept off our feet by a tempest—in a teapot! We suffer a whole day to be utterly spoiled by something to which we should have paid no attention. We permit ourselves to be cruelly hurt by things which were not in the least intended to hurt us. We are so intent upon goods which we do not have that we derive no satisfaction from goods which we do have. We pity ourselves when we ought to forget ourselves in earnest effort to promote something that is greater than ourselves. A proper perspective is something which we all need. And may we not get it through prayer? Let any man make an honest and earnest attempt to look at life through the eyes of God and great things will begin to appear great; yes, and small things will begin to appear small. In prayer a man may turn his attention away from lesser things and fix it upon important things. If he does, he will presently secure a proper perspective; and when he is able to see life steadily and see it whole, what a vast relief he will experience from petty cares and annoyances, what a marvelous increment of courage and poise and power!

Prayer does unquestionably get results in the life of the person who prays; not always, to be sure, for everything depends upon the attitude of the pray-er. But given the right attitude on the part of the person praying, prayer will create unity in his life, it will make him more heroic, more productive, better poised. And if that were all that prayer was able to accomplish, the practice of it would be abundantly justified; but that is not all that prayer is able to do.

How profoundly true that ancient observation of Saint Paul, "No man liveth unto himself or dieth unto himself." Whatever affects the individual affects at least to some extent the human group to which he belongs. To his own generation Thomas Carlyle endeavored to make this clear by telling the story of an old Irish widow who, in dire distress, appealed to her neighbors for help, but was denied it. Whereupon she sickened and died, but not before she had infected the whole neighborhood with typhus fever, of which seventeen other persons eventually died. The plain-speaking Mr. Carlyle was impelled to add, "She proved her sisterhood. Her typhus fever killed them. They were her brothers even though they denied it." Today, a distinguished British scientist is trying to bring home the same truth to his generation by insisting: "As long as we maintain slums and dusty occupations we shall have foci from which the tubercle bacillus will attack the well-to-do. As long as we have families of six in a single room we shall be unable to prevent the spread of diphtheria or measles." And what a terrific illustration of human solidarity is furnished by a world war. Early one morning in 1918, as I entered the railway station at Nancy, in the dimly lighted waiting room I encountered a soldier in the blue uniform of a French officer. But over his shoulders was a huge cape, spotlessly white; over his head was a crimson hood, and the face which appeared beneath it bore the tawny hue of the African sun. He was a Moroccan, drawn into the white man's war. Another day, as I stood at a railway crossing waiting for a troop train to pass, the train stopped, and from those luxurious war-time coaches marked "Quarante hommes, huit chevaux" yellow-skinned members of a Chinese labor battalion called to me in a strange bedlamic mixture of Chinese, English, and French. Under modern conditions how very much more true is that ancient saying, "No man liveth unto himself or dieth unto himself."

Prayer, therefore, has social consequences. Its benefits are not confined to the person who prays. It does not merely change the life of the individual. Through changed individuals it begins to refashion the life of the world. It must, of course, be frankly confessed that the social benefits of prayer are not always easily detectable. Even in days when prayer meetings were more largely attended than they now are one might, in many communities, have looked in vain for any notable social results from prayer. But the absence of significant social consequences should never be counted against prayer itself. It should rather be attributed to the narrow vision and somewhat selfish individualism of those who pray. When the burden of human praying is "O Lord, give me this or that," it is hardly to be expected that society should derive any benefit from it. But let men pray for ability to pull themselves together in order that they may make a better go of life; let them pray for courage to say what ought to be said and to do what ought to be done; let them pray for clear vision—"light, more light"; let them seek through prayer to turn away from lesser things and fix their attention upon the supreme thing. Will prayer in that event have social consequences? It is bound to have them. Would it be too much to say that the prayers of Jesus have changed the moral climate of the world? In prayer the Master made his great decision. In prayer he gathered strength and courage to do the thing which he had been commissioned to do. Because of what prayer did for him the whole world of men is becoming a different world.

If, then, the question be raised, What is the good of praying? must not the answer be, It all depends upon what you hope through prayer to accomplish. When it comes to the so-called world of nature, prayer not only does not get results but ought not to be permitted to get them, save indirectly by fortifying the human spirit in its great attempt to master its physical environment. But when it comes to the world of men, the power of prayer to get results is indisputable. If what you are chiefly concerned to do is to make the most of your own life and to secure for your fellows a favorable opportunity to make the most of their lives, then not to pray would be to leave unused the very greatest of available powers.

VIII

CHRISTIANITY AND RESPECTABILITY

TODAY, whenever someone says to a convivial company, "Let your conscience be your guide," there is apt to be a laugh. Why the laugh? Is it not because every member of that jovial group entertains a very lively and not ill-founded suspicion that conscience is not an altogether reliable guide? The cynical laugh is produced by the knowledge that before the evening is over, somebody, with only his conscience to guide him, will probably make a fool of himself.

In that which we call conscience, there are, it appears, two factors. There is, first, the conviction that one ought to do what is right; and then, there is an accompanying judgment as to what is right. Both factors are obviously essential to moral experience and achievement. If conscience should say to us, "Here is something which is right," and fail to add, "You ought therefore to do it," how ineffectual it would be! And if, on the other hand, conscience should say to us, "You ought to do what is right," but fail to give us any information as to what is right, how equally ineffectual it would be! But this necessity which is laid upon conscience to decide what is right under circumstances which, as often as not, are very complicated, precludes the possibility of conscience ever becoming an infallible guide.

The conviction that a man ought to do what is right always and everywhere is, of course, axiomatic, self-authenticating, beyond dispute. If anybody begins to dispute it, the thing to do is not to argue with him, but to send for the police and have him searched. Not so, however, the judgment as to what is right. At that point you have many chances to make a mistake. With utter honesty St. Paul could say, "I have lived before God in all good conscience until this day." Yet at one time in his life he had conscientiously done something which he was later with his whole soul to deplore. He had believed that he ought to hunt down Christians, men and women both, and clap them into prison. He had done this with rigor and vigor. Under the circumstances, the rigor and vigor were probably commendable, but what must be said of the judgment?

Now the fact can hardly be denied that a man's moral judgment is very largely influenced by the moral sense of the community in which he lives. If he lives in a community that sanctions foot-binding, he is very apt to have his daughter's feet bound. If he lives in a community which sanctions child marriage, he is very apt to have her married at a very early age. If his community sanctions polygamy, he is apt to be a polygamist. If it sanctions slavery, he is apt to be a slave holder. And in all good conscience, too! In the year 1860, the conscience of the Southerner told him that slavery was right, because that was the conviction which generally prevailed throughout the South; and the conscience of the Northerner told him that slavery was wrong, because that was the conviction which generally prevailed throughout the North. There were, to be sure, some persons in the South whose conscience was troubled by slavery, and some persons in the North whose conscience was undisturbed by it. It is only fair for us to remember that Robert E. Lee had freed his slaves in Virginia when Stephen A. Douglas was saying, in Illinois, that it made no difference to him whether slavery was voted up or down. But, generally speaking, a man's judgment in respect to the moral character of negro slavery was determined by the moral sentiment of the section of the country in which he had been born and brought up.

Nor is the situation with respect to moral judgment any different today. My judgment as to what is right for a man in my profession to do is very largely influenced by what men in my profession actually do. Your judgment as to what is right for a man to do in business is bound to be influenced by what men in business actually do. In any social group, whatever is commonly done is commonly condoned. In political circles, if petty graft is generally winked at, the conscience of the average politician does not protest very rigorously against it. On college campuses, if "petting" is almost universally indulged in, it is only the occasional student whose conscience is disturbed by it. In social circles where cocktails are considered to be an indispensable preparation for the enjoyment of a good dinner and a pleasant evening, it is only the very exceptional individual who is "queer" enough to refuse them. In circles where smoking on the part of women is generally countenanced, even nice old grandmothers have been known to risk at least one "cough in a car-load."

Very few persons look with suspicion upon any idea or practice which has been accepted by the group to which they belong, or view with favor any idea or practice which is frowned upon by the group to which they belong. There is an old saying that possession is ninety-nine points of the law. Might it not also be said that common practice is ninety-nine points of respectability? *Respectability is conformity to whatever is regarded as right and proper by the major portion of the particular group to which you belong.*

It is obvious that respectability makes no uniform demand. When it comes to such virtues as honesty and politeness, a good deal depends upon your racial inheritance. If you happen to belong to one of the Teutonic families, respectability requires you to tell the truth even under circumstances where it is a bit difficult to tell the truth and be polite. But if you happen to belong to one of the Latin families, respectability requires you to be polite even under circumstances where it is difficult to be polite and tell the truth. A Scotchman feels that he has done enough if he has told the truth. A Frenchman or a Venezuelan feels that he has done enough if he has been polite. If the group to which you belong is one by which the drinking of intoxicating liquors is held to be sinful, respectability requires you to be a total abstainer. But if it is one by which the drinking of intoxicating liquors is held to be morally blameless, respectability requires you to do what? Today, it requires you to use liquors in moderation, but the time is not very far past when, as a member of such a group, you might have gotten gloriously drunk without diminishing in the least your claim to respectability. When it comes to theological matters, a good deal depends upon your social connections. If you are surrounded by so-called fundamentalists, not only intellectual but moral respectability requires you to accept, without any mental reservations, such doctrines as the Verbal Inspiration of the Scriptures and the Virgin Birth of Christ. If you are surrounded by so-called modernists, at least intellectual respectability requires you to separate yourself from certain traditional religious beliefs. And when it comes to your political or your economic opinions, how very much depends upon your social status! If you belong to the so-called upper classes, you can hardly be respectable and vote the socialist ticket. If, on the other hand, you belong to the so-called lower classes, you can hardly be respectable and not be in some sense a socialist.

It is obvious that respectability makes no uniform demand. Is it not equally obvious that it makes no heroic demand? In any case, respectability is simply the expression of the crowd mind, and certainly it requires no great amount of courage to go along with the crowd. To be an out and out prohibitionist among people clamoring for light wines and beer, or to be a modificationist among thoroughgoing prohibitionists would require a little courage. To be a modernist among fundamentalists, or a fundamentalist among modernists; to be a socialist among capi-

talists or a defender of the capitalistic system among so-
cialists; to be a pacifist among militarists or a militarist
among pacifists would require a good deal of courage. But
to conform to whatever is regarded as right and proper by
the majority of the group to which you belong; to be, in a
word, respectable, requires no courage at all. It is merely
to think what your crowd is thinking, to say what your
crowd is saying, and to do what your crowd approves.

Nevertheless, there is a good deal to be said for respectability. If it makes no uniform demand, and no heroic
demand, it at least makes some demand to which the
average individual feels obliged to measure up. Respectability is, indeed, a kind of adjustment to your environment,
not to your total environment as we shall see later on, but
at least to your local environment, and any man who ad-
justs himself to his local environment can manage to get
along fairly well in this world. He will not run counter
to the law; he will keep out of jail. He will not run counter to public opinion; he will keep out of trouble. If he
happens to possess a flair for finance he may make a lot
of money. If he happens to possess unusual executive ability he may be entrusted with the management of great institutions. If he happens to possess gifts which appeal to the
imagination of the multitude, or are useful to the holders of
power, he may be elevated to high political position; he
may be permitted to sit in the seats of the mighty, envied
by many, respected by most. Respectability is not to be
despised. In many cases it represents a hard-won moral
achievement. It stands for a goal which the race has

reached only very slowly and very painfully. To say of some man that he is at least respectable is, after all, to say a good deal. It is certainly better to measure up to the requirements of respectability than to fall below them. It is better to be respectable than to be disreputable.

But is respectability enough? Viewing the matter historically, we can, I think, readily see that respectability alone would never have brought civilization up to the point which it has now reached. In a society which sanctioned polygamy, respectable men married only as many women as the law permitted, and retained them or divorced them as the law required. But it never occurred to them to ask, "Is polygamy the highest and loveliest form of family life which civilization might conceivably evolve?" In a society which sanctioned slavery, respectable people treated their slaves with a good deal of kindness. They did all they could to minimize the cruel aspects of human bondage. But it never occurred to them to question whether the institution of slavery had been ordained by God, whether perchance it was not being condemned by God. Respectability conforms to existing standards of right, but never asks whether these standards are themselves right. In a world composed entirely of merely respectable persons civilization would stand still, precisely for the reason that it would never occur to anybody to suppose that there could or should be any advance.

There is a story connected with the British landing at Gallipoli which is highly significant. On one of the barges being used by the landing party were two chaplains, one a

Wesleyan, the other a Roman Catholic. As the men on that barge disembarked and were wading to the shore, one of them was shot down. The Wesleyan started to go to his assistance. His fellow chaplain sought to dissuade him, saying, "You must not think of it. It is sheer madness. You are going to certain death." But the Wesleyan disengaged himself from the other's grasp. "I have got my orders," he said. "They came from a higher command than yours." As he reached the shore and was stooping over to assist the wounded soldier, he himself was shot dead. Immediately the priest sprang after him. The officer in charge of the landing party cried, "Stop. I forbid you to go. We are losing entirely too many men." But the priest went on, stopping only long enough to explain, "You heard what my Protestant comrade said. I, too, have gotten my orders from a higher command." Is not that story a significant parable of human progress? Human progress has been made only when some man, taking his orders from a "higher command" than the contemporary conscience, has dared to go beyond the requirements of respectability.

Now, many of us who profess to be Christians are, after all, little more than respectable persons. To whatever is considered right and proper by our own social group we conform. We think what our crowd thinks, and say what our crowd says, and do what our crowd approves. And yet, we are the professed disciples of a man who said to his contemporaries, "Except your righteousness shall exceed the righteousness of the Scribes and Pharisees (eminently re-

spectable persons) ye shall in nowise enter into the Kingdom of God"; and who said, "For if ye love them that
love you, what reward have ye? Do not even the publicans
the same? And if ye salute your brethren only, what do
ye more than others? Do not even the gentiles the same?
Ye therefore shall be perfect as your heavenly father is perfect." Beyond dispute, Jesus called for something more
than respectability. He insisted that it is absolutely impossible to build a heaven on earth with people who are
content to do nothing more than the majority of folk
are willing to do.

I suggest therefore that we dare to put to ourselves that
searching question of the Master, "What do ye more than
others?" We may well begin with the precise situation
in which this question was raised. If you love only people
who love you, if you salute your brothers only, what do you
more than others? In order to be respectable we must, of
course, be kind to people who are kind to us. We must
not hurt anybody who belongs to our own social group.
But in order to be respectable it is not necessary for us to
be kind to people who are unkind to us; nor is it necessary
for us to refrain from practices and policies which, in certain indirect but none the less vital ways, do hurt people
whom we never see. There are young men who wouldn't
think of going too far with any girl who belongs to their
own social group, but who may and do, without any loss
of caste, go entirely too far with girls who belong to a
different social group. There are older men who could not
be hired to hurt anybody who moves in their own social

circle, but who may and do, without any loss of respect, consent to practices which make life hard for thousands of men and women and little children whom they do not personally know.

Nothing is more characteristic of respectability than its habit of limited concern. The respectable man is concerned for his wife and children. If his father and mother are still alive, he is concerned for them. He is concerned also for his friends and business associates. He is concerned for his country when he thinks of it, not in relation to all its citizens, but in relation to those who constitute his own social group. But there his concern stops. He is not concerned for all sorts and conditions of men. He is not concerned for mankind. Such a man may be altogether honest in his belief that he is a Christian, and may keenly resent the suggestion that he is not. But how will he meet that searching question of the Master, "If ye love them that love you . . . if ye salute your brethren only, what do ye more than others? Do not even the very pagans the same?"

In this same connection Jesus said, "Give to him that asketh thee." And it is easily possible to make this saying of his appear ridiculous. One may conjure up a number of situations in which it would be sheer folly to give to him that asketh thee. It is only fair, however, to remember that when Jesus flung out that great word, "Give," he was not delivering a lecture on the theory and practice of benevolence, he was presenting a challenge to the hearts of men. He was asking men to "face up," as we now say, to the need of the world and then, in heaven's name, to do something to relieve it. If he had stopped to hedge his statement about with all sorts of qualifications, if he had taken time to point out the undeniable danger of unintelligent and indiscriminate giving, the world long since would have forgotten what he said. But, "Give," said he, and his word is immortal. Men remembered it throughout the first century. They did not forget it in the second century, and in our twentieth century it is still challenging the hearts of men.

The privilege of giving is not confined to the giving of money, but money needs to be given. With money you can build and maintain hospitals that will minister to the physical ills of men. With money you can establish schools and colleges—circles of light, centers of culture, fostering mothers of the intellectual life. With money you can build and maintain churches, the very humblest of which will suggest to weary and heavy-laden folk that, beyond the world which reveals itself to the senses, there is a world of spirit to which they may turn in hours of need and find rest and comfort and peace. With money you can go to the ends of the earth with the illuminating and up-lifting gospel of Christ; or you can send a representative who will labor to lift a civilization out of superstition and selfishness into a more abundant life. With money you can do all of these things; without it you can do none of them. Money undoubtedly needs to be given.

But notice in this connection a very significant fact. In the world today, you can be perfectly respectable and not

give very much. Some people may think that you are
not as generous as you might be. A few may go even so
far as to say outright that you are inclined to be parsimoni-
ous. But nobody will say or even think that you are not
respectable. Not even yet do the canons of respectability
require a man to be very generous in the giving of money.
It is still possible to be respectable and stingy. Are there
not thousands of perfectly respectable persons, with incomes ranging from five to fifty thousand dollars a year,
who consider that they have discharged their full debt
to society when they have made a pitiful subscription to
some church or charity? Are there not tens of thousands
of perfectly respectable persons whose position with respect to giving is not, "What is the very most that I could
give," but "What is the very least that I can manage
to give and get by?"

Suppose, then, that some of us who profess to be Christians take a very similar position. Suppose that we, too,
are in the habit of asking, not, "How much could I give,"
but, "How little may I give and not be too severely criti-
cized?" In that event, what do we more than others?
Wherein are we different from the multitude of respectable
folk outside the churches who make no claim to be followers of Christ?

He who said, "Give to him that asketh thee," gave
something more than money; he gave himself. There is
need that a man should give his money. There is an even
greater need that he should give himself. To realize the
truth of that statement, all you need to do is to let your

imagination conjure up a world in which nobody was willing to give himself—no preacher, or teacher, or physician, or nurse, or settlement house worker, or anybody else. What a world that would be! The name of it would be hell.

At this point the nature of the Christian demand is beyond dispute. "Not to be ministered unto, but to minister" —that is the Christian demand, and there are no reservations in its application. Christianity requires a clergyman to think more of his congregation than of his salary. It demands of a teacher that he shall think more of his pupils than he does of his pay check. It demands of a physician that his first concern shall be, not his fee, but his patient; and it demands of a business man that his first concern shall be his responsibility to the community, not his own personal profit. When, in that notable address which he delivered at the dedication of the Harvard School of Business Administration, Mr. Owen D. Young declared that "the ministers of our business, like the ministers of our churches, should appreciate their responsibility," he was voicing the Christian demand.

But that is not the demand of respectability. Respectability does not require you to go into the business or professional world "not to be ministered unto but to minister." When the head of a great sugar corporation says, "It is, I think, quite fair to get out of the consumer all that you can consistent with the business proposition," there may be some people who wish that he had not said it, or at least that it had not gotten into the newspapers, but nobody feels constrained to remark that he is not respectable. It is still possible to be respectable and selfish. Suppose, then, that when it comes to the point where we touch life most deeply and continuously, namely, at the point of our job, some of us who profess to be Christians are motivated, not by a desire to give and serve, but only by a desire to get all that we can for ourselves. What in that event do we more than others? Are we not governed by the same motives, swayed by the same passions, devoted to the same ends as are the great majority of respectable folk who make no profession of Christianity?

Consider one more situation to which this question of Jesus applies. I should like to quote again from that notable address by Mr. Owen D. Young:

Perhaps some day we may be able to organize the human beings engaged in a particular undertaking so that they truly will be the employer buying capital as a commodity in the market at the lowest price. It will be necessary for them to provide an adequate guaranty fund in order to buy their capital at all. If that is realized, the human beings will then be entitled to all the profits over the cost of capital. I hope the day may come when these great business organizations will truly belong to the men who are giving their lives and their efforts to them, I care not in what capacity. Then they will use capital truly as a tool and they will be all interested in working it to the highest economic advantage. Then an idle machine will mean to every man in the plant who sees it an unproductive charge against himself. Then every piece of material not in motion will mean to the man who sees it an unproductive

charge against himself. Then we shall have zest in labor, provided the leadership is competent and the division fair. Then
we shall dispose, once and for all, of the charge that in industry
organizations are autocratic and not democratic. Then we
shall have all the opportunities for a cultural wage which the
business can provide. Then, in a word, men will be as free in
cooperative undertakings and subject only to the same limita-
tions and chances as men in individual businesses. Then we
shall have no hired men. That objective may be a long way
off, but it is worthy to engage the research and efforts of the
Harvard School of Business.

Here is a man who is not content to take and leave the
world as he finds it. He is trying to visualize a somewhat different and better world. Is not that undeniably
what Christianity would have a man do? "After this
manner pray ye, Thy Kingdom come, thy will be done,
on earth as it is done in heaven." Could any man sincerely
offer that prayer and not sometimes try to visualize a somewhat different and better world?

But respectability does not ask a man to offer any such
prayer as that. It is perfectly possible to be respectable
and be content with things as they are. Are you a professional man? You need not even try to elevate the
standards in your profession. Are you a business man?
You need not even venture to ask whether it would be
possible or desirable to build business on a somewhat different foundation from that on which it now rests. Suppose,
then, that some of us who profess to be Christians never
permit ourselves to question the legitimacy of the existing

order, never allow ourselves to visualize a somewhat better order. What in that case do we more than others? Wherein do we differ from the multitude of men who live and die content to leave the world as they found it?

Respectability calls for conformity to existing standards. Christianity calls for a lifting up of standards. Respectability bids you go the first mile which the law requires you to go or public opinion constrains you to go. Christianity bids you go the second mile which only a daring idealism imposes. Respectability says, "Be as good as the average." Christianity says, "Live above the average. Be better than the average man is content to be. Do more than the average man is willing to do."

As a matter of fact, the Christianity of Christ has dared to say to all sorts and conditions of men, "Ye therefore shall be perfect as your heavenly father is perfect." Some one may be thinking that that is going a bit too far, that that is an absurd, impossible, quixotic demand. But stop for a moment to consider what it means. We said a while back that respectability means adjustment to one's environment; but we were careful to add, "not to one's total environment." A man's total environment is not, after all, that little group of human beings with whom he daily associates. His total environment includes all the greatest and noblest lives that are being lived in this world. It includes all the greatest and noblest lives that have ever been lived in this world. It includes the very best that has ever been thought and done in the world. A man's total environment is God!

By adjusting yourself to your local environment you can manage to get along fairly well. You can keep out of jail, avoid trouble, make money, hold office, inspire envy, and command respect. But unless and until you adjust yourself to your total environment—God—you can never climb to life's highest peak and know the joy and the peace of Christ. How very disappointing the New Testament would be if it did not contain that heroic challenge, "Ye, therefore, shall be perfect as your heavenly father is perfect."

Among the solid certainties of life are these three. First: the one hope of social progress lies in the possibility that increasing numbers of men and women will dare to go beyond the requirements of respectability; that they will see something which the multitude of men has not yet seen, and go after it. Second: the determination to go after something better always has involved, and always will involve, the possibility of sacrifice. In one of his stimulating essays, John Brierly calls attention to the fact that the prisons of the world have, historically, housed two types of people, the worst and the best. He refers by way of illustration to those three crosses on Golgotha, two of which held the bodies of thieves, the third the body of God's Messiah. The thieves were there because they had fallen below the requirements of respectability. Jesus was there because he had risen above them. But third: the determination to go after the best involves also the possibility of a peace and joy and inner content which merely respectable people never know. In pulpit or pew, on college campus or board of trade, the man who goes after the best may taste a little of the bitter sweat of Gethsemane and know a little of the awful loneliness of Calvary; but in the end he will experience the triumph of an Easter morning!

For many of us, perhaps, the most searching and important of all questions is just this: Am I purposing to be merely a respectable person, or, God helping me, am I purposing to be a Christian?

IX

REFORMER, REFORM YOURSELF

NO doubt you will quote to me this proverb, "Physician, heal thyself." Luke 4:23.

The meaning of this ancient proverb is perfectly obvious. Anyone who professes to be able to heal other people ought to be able to heal himself. Anyone who is always preaching to other people ought occasionally to preach to himself. Anyone who is trying to reform the world ought certainly to reform himself. Let the physician take his own medicine. Let the parson practice what he preaches. Let the reformer begin with himself.

Now, the number of would-be reformers in this world is certainly very large. It is probably equal to the total adult population of the globe. Is there any husband among us who is not seeking to reform his wife, or any wife who is not seeking to reform her husband? Are there any parents who are not seeking to reform their children, or any children fourteen years of age and upwards who are not seeking to reform their parents? Is there any teacher who is not seeking to reform some of his students or any student who would not like to reform some of his teachers? And of course there is no preacher who is not seeking to reform his congregation and no congregation who would not count it all joy to reform their preacher.

This universal desire to make over those about us is due in part to the well-known fact that like craves like. We like to have people agree with us and dislike to have them differ from us. Among the things that every woman knows is that a declaration of intellectual independence is apt to produce a civil war. The so-called attraction of opposites that is supposed to lead to many a marriage does not apparently include opposite opinions on live issues. We can hardly endure the thought that any body who is intimately associated with us should entertain an opposite opinion on a live issue. His apparent conviction that he is right and we wrong nettles us; it appears to be too serious a reflection upon our own judgment. So we try to bring him around to our way of thinking. We try, that is to say, to reform him; and if we succeed, we believe that a great victory has been won for the cause of truth and righteousness.

There is also another and perhaps worthier reason for this universal desire to reform people. Undoubtedly a great many people need to be reformed. It is only the simple truth to say that they are not all that they ought to be. They are lazy, or thankless, or thoughtless; they are conceited, or petty, or domineering; they are timid, or selfish, or dishonest. Can we afford to stand by and do nothing? We can not. For their own sakes, as well as for the world's sake, these mal-formed individuals ought to be reformed.

Nor is it only individuals who stand in need of reformation. Without very much fear of contradiction one might venture to say that there is no institution today that would not profit by the right kind of reformation. Consider the church, for instance. A few years ago I published a little book under the title, "What Must the Church Do To Be Saved?" and at least two high-placed ecclesiastics did me the honor to take it seriously and to denounce it in public. One of them, who afterwards acknowledged that he hadn't gone to the trouble of reading the book, maintained that the title alone was enough to damn it. But nobody, I take it, would venture to say that any church today is a perfect incarnation of the spirit of Jesus. And what shall be said of schools, and colleges, and businesses, and industries? What shall be said of France, and Germany, and Great Britain, and the United States? Could it be successfully maintained concerning any one of these great human institutions that it is all that it ought to be?

The number, therefore, of would-be reformers is not to be wondered at; nor is it to be deplored. We ought to be glad and thankful that so many persons are eager to make this world of ours a little better place in which to live. We ought even, no doubt, to be glad and thankful that so many persons are eager to make us a little easier to live with. Were it not for the presence of a multitude of folk who are never satisfied with it and who are ever trying to change it, the world would be worse than it is. Were it not for a few persons who are never satisfied with us, we ourselves, no doubt, would be worse than we are.

But reformation, like charity, begins at home. If it does not begin there, it is not likely to get anywhere; because, for one reason, the reformer himself is partly the product of the very situation which he is eager to reform. No man can live continually in an imperfect society and remain totally unaffected by its imperfections. Its misconceptions color at least to some extent his own thinking. Its prejudices influence at least to some degree his own attitudes. Its injustices leave at least some mark upon his own spirit. The world which undeniably needs to be reformed includes among other persons its would-be reformers. If ever the world as a whole is to be made over they too must be made over.

There is, moreover, a certain incongruity in the spectacle of an unreformed reformer attempting to reform other people. There is, indeed, so great an incongruity that his efforts are likely to prove unavailing. What he is speaks so loud that people cannot hear what he says. There are many parents who would like to reform their children; yet the chief trouble with many children is their parents. If the parents were different, the children would be different. A boy under provocation uses the same tone in addressing his sister which many more times than once he has heard his father use in addressing his mother. Whereupon, his father says to him sharply, "You can't speak to your sister like that. I won't have it." And the boy thinks, if he does not say, "But you talk like that to mother." Not long ago an "eighth-grader" came to school with a bottle— not a milk bottle! The principal, who knew his business, said nothing to the boy; but what he said to the boy's father and to the fathers of certain other boys in that school was precisely what needed to be said. Concerning any parent who is attempting to correct in his children the very faults which in his own life he leaves uncorrected, would it not be fair to observe that what he is speaks so loud that the youngsters cannot hear what he says? And would it not be perfectly right and proper to make a similar observation concerning temperance reformers who in their denunciation of people who hold an opposite opinion use exceedingly intemperate language? And concerning peace advocates who advocate peace in a manner and spirit which are provocative of strife?

David Noyes Wescott's famous character, David Harum, used to advise: "Do unto others as they would do unto you and do it first." But David Harum was talking about horse-trading, whereas we are talking about reforming, and for all would-be reformers would not this be good advice: Be what you want other people to be and be it first? To the distinguished English missionary, Mr. Charles Andrews, Mahatma Gandhi one day remarked that the great difficulty with westerners is that they start doing before being. It would, no doubt, have been a little less polite, but none the less true, had he remarked that the chief trouble with us is that we start *talking* before being. Would he not indeed have remained quite within the bounds of truth had he ventured to suggest that, unconsciously perhaps, we have even *substituted* fine talking for fine living? We have said, for example, a great many fine things about the fatherhood of God and the brotherhood of man, and then we have exploited or snubbed, or, at best, patronized persons of another color. We have likewise said a lot of beautiful things about unselfishness and love and forgiveness, and then what haven't we done in repudiation of these noble sentiments? What Gandhi politely hinted at, the wisest and best of our own missionaries are now saying openly and bluntly, namely, that what we are speaks so loud that the East cannot hear what we say. If we really desire to christianize the Orient, we must begin living Christianity, not merely talking about it. We must be what we want Orientals to be and be it first. Today, not without reason, might the East say to the West, "Reformer, reform yourself."

To certain would-be reformers Jesus once put a question which was at once serious and humorous. He said to them, "Why beholdest thou the mote in thy brother's eye and considerest not the beam in thine own eye?" The humor of this question is more clearly brought out by Professor Moffatt who translates, "Why do you note the splinter in your brother's eye and fail to see the plank in your own eye?" And the Master went on to suggest to these would-be reformers that if they would first take the planks out of their own eyes they could see better how to take the splinters out of other people's eyes.

That many of us who are eager to reform others do fail to see that we ourselves need reforming, it would be hard to deny. "Isn't it too bad," we say, "that he is so terribly conceited?" and never suspect that there is any conceit in ourselves. Or we sometimes say, "What a pity it is that he who has so much gives so little," and fail to realize that we ourselves, in proportion to what we have, give very little. How often, too, do we condemn in others what we condone in ourselves. When somebody else loses his temper we reflect that he ought to have exercised a little more self-control. When we ourselves lose our temper we reflect that we have come home very tired; we have been working very hard; we have, indeed, been slaving day and night for people who might have shown a little more consideration. Why other people should occasionally exhibit irritability and peevishness we simply cannot understand. Won't they ever grow up? They are certainly old enough to stop acting like spoiled babies. But when we ourselves "do the baby act," people ought to remember that we have a head-ache, or that we are hypersensitive. Oh, hypersensitiveness, how many ugly faults are maintained in thy name!

Why do we thus see the splinter in our brother's eye and fail to see the plank in our own eye? Is it because we are brazen, unblushing hypocrites? Not at all. Bad as we are, we are not that bad. Is it not rather because, when it comes to our own faults, we have a real mental blind spot? A well-known advertisement has persistently warned us that we may have something very objectionable and not know that we have it—something so objectionable that it may militate against employment, love, marriage, and social success. Well, the awful possibility that we may have something very objectionable and not know that we have it is not confined to the one thing mentioned in the advertisement. We may, for instance, have a bad disposition and not know that we have it. We may have fallen into the habit of nagging people day after day and honestly resent being told that we do it. We may be indulging in the expensive and debilitating luxury of self-pity and never suspect that we are feeling a bit too sorry for ourselves. We may be conceited and honestly believe that we are humble. We may be obstinate and suppose that we are courageous. And who ever suspects that he is opinionated, or narrow-minded, or snobbish? Who ever suspects that he is severe in his judgments of other people and lenient in his judgment of himself? We have, undoubtedly, a mental blind spot that keeps us from seeing the plank in our own eye.

What then can we do? We could, if we were so disposed, listen occasionally to the kindly criticism of our friends. But seldom if ever are we so disposed. Even though we have invited criticism we do not like it when we get it. We resent it, are hurt by it; and immediately we place ourselves on the defensive. Instead of considering the possibility that what has been said to us in all kindness may be true, our instantaneous reaction is, "It can't be true of me, and it is most unkind of her to suggest it." Let any wife say to any husband that he might have spoken or acted differently, and the response is likely to be, "As usual, I am the one to blame!"

The psychological fact of the matter probably is that in order to carry on at all in this world, it is necessary for us to develop a certain amount of self-confidence and self-esteem. If we utterly distrusted ourselves we would hardly have enough courage to face what we have to face and do what we have to do. It is, therefore, something of a shock to be told that we are not all that we supposed we were. If we are not as big or as good as we thought we were, how can we meet the demands of life? Criticism appears to threaten that whole mechanism of self-confidence and self-esteem which we have carefully built up as a means of protecting ourselves against the slings and arrows of outrageous fortune.

The danger however is only in appearance, not in reality. If we have anything objectionable in us and do not know that we have it, the sooner we find out that we have it the better for all concerned. Nothing is ever finally lost by a frank, brave facing of facts, even though they be unpleasant facts about one's self. That great saying of Jesus, usually quoted in another connection, is applicable likewise in this connection: "Ye shall know the truth and the truth shall make you free." A knowledge of the truth concerning ourselves might conceivably set us free from many a cramping limitation and enable us to become a bigger and better person than we now are. If only we could get rid of the idea that there is some awful stigma attached to any acknowledgment that one has been in the wrong! If only we could get hold of the idea that what old-fashioned people call "confession of sin" and "hearty repentance" is but a normal and necessary part of one's intellectual and moral development! A frank confession that in certain specified particulars he has been at fault, accompanied by a sincere desire for improvement in those particulars, far from diminishing a man's self-respect, ought immeasurably to increase it; for what it means is that he is big enough to acknowledge a limitation and brave enough to undertake its correction.

Just here, however, appears the very disturbing question whether it is really possible for a mature person to effect any radical change in his life. Granted that you are not all that you ought to be and not all that you supposed you were, what are you to do about it? What can you do about it? A few days ago I read an advertisement which ought, no doubt, to have given me a great deal of encouragement. It assured me that at the special low price of only three dollars I might purchase a volume which would tell me how to become a fascinating force in social life, a powerful, dynamic, commanding figure in my profession, a more popular, more prosperous, more gloriously successful person than I ever supposed I could be. And accompanying this startling statement was the author's express guarantee that if within five days of the receipt of this marvelous volume I did not experience a decided change in my personality I would not owe him a cent. I was tempted to buy the book. (I had three dollars.) I was also tempted to communicate with the Postmaster General of the United States and with the Society for the Prevention of Cruelty to Animals. When I considered all the poor, ambitious, pathetically credulous people who must be buying this book (else how could the author afford to publish a full page advertisement in a leading magazine?) I felt, like the would-be reformer I am afraid I am, that something ought to be done about it. But my complete scepticism as to the value of any such remedy as this advertisement describes leaves me still confronted by the question: Is it possible for a man as old as I am to effect any radical change in his own life? If one is opinionated, or conceited, or lazy, or selfish, or narrow-minded, is there any ghost of a chance that he may remodel himself to any appreciable degree?

Well, the old saying that manners make the man is now being revised to read: "Habits make the man." If you have formed the habit of always being late, or of always finding fault, or of always making excuses for yourself, or of always putting off till tomorrow what ought to be done today, or of always looking on the dark side of things, then you are the sort of person whom such habits produce. One of the most confident convictions of modern psychology is that a man is precisely what his habits are. That conviction not only affords us a relatively simple definition of such terms as "self" and "personality," it gives us a fairly clear understanding of how to change one's "self" or "personality." If a man is what his habits are, obviously the way to change the man is to change his habits. The question, therefore, with which we are really confronted is just this: Is it possible for a mature person to change his habits? Is it possible for him to form new habits, the sort of habits which he ought to form?

Now, the possibility of forming new physical habits is generally conceded. Even after forty, a man may learn how to play golf. He may develop all the queer, funny, and peculiar physical habits which must be formed by anyone who would take a slender stick and drive a small ball in the right direction. During the past quarter of a century hundreds of thousands of adults have learned to drive motor cars. They have developed all the new physical habits which the driving of a motor car calls for. Recently, in order to test one of his own pet theories, the President of an eastern university, who had never before drawn a bow across strings, undertook in sixty days to learn how to play the cello, and was actually able at the end of two months to play fairly well such compositions as Händel's "Largo" and Massenet's "Elegy." Beyond dispute, we may, even in middle life, form new and desirable physical habits.

Why then should it be considered impossible to form new mental habits? Mental habits, no doubt, may not be so easily formed. But by the same process by which one forms a new physical habit might he not form a new mental habit? In order to play a good game of golf a man must exercise self-control. If he can exercise self-control on the golf links when he is dealing with a rubber ball, what is to prevent him from exercising self-control in his office when he is dealing with his subordinates, or even in his home when he is dealing with his wife and children? By the same process by which he acquires ability to control his muscles might he not acquire ability to control his temper? In order safely to drive a motor car through a traffic jam a man must continually look out for other motorists and pedestrians. He must be careful not to run

into them or over them. And if he can look out for other
people when he has a motor car under his control, could
he not look out for other people when he has a big business
under his control? By the same process by which a man
acquires the ability to make his way through traffic without running over anybody, might he not acquire the ability
to make his way through life without running over anybody?

The reason why we do sometimes form new and desirable
physical habits and do not more often form new and desirable mental habits is just because, in the one case, we
make a determined and persistent effort to succeed and,
in the other case, we do not try very hard. If only we were
as resolutely determined to make a success of our home
life as we are of our golf game, our children before long
would be saying, "What has happened to father? He is
so different!"

Reformer, reform yourself. It is not an unreasonable
demand. It is a demand which should and can be met—
with the aid of religion. In order to form new mental
habits a man needs religion because, for one reason, he
needs a strong and compelling desire to form them. As
we remarked a moment ago, we do form new physical
habits because we want to form them and try hard to
form them, and we fail to form new mental habits because we do not to the same degree either want or try
to form them. For the building of a new personality, a
gloriously better personality, the first and all-essential re-
quirement is a strong and compelling desire for such a

personality. Can religion produce such a desire? It can.
The Book of Job, which Tennyson pronounced the greatest poem in any language, ends in these words:

> I had heard of thee by the hearing of the ear;
> But now mine eye seeth thee:
> Wherefore I abhor myself,
> And repent in dust and ashes.

A man may, perhaps, see God without abhorring himself,
but can any man see God without wishing that he were a
somewhat better man? Let us suppose that what is meant
by "seeing God" is something like this: A selfish, self-centered, somewhat cynical and somewhat unhappy individual
meets someone who gives him a jolt—a teacher, perhaps,
who says: "Harvard University pays me for doing what
I would be only too glad to do without pay if I could
afford it"; or a medical missionary like Albert Schweitzer
who is seeking in Africa to reduce the amount of human
pain; or a devoted settlement-house worker like Miss Jane
Addams, who is seeking in Chicago to lift human life to
higher levels; someone who is manifestly unselfish and
manifestly happy too. He is obliged, therefore, to acknowledge that there is in this world such a thing as unselfishness. Indeed, once his eyes are open, he begins to
discover that there is, after all, a vast deal of loving-kindness
and self-forgetfulness. And presently he begins to suspect
that that is what lies deep down in the heart of the world;
that that is the secret of life, of joy and of peace. Such a
man has at last "seen God"; and if he does not despise him-

self, surely he will at least wish that he were a little more like that which his eyes have seen.

Religion renders a further service which is greatly needed. It helps to create an environment in which new and desirable mental habits may be formed. The best way to learn how to speak French or even good English is to associate with people who do speak it. The best way to acquire culture is to associate with people who have it. The best way to acquire the mental attitudes which Christianity calls for is to associate with people who have those mental attitudes. It would be going much too far to say that a man is altogether shaped by his environment. For every hundred instances which you can find where environment has shaped a man, surely you can find at least one instance where some man has shaped his environment. But the fact remains that all of us to some extent, and most of us to a large extent, are shaped by our environment; and for a multitude of folk this fact would be disheartening enough if their local, physical and social environment were the only environment in which they could live. But it is not. Beyond that narrowly circumscribed local environment lies the possibility of a far vaster environment which the imagination may create. Beyond that physical environment with its mean streets and shabby dwelling houses lies the possibility of a lovelier environment which the soul may create. Beyond that social environment, formed it may be by human pettiness and prejudice and passion, lies the possibility of an environment such as the saints of the centuries have formed. And notice: it is out and up into this vaster, lovelier, more inspiring environment that religion lifts a man. Do you live in a small town? Religion may extend your horizon. It may enable you to stand with Arnold Toynbee in the slums of London, or to travel with David Livingstone through the heart of Africa, or to visit the sick with Wilfred Grenfell along the coast of Labrador, or to labor with James Thoburn in the villages of India. Do you live on a narrow street in a run-down neighborhood and up on the "third floor back"? Religion may transport you. It may take you to the city of God, a city which is yet to be built, but which you may see even now through the eyes of faith, and in the building of which you may find refreshment for your thirsty spirit. Do you live among people whose taste is poor and whose standards are low? Religion may come to your assistance. It may enable you to live with the finest spirits of all the ages. Would it not, then, be altogether right and proper to say: *Reformer, reform yourself with the aid of religion?*

X

CHRISTIANITY IN A MACHINE AGE

SOME time ago, influenced more by curiosity than by hunger, I went into a small restaurant whose window advertisements informed me that all the food which was cooked there was prepared without the intervention of the human hand. It proved to be fortunate that I was more curious than hungry, but the experience was interesting and, I think, significant. Today, a perfectly enormous amount of work which used to be done by human hands and legs and backs is being done by machinery. To an extent which few if any of us fully appreciate, western civilization is machine-made.

Now, concerning a machine civilization there are many things to be said, and by no means all of them are uncomplimentary. A distinguished Chinese has recently told us that he discovered the border line between the civilizations of the East and the civilization of the West when, on his way to Europe, he arrived at Harbin in northern Manchuria. There are, it appears, two Harbins, one a native Oriental city, the other a Russian westernized city. Through the native Harbin he passed in a jinrikisha, propelled by man power. Through the Russian Harbin he passed in a taxicab, propelled by machine power. And he says that he, for his part, cannot see any particularly noble kind of spirituality in a civilization which tolerates such a terrible form of human slavery as the jinrikisha, or any particularly ignoble kind of materialism in a civilization where, thanks to science and machinery, the multitude of men have at least some time and strength to seek after the higher values of life.

In the medieval, hand-made civilizations of the East you have, so far as the masses of the people are concerned, abysmal poverty, scourging disease, and awful illiteracy. In the modern, machine-made civilization of the West you have a falling death rate, a growing literacy, and a common man who probably possesses more in the way of physical comfort and of cultural opportunity than was possessed by the common man in any other civilization known to history.

Nevertheless, there are in western civilization certain very grave dangers, of which one is the danger that men may lose sight of spiritual realities.

It seems to be natural, if not inevitable, that human beings should think of Reality in terms of the dominant factor in their environment. Ancient man, living in a world of autocrats and slaves, pictured his God as an omnipotent, capricious tyrant. Medieval man, living in a world of feudal lords and serfs, pictured his God as a mighty potentate of a feudalistic character. When, after the Protestant Reformation, western society lost its unity, the birth of nationalism influenced men's conception of Reality to such an extent that a British sea captain, when being pursued by a Dutch man-of-war, felt sure that the wind would change in his favor, for, said he, God cannot desert a fellow countryman. The appearance of political democracy likewise registered itself in a congenial conception of Reality. The monarch of the skies was shorn of much of his power and made responsible to some extent to the wishes of his subjects. Men who refused to submit to taxation without representation refused also to submit to damnation without explanation.

Today, once more, the dominant factor in man's environment is influencing his conception of Reality. A machine-made civilization is producing a mechanistic theory of life and the world. In some quarters we are being told that man himself is but a highly complicated machine, differing from other machines in degree but not in kind; able, to be sure, to reproduce himself and to some extent to repair himself when he gets out of order, but possessing no more of real freedom than is possessed by an automobile. Some, indeed, would have it that we must think of the universe itself as a kind of infinite machine.

Scientists themselves frankly admit that science in the main is concerned with but one aspect of Reality, that which is associated with time and space and may, therefore, be called its material aspect. But the tendency today is to assume that the material aspect of Reality is just about the only aspect which Reality has to present. Medical students who are pre-occupied with anatomical studies are likely to forget that a man is, after all, something more than flesh and bones and blood. A generation that is pre-occupied with machinery, and all those wonderful things which machinery is able to produce, is likely to assume that the aspect of Reality which is given in a machine is, if not the only aspect, at least and by far the most important one.

This daily occupation of our minds with the machine and its products is producing in us certain deplorable effects. It is, for one thing, causing us more and more to place our trust in mechanistic forces. The disposition to rely upon physical force is, to be sure, no new thing under the sun. Hundreds of years before the birth of Christ, a lone Hebrew prophet cried out, "Woe to them that go down to Egypt, that rely upon horses, and trust in chariots." But the temptation to rely upon horses and trust in chariots has become exceedingly great in an age which has produced cruisers and aeroplanes, machine guns and lethal gas. And if anyone feels disposed to ask, "Well, what of it?" the reply is that in the judgment of many persons whose opinion is entitled to be taken seriously this tendency to rely upon physical force is becoming alarmingly dangerous. It may result in the destruction of western civilization.

We refuse to rely upon spiritual forces because we are blind to spiritual realities. And our blindness to spiritual realities may sap our faith in the worth of life. Significantly enough, a machine-made civilization has produced an instrumental theory of knowledge. According to this instrumental theory, knowledge is not nor ever will be acquaintance with Eternal Truth. There is no Eternal

Truth with which one may become acquainted. Knowledge is simply a useful instrument for managing one's environment. And Bertrand Russell, who feels inclined to believe that this instrumental theory of knowledge may turn out to be true, also feels inclined to believe that it will eventually undermine all incentive for scientific pursuit. If there is nothing of any fundamental importance to find out, nothing eternally valid to be validated, why all the pother of scientific pursuit?

Nor is this the only question that is likely to be asked by people who lose sight of spiritual realities. The machine is powerful but it is not permanent. Every machine is destined soon or late to be scrapped. And the products of the machine, interesting and diverting though they are, possess nevertheless no permanence, nor any power permanently to satisfy the deepest longings of the human heart. Picture, then, a generation of men and women becoming increasingly absorbed in those material goods which machinery is able to produce, making incidentally the discovery that no number of machine-made products is able to heal a broken heart, and then one day waking up to the fact that there is, so far as they can see, nothing in all the world that is destined to endure. Is it not altogether likely that such men and women will presently be asking, not only concerning scientific investigation, but concerning any form of human striving, "What's the use?"

Here, then, is one grave danger in western civilization. Men may lose sight of spiritual realities, refuse to rely upon spiritual forces, and eventually suffer a disastrous loss of faith in the worth-whileness of the whole human adventure.

Another danger is that the machine may come to be thought of as possessing more importance than the man who operates it. Dependent as we now are upon machine production for so many of those conveniences which we have learned to look upon as necessities, we may fail to realize that we are even more dependent upon our fellow men. During recent years science has been able to perform miracles, but there is one miracle that not even science is likely to perform, namely, the production of a machine which will operate itself. I have all the small boy's fascinated delight in a locomotive. I never see a steaming locomotive without experiencing a thrill. But no locomotive ever built has been able to run itself. Venture, then, to imagine what would happen in this or any other country if all the engineers of all the locomotives of all the railroads should declare and make effective a general strike. We are indeed dependent upon our machines, under present conditions almost tragically so. But we are even more dependent upon our fellow men, as we are destined to find out if we fail to provide the human operators of machines with enough incentive to go on operating.

The danger of which we are now thinking has been pointed out in one of the most significant dramas which has appeared in recent years, "Rossum's Universal Robots." A great physiologist named Rossum discovers a substance which behaves like living matter, although its chemical composition is somewhat different. With this substance his son, a practical engineer, succeeds at last in producing a creature who looks and labors like a man. This creature, called a robot, is then manufactured by the thousands and sent to every country on the face of the earth to do the work of the world. Robots are intelligent, in some brands marketed at a higher price extraordinarily so, and before long they are found to be performing every operation which human beings have historically performed. But they are neither regarded nor treated as men, and when they are damaged beyond repair, they are scrapped like any other machine.

The robot, however, becomes too valuable to his human owner to be allowed needlessly to injure himself, and in order that he may not foolishly thrust his hand into a revolving wheel, he is made sensitive to pain. His sensitiveness to pain causes him to become so nearly human that he desires, and presently demands, to be treated as a man. By this time his manufacturers have become alarmed. They realize that this robot, physically more powerful than his human owner, and in some cases more intelligent too, may one day decide to unite with his fellow robots to secure the mastery of the world. An eleventh hour attempt is made to turn out national robots, speaking different languages, feeling different loyalties, in the hope that in any crisis these national robots may be persuaded to fight against one another rather than to unite against their human owners. This attempt, however, proves to be futile. The robots of the world do unite and destroy the civilization which produced them. A terrific parable, is it not?

During the past one hundred years we have been trying to lift illiteracy from the mind of the race. We have been going in for popular education. Some of us have even been dreaming of universal education. And, thanks to the educational process, the masses of mankind are beginning to experience wants, desires, ambitions, hopes which the multitude of men have never before known. How inevitable, then, a growing demand on the part of human beings who are becoming more sensitive that they shall be treated no longer as slaves or serfs or parts of machinery, but as men! And how very blind all persons of privilege who fail to see that this demand will have to be granted if production is to go on.

A third danger in a machine civilization is the danger of nervous exhaustion. Thanks to science and machinery, we of this generation possess more leisure than the men and women of any preceding generation were able to command. But what do we do with this unprecedented leisure? We certainly do not use it leisurely. Most of us use it feverishly. Many of us use it noisily. Not a few of us use it to "make whoopee." (For the benefit of any unenlightened member of the older generation, let me hasten to explain that "making whoopee" is the modern equivalent of "raising Cain.") When the day's work is over, how many persons belonging to our generation proceed in one way or another to make whoopee! And why? Because, for one important reason, they are the victims of jaded nerves—the sort of nerves that large scale machine production is likely to produce, not only in mechanics but in foremen, superintendents, and high-placed executives. As a matter of fact, the people today who appear to be making most whoopee are not those who have small salaries but those who have large incomes. The rich, certainly, no less than the poor are caught in the whirl of the machine; and beyond dispute a machine-driven civilization is altogether the most nerve-racking civilization which has ever appeared on this planet.

After you have been "stepping on it" all day you find it a bit difficult to settle down at night. Your nerves are all on edge. You crave excitement. You feel the need of a stimulant—coffee, tobacco, "hooch," a "wild party," something with a "kick" in it. Is not this, perhaps, the most interpretive of all explanations of modern whoopee, cubist art, and noisy jazz? Given the machine with its constant demand for speed and its frequent accompaniment of noise, and fatigue-poisoned bodies and minds are likely to crave crude excitements. After your typical "go-getter" has been going all day, with the understanding that unless he gets more orders this month than he got last month his territory will be taken away from him and given to someone else, it is hardly to be wondered at that when night comes he finds it extremely difficult to derive enjoyment from anything so leisured and quiet as a rewarding book or conversation.

The machine is getting on our nerves. It is making us irritable, and sometimes despondent.

But all this being conceded, what is to be done? Should we scrap the machine in order to avoid the danger that the machine may scrap us? However great that danger may be, my own guess is that we shall never scrap the machine. We shall never have the courage to do that. We are too dependent upon our machines for the conveniences of life. Let New York's subways be blocked for twenty-four hours, or Chicago's elevated trains be stopped, or Gary's steel mills be closed down, and millions of people will discover quickly enough how dependent they are upon the machine. But if we do not scrap the machine, we must make it our servant and refuse to let it become our master. As our servant, it may uplift us; as our master, it may destroy us. And my own belief is that the one only way in which we may hope to make the machine our servant is to take seriously the Christianity which we profess.

We need to become Christian in our thought of the universe in which we live. When it comes to the fundamental nature of the universe we can, at best, only form mental pictures which are confessedly inadequate. But we need to believe that a more adequate picture of what lies at the heart of the world may be found in a great human soul than may be found in any machine; that when a man stands face to face with life's final fact he will be nearer the truth if he repeats the words, "God and Father of our Lord Jesus Christ," than he will be if he repeats the words, "Infinite Machine." At this point, to be sure, someone may insist that even a great human soul, so-called, is, after all, but a highly complicated machine. But this surely represents an unproved hypothesis. If anyone chooses to believe it, I for my part would not have him arrested—except by the possibility that it may turn out to be stuff and nonsense, one of the temporary aberrations of an immature science which is still childishly fascinated with huge and powerful mechanical toys.

As a matter of fact, some of the very greatest of living scientists do not believe that there is no essential difference between a man and a machine. They believe that in all living forms there is at least some small power of choice, that this is, indeed, the secret of the whole evolutionary process, and that in man this power of choice, which no machine ever did or will possess, has become so great that, as Professor Mather has not hesitated to say, when a man makes up his mind he changes the course of history. It is, therefore, still pertinent to ask: Are we living in a universe whose fundamental nature is revealed in machines or one whose fundamental nature is revealed in great human souls?

That we need to believe the latter rather than the former goes, I think, without saying. And surely it is evident that our need is dictated by something far more important than any ecclesiastical concern. It is not that we need to become Christian in our thought of the universe in order to keep our churches going. It is rather that we need to do so in order to keep ourselves going. Venture to believe that the universe, including man himself, is but a machine, and you will find it increasingly difficult even by whistling to keep up your courage. But venture to believe that truth is not merely a convenient instrument but an eternal reality, that beauty is at once a human appreciation and a divine revelation, that love transcending mere sex interest and passion is something which the universe itself is striving to achieve, at least in human life, and you have something to live on, yes, and something to live for.

What is there to prevent a man from making the Christian faith his own? Any single fact which has been brought to light by modern science? No. What stands today in the way of the Christian faith is not our science but our lingering inhumanity to man. Every time you treat a human being as though he were not a man but merely some useful kind of machine you find it more difficult to believe that the universe itself is anything more than a machine. Every time you put your trust in physical forces you find it more difficult to believe in spiritual realities. We pay for our social cruelties by the loss of our religious convictions. We pay for our slums and our dirty, ugly factory towns by the obscuration of our vision of God. We pay for our trust in battle ships and bayonets, and our all too frequent willingness to use them for selfish ends, by losing sight of those spiritual verities and glories which alone have power to help us when our hearts begin to ache. The significance of the universe, if it has any significance, is, so far as we earth dwellers are concerned, revealed in men. To the extent that men appear to be significant the universe appears to be significant. To whatever extent we cause men to appear insignificant we find it difficult to believe that the universe is significant.

If, then, we say, "Let us look to the machine and its products," and do not say with far greater earnestness, "Let us look to the human operator of the machine and to his wife, his children," we shall be running not merely one great risk but two. There will be the risk that, having deprived this indispensable human operator of our machines of enough incentive to go on operating, production will begin to fall off. And there will be also the further danger that, having treated our fellow man, not as though he were a little lower than the angels, but rather as though he were a little lower than the machine which he operates, we shall have deprived not only him but ourselves of that all-essential faith in God which is so dependent upon faith in and respect for mankind.

In that powerful drama to which I referred a moment ago, the robots of the world destroy the civilization which produced them. Mercilessly they kill every human being with but a single exception—the one man who has always protested against their manufacture. Him they let live; and when one day they make the awful discovery that in the universal destruction which they have brought about the very secret of their own manufacture has been destroyed, they appeal to him to re-discover it. He tries to do so, but fails. And he and they are just on the point of giving up in despair when two of the robots, one man-like, the other woman-like, begin to reveal a dawning appreciation of beauty and a dawning affection for each other. The drama ends with the enormously important suggestion that the very greatest of all our human needs is not anything which machinery can produce, but rather beauty and love, those spiritual values which Christianity urges men to seek first.

It may further be said that the way to secure genuine and lasting relief for jaded nerves is not to make whoopee. One may be ever so gentle in his judgments of those of his fellows who can, apparently, find no better way in which to use their leisure than to go out and raise Cain. One may fully appreciate the fact that they are the victims of nerves that are worn to shreds by the speed and noise of a machine-driven civilization. One may suspect that the very worst kind of modern jazz, the kind that turns an orchestra into a group of circus performers, is an expression of nervous hysteria. One may believe that cubist art, crazy and meaningless though it appears to be, is probably a violent protest against the hypocrisies and cruelties of a civilization in which far too many human beings are ruthlessly sacrificed to the demands of the machine. But unless one is himself as blind as a bat he can hardly fail to see that in the making of whoopee his fellows are failing to find the relief which they seek.

It is, however, impossible to help them merely by protesting against what they are doing. One may protest until he is blue in the face and they will go on throwing wilder and wilder parties unless they can be made to see with Jesus that a man's life does not consist in the number of things which he possesses. My own belief is that the only way to secure relief for the jaded nerves of a machine-driven civilization is to change the character of human ambition from lust to possess something into eagerness to create something.

A telephone operator whose chief ambition is to possess and wear clothes that are cheap, factory-made imitations of the clothes worn by the wives and daughters of the rich may, at the close of her grueling day, be sorely tempted to go to a wild party. And if she does go, she will come home at two or three o'clock in the morning more weary and discouraged than she was when she went. But suppose some telephone operator should become eager to create something and should definitely set aside a part of her leisure time for that purpose. In almost any kind of creative activity would she not find a genuine relief for jaded nerves? Would she not find the same sort of satisfaction which the artist knows, and the man of science? Would she not, indeed, presently discover those mighty spiritual realities which reveal themselves to creative minds? And if only her example were followed by others, if only increasing numbers of persons should develop an eagerness to create something, is it not at least conceivable that bye and bye a whoopee-making civilization would develop a capacity for spiritual enjoyment and begin to experience the peace of God?

For twenty years I have been in a position where I was expected to stand for Christianity, and I think I may say with a reasonable degree of honesty that I have stood for it during all of those years. But never with such overwhelming conviction as I do today. My present belief is that Christianity is not merely one of the ways but the one only way in which we may escape nervous exhaustion, suicidal strife, and eventual despair. I am personally convinced that in Christianity alone may we find the faith and courage which we so desperately need to master the machine.

XI

RELIGION AND ART

NOW abideth truth, beauty, goodness, these three; and the greatest of these is—which? A scientist might answer "truth"; an artist, "beauty"; a saint, "goodness." But in any case we cannot afford to get along without any one of these three. Life without truth would be chaos, without beauty would be deformity, without goodness would be hell. As a matter of fact, truth and beauty and goodness interpenetrate. Mathematics is not only true but beautiful. The Sistine Madonna is not only beautiful but true. The soul of a Phillips Brooks is not only good but beautiful.

Now, if religion is to be what clearly it ought to be, the worship of the highest, it must come to terms with these three supreme values.

It must come to terms with truth. This does not mean that religion must accept immediately every proposition which is advanced in the name of science. It certainly does not mean that religion must accept those occasional pronouncements made by certain scientists who, not content with the finding of facts, venture to offer interpretations of facts which outrage religious feeling. The finding of facts is the province of science. The interpretation of facts is the province of philosophy. There is, of course, no reason under heaven why a scientist should not occasionally take an interesting excursion into the province of philosophy; but if he does, he ought clearly to understand that he is speaking, now, not as a scientist, but as a philosopher, and that his philosophy must take its chance along with other competing philosophies which likewise claim to interpret the facts of life. What is meant by the assertion that religion must come to terms with truth is that whenever facts are definitely established religion must loyally accept them and make whatever adjustments in its thinking the facts appear to demand.

Religion no more than science is destined to lose anything by accepting truth. When Einstein discovers some aspect of truth which upsets certain scientific calculations, nobody feels called upon to say that science has been discredited. When somebody discovers some aspect of truth which upsets certain theological dogmas, why should anyone feel called upon to announce that religion has gone down to defeat? The finding of truth is the glory of science; the acceptance of truth is one of the glories of religion. It is one form of loyalty to God.

And surely it is obvious that religion, if it is to be the worship of the highest, must come to terms with goodness. This does not mean that religion must endorse and seek to promote whatever may be regarded as goodness by any given generation. In the "goodness" of first century Pharisees, seventeenth century Puritans and nineteenth century Victorians, there was a good deal that wasn't very good. In much which historically has passed as goodness, there has been considerable cruelty, uncharitableness, and intolerance. It has happened more than once in human history that publicans and harlots have been somewhat nearer to the Kingdom of Heaven than smug, self-satisfied Pharisees and Puritans. When, therefore, one says that religion must come to terms with goodness, he does not mean that it must come to terms with conventional goodness. Religion must persistently challenge conventional goodness in the name of a better goodness. It must become the vision in which men shall be able to penetrate farther and farther into the meaning of goodness.

What if popular religion had always come to the support of prophetic vision? What if the tremendous power of the religious sentiment had always been placed behind the demands of that more than conventional goodness which prophetic vision had discovered? How differently history would read! What has been written has been written and cannot now be altered. But in respect of what may be written, is it too much to hope that more and more even popular religion will come to the support of the higher ethical demand?

And religion must come to terms with beauty. There is some reason to believe that most if not all of prehistoric art was inspired by beliefs and emotions which were essentially religious. Undoubtedly religious are many of the dances, songs, and paintings of existing primitive peoples; and it is of course beyond dispute that much of the world's greatest art drew its inspiration from religion. Concerning Europe's great cathedrals, Mr. G. Baldwin Brown has said: "Of the general artistic effect of these vast structures at the time of their glory, when the interiors, often now so cold and bare, were glancing with gold and colour, and were hung with gorgeous eastern stuffs, we can form but an imperfect idea; but it is probable that nothing more artistically beautiful has ever been seen." And what shall be said of Greek statues or of Italian paintings?

But, as everybody knows, during the post-reformation period, religion in some countries became afraid of art, turned against it, and cast it out. In Switzerland, beautiful paintings were pronounced idolatrous and banished from the churches. In England, and especially in Scotland, "artistic treasures of indescribable beauty were ruthlessly destroyed." How are we to account for this apparently inexcusable vandalism? Much of it no doubt was sheer, bitter revolt against a church which had become morally discredited, and against everything associated with that church, including lighted candles, burning incense, pictured madonnas, sculptured saints, and stained glass windows. In the thought of the revolters these beautiful, artistic treasures were no longer symbols of the ineffable and the eternal; they had become merely the pomp and circumstance of a discredited ecclesiasticism. Nor need we hesitate to suppose that among the revolters were occasional vulgarians who found the vulgarian's savage delight in sheer destruction.

But clearly there is something else to be said. One recalls with a start that the revolters numbered among them also some of the moral heroes of the race. These men who became afraid of art, and fearful even of that beauty which is the soul of art, were not by any means all vulgarians. In England, and later in New England, they produced a spiritual culture to which no one may point with justifiable scorn. Obviously, then, there must have been for their revolt some deeper and more significant reason than any we have yet named. What was it?

Well, if you had lived toward the close of the Middle Ages in some medieval town with a great cathedral in it, and had seen on the one hand a form of worship indescribably rich and beautiful, and on the other a kind of life indescribably ugly and corrupt, you might conceivably have come to the conclusion that the world needs something more than beauty to save it from destruction. You might even have come to entertain considerable doubt as to the legitimacy of the marriage of religion to beauty. You might have found yourself asking, "Is there not perhaps in art a positive peril to the spiritual life, something which satisfies the senses but drugs the soul to sleep?"

A modern Quaker [1] says that he is frankly afraid of stained glass windows, and lovely organ music, and beautiful anthems sung by white-robed men and boys. He admits that all this produces a certain hypnotic effect upon the worshipper, that it is beautiful and restful and soothing. His objection to it is that it stops there, that it does not awaken the conscience, does not quicken moral intuition, or strengthen moral resolve. He calls attention to the fact that the Orthodox Greek Church in Russia was at once the most ornate and splendid in its ritual and the most

[1] J. W. Graham, in "The Faith of a Quaker," p. 178 f.

corrupt in its morals; that for centuries it had been in alliance with a barbarous despotism and had carried on religious persecutions for political reasons.

There is undoubtedly a danger in art. The materials which the artist uses in the production of art are far more tractable than are the materials which must be used by the prophet and the pioneer in the production of a nobler social order. It is very much easier to realize an ideal in art than it is to realize an ideal in society. A beautiful painting can be produced at far less cost than a beautiful life. A splendid cathedral can be erected at far less sacrifice than a splendid civilization. There is, therefore, the ever-present temptation for men to avoid the gruelling toil, bitter disappointment and long delay which social creation involves and rest content with artistic creation.

That, I suppose, is the reason why from the days of Amos and Micah until now the prophet has always looked with distrust upon gorgeous temples and elaborate rituals. He has seen men erecting beautiful churches and permitting their fellows to live in ugly slums. He has seen them embellishing their forms of worship, producing a religious pageantry which has made of the celebration of religion the most gorgeous and dramatic of all celebrations, and at the same time allowing their economic life to become ruthless and their political life to become corrupt. He has, therefore, been afraid that artistic interest would side-track social concern, that devotion to the ends of art would be accepted as a substitute for devotion to the ends of personal righteousness and social justice.

There is also in art the danger of a premature and, therefore, superficial and unlasting satisfaction of certain deep and legitimate human desires. We all want to be happy. We all want to have a little real peace before we die. And there is only one way to achieve either happiness or peace—the long, hard road of moral discipline. No man has ever achieved a great and lasting happiness except in the pursuit of ends which transcended his own individual hopes and ambitions. No man has ever achieved a real and abiding peace except as a result of moral adjustments which enabled him to be at peace with himself.

But a superficial kind of emotional satisfaction may be secured through the short-cut of art. One may listen to great music, or look at great paintings, or sit for an hour in a great cathedral, and feel for the time being that all is well with himself and the world. One may experience a sense of repose which he may all too easily mistake for the happiness and peace for which his soul longs. If one has easy access to the ministrations of art, he may even form the habit of resorting to them, very much as the drug addict resorts to drugs, as a means of securing an immediate relief from worry and pain and a momentary stimulation.

There is, therefore, in art the further danger that men may be led to seek an apparently quick and easy satisfaction of deep desires which can never be permanently satisfied except by moral discipline.

But now abideth not only truth and goodness but beauty; and however dangerous beauty may be, we cannot afford to get along without it. Religion, certainly, cannot afford to ignore it. The time is coming, if indeed it is not already here, when persons who crave beauty will not consent to worship in churches which both without and within are hopelessly ugly. And even though they should consent to do so, a religion which refused to avail itself of the service of art would seriously and needlessly impoverish itself.

Not long ago, a group of young women were celebrating a holiday. In festive mood, they paid a visit to the new chapel of the University of Chicago. They went in hilarious. They came out reverent. One of them, whose professed indifference to religion was known to the others, remarked as she came out, "It is curious what a place like that does to you." It is curious; or is it? Not when you consider the fact that music and art can say some things which no man through the medium of speech has ever been able to say.

Nor is this utterance of the unutterable the only service which art may render to religion. Art may vitalize truth, make it more powerful and persuasive. Consider the difference in effect between a prosaic and a poetic statement of the same fact. Here is a fact which I shall state first in plain, unadorned prose: for thousands upon thousands of years human beings have believed in God and derived at least some degree of comfort from their religious faith. Now let me state this self-same fact in poetry, using for the purpose a great Hebrew Psalm and a great Christian hymn:

Lord, thou hast been our dwelling-place in all generations.
Before the mountains were brought forth,
Or ever thou hadst formed the earth and the world,
Even from everlasting to everlasting, thou art God.

O God, our help in ages past,
Our hope for years to come,
Our shelter from the stormy blast,
And our eternal home!

How very different the effect! How very much more
pronounced the emotional response! How very much
more vital and meaningful the fact which has been stated!
That is the service of art.

We have frankly admitted that devotion to art may be
accepted as a substitute for devotion to social welfare; but
it need not be. On the contrary, art itself may stimulate
social passion. "Let me write the songs of a nation and I
care not who writes its laws." Think of what the hymn beginning, "A mighty fortress is our God" did for the Reformation. Think of what the Marseillaise did for the French
Revolution. Think of what any national anthem does for
a nation. If only we had more songs that would embody
the dawning social vision and voice the developing social
passion of our time! The present dearth of hymns that
express and vitalize the thoughts of living prophets is nothing less than tragic. At this point religion is suffering
terribly from the lack of art—art that would take these
prophetic visions and hopes and carry them with passion
into the hearts of men. You may talk about international
peace until you are almost literally blue in the face and
accomplish little if anything. Even when you secure the
consent of men's minds, you do not deeply stir their hearts
or galvanize their wills into action. But get men to sing
about peace. Set Thomas Curtis Clark's noble little poem,

"Who Goes There?" to Edvard Grieg's haunting music, "Aase's Death," and let men sing:

> Who goes there in the night,
> Across the storm-swept plain?
> We are the ghosts of a valiant war,
> A million murdered men.
>
> Who goes there, at the dawn,
> Across the sun-swept plain?
> We are the ghosts of those who swear,
> It shall not be again.

The difference in effect between a poem such as that and any ordinary discourse on the subject of peace strikingly illuminates this further service which art may render to religion.

We have taken note of the fact that the materials which the artist uses are more easily managed than are the materials which must be used by the prophet and the pioneer. We have suggested that this, perhaps, is the reason why men are tempted to rest content with the achievement of an artistic triumph instead of striving in sweat and blood to secure a social triumph. But a great artistic triumph might conceivably produce an exactly opposite effect. Is it not possible that it might encourage men to believe that what they have been able to do with paint and glass and stone they will be able some day to do with ideas and ideals? Beauty undoubtedly contributes to the joy of life. It enhances the value of life. It produces not only certain psychological effects but even certain physiological effects. It makes men feel stronger; it may even make them actually stronger. Is it not, then, at least conceivable that out of some great artistic triumph might come, first, an increase of joy, and then presently an increase of faith in the possibility of every kind of social progress and a more determined resolve that the whole of life shall be made as beautiful as the great creations of art?

I have just used the expression, "the great creations of art." Art *is* creation. Creation is involved in the production of art. It is involved even in the interpretation of art. When Fritz Kreisler plays a masterpiece, is he merely reproducing? No, the musical score may be the creation of Bach, but the interpretation is the creation of Kreisler. Is there not at least some degree of creation involved even in the enjoyment of art? In order fully to enjoy a great work of art, the listener or spectator must enter to some extent into the creative travail of the artist. Art, that is to say, not only is creation, it inspires creation. Even in the spectator, if he be at all sensitive, it produces a desire to create something.

Now this desire to create something is surely one which religion ought to foster. What is the trouble with the world? Once upon a time, Lincoln's young sons were heard quarreling. Someone asked their father what the trouble was. "Oh," replied Lincoln, "the trouble with them is just the trouble with the world. They have between them seven walnuts, and each boy wants four." One of the biggest of all the world's troubles is just this lust to possess something, and something more than the other fellow has. Out of it comes most of the bitterness and strife which curse the world. But just suppose for one exciting moment that most people were eager not merely to possess something but to create something. What a wonderful increase of production, enabling even the masses of men to secure at least the physical equipment for a happy life. Yes, and what a wonderful increase of joy; it is more fun to create something than it is merely to possess something. Given, then, here and there and everywhere a desire to create, and instead of a materialistic civilization with its awful extremes of wealth and poverty, and its attendant bitterness and strife, there would presently appear an artistic civilization in which all sorts and conditions of men would experience more of the joy of life. Religion should develop the desire to create; and in its attempt to do so, does it not need the service of art, that great art which makes everyone who comes under its influence feel that he too would like to be an artist?

To thoughtful minds the world around it is becoming ever more apparent that civilization cannot permanently endure divided, as it now is, into races that look down upon one another, nations that fear one another, and classes that hate one another. A world which economically has become a neighborhood must spiritually become a brotherhood, or what we call civilization will crash.

During the Middle Ages, notably in the thirteenth century, western civilization secured a very considerable degree of unity under the influence of one great political organization (the Roman Catholic Church), one great confession of faith (the Creed of Nicæa), and a widespread interest in architecture and art. In this twentieth century we must strive to recover that thirteenth century unity, but in another and nobler form. The unity of the thirteenth century was largely the result of compulsion. It was a unity imposed by a politico-ecclesiastical organization which had the power to impose it. Today, no organization possesses such power. Some of us believe that no organization ought to possess it. The unity of the future must be the result of the free choices of free men. It must be something more than a political unity. It must be a unity of spirit. The achievement of that kind of unity is now the great task of religion. A religion which says that God is one, and that beside him there is no other, cannot rest content until society too is one. Religion must bring all sorts and conditions of men together and lift them all up to God. Can religion even hope to do this without the service of art? Of the three great powers which religion used to bring men together in the thirteenth century, only one remains. The power of one great politico-ecclesiastical organization is no more. The power of a universally accepted creed is no more. But the power of art remains, and while it is not by any means the only power which religion may and must use in its attempt to secure unity and peace for the world, surely it ought not to be ignored. Music is a language that all the races of men can understand. A great cathedral is a symbol of realities of which all men at least dimly desire to become aware.

Religion, then, must come to terms with beauty. It must learn to use beauty as a means of uttering the unutterable;

as a means of vitalizing truth and carrying it with passion into the hearts of men; as a means of increasing human faith in the possibility of a better world; as a means of producing that desire to create something without which no better world will ever be built; as a means of uniting men out of all nations and tongues and tribes and of lifting them up to the vision and love of God.

XII

THE PROHIBITION PROBLEM

CONCERNING national prohibition there are certain facts which it seems to me we ought frankly and fairly to recognize.

It has frequently been charged that the Eighteenth Amendment was the outcome of a war-born hysteria, that had America not entered into the World War, national prohibition would never have come to pass. It is, however, a fact that before the United States entered the World War thirty-three of the forty-eight states had outlawed the liquor traffic, and that in even the wettest of the remaining wet states there were numerous counties and municipalities which were at least officially dry. The war undoubtedly hastened the coming of national prohibition. It opened men's eyes to the awful wastage involved in the liquor traffic, wastage not only of materials but of man power. But the assertion that the Eighteenth Amendment would never have been adopted had the United States stayed out of the Great War strangely overlooks the fact that before 1917 the liquor traffic had been outlawed by all but fifteen of forty-eight states, and by all but three hundred and five of two thousand five hundred and forty counties. Undeniably, an increasingly vigorous movement looking toward national prohibition as its ultimate goal had been under way in this country for at least fifty preceding years.

It has also been charged that the Eighteenth Amendment even at the time when it was adopted did not represent the desire or conviction of the vast majority of the American people; that it was "put over" by political pressure exerted by a relatively small but determined, well-organized and none too scrupulous minority. But what are the facts? The Eighteenth Amendment received the largest vote ever given to any amendment to the Constitution of the United States. Indeed, it received a very much larger proportional vote than was given to the Constitution itself. In our National Congress, more than two-thirds of the Lower House and more than three-fourths of the Upper House voted for it.[1] In our State Assemblies more than three-fourths of the members of the Lower Houses and considerably more than four-fifths of the members of the Upper Houses voted for it.[2] The amendment was finally ratified by all but two states—Connecticut and Rhode Island—and the population included in the forty-six states which did ratify it was 98.2 per cent of the total population of this country. There were 6,839 persons who had a direct opportunity to vote upon this amendment. Of these, 5,426, nearly 80 per cent, voted for it. Is it conceivable that four-fifths of the politicians of this country would have voted for a measure which they had reason to believe was repugnant to the vast majority of their constituents, and desired by only a relatively small minority? Is it conceivable that

[1] The vote in the Senate was 65 for and 20 against; in the House of Representatives, 282 for and 128 against.
[2] The vote in the lower houses was 3,782 for and 1,035 against; in the upper houses, 1,310 for and 237 against.

if, at the time of its presentation, the Eighteenth Amendment had not been wanted by the vast majority of the American people it would have been adopted?

It has also been charged that national prohibition represents a puritanical revolt against the use of intoxicating liquors on the part of queer, hard, strait-laced individuals who had persuaded themselves that even a moderate use of light wines and beer, not to mention distilled liquors, was physically harmful and morally wrong. Well, national prohibition was advocated by a militant and somewhat bigoted type of puritanism, but could anybody seriously and sincerely claim that the Eighteenth Amendment was added to the Constitution of the United States at the sole dictate of a spirit that might be symbolized by a lean, hard-faced fanatic, clothed in top hat, white tie, Prince Albert coat, and carrying an umbrella?   Is it not a fact that long before we had nation-wide political prohibition, we had nation-wide industrial prohibition?   Is it not a fact that every great railroad system in the United States had forbidden its employees to use intoxicating liquors either on or off duty, and had even gone so far as to declare that the mere frequenting of places where such beverages were sold was a sufficient cause for dismissal?   Is it not a fact that in the interest of safety and of efficiency one great industry after another had, before the adoption of the Eighteenth Amendment, established prohibition within its own organization?   And is it not also a fact that increasing numbers of people, who were themselves by no means teetotalers, had, nevertheless, come to the conclusion that the American saloon was a huge liability and a terrific menace? In one local option campaign after another, had not thousands upon thousands of drinking men voted "dry"?

In order to answer the question, "Why the Eighteenth Amendment?" one must point to something more than a strait-laced puritanism. One must point to an alert and anxious industrialism which had discovered that it was being continually handicapped by the carelessness, irregularity, and general inefficiency brought about by the presence of the ubiquitous saloon in which employees cashed their pay checks, squandered their earnings, muddled their brains, and rendered themselves unfit for steady employment. And certainly one must point to a lawless institution which had battened upon the weakness and misery of men, resisted any and all attempts to regulate its operations, leagued itself with vice, lent itself to crime, sought and found protection in political corruption, and finally brought down upon itself the accumulated wrath of an outraged people. To disregard such facts as these is not only to misread the past but to render oneself incapable of offering intelligent guidance for the future.

Now, the present situation is bad enough, but it is not as bad as it is sometimes painted. Some persons are saying that more liquor is being drunk in this country today than was ever drunk before. Some of these same persons are saying that, owing to the difficulty of obtaining liquor, there is an increase in the number of persons resorting to drugs! The fact of the matter is, of course, that nobody knows, or has any means of finding out, just how much liquor is being consumed today.

The assertion is frequently made that men who used to drink wine and beer are now drinking whiskey and bad whiskey at that. Well, in 1914 the amount of hard liquor that was poured down American throats totalled 103,000,000 gallons. The United States Prohibition Commissioner has estimated that in 1925 possibly as many as 15,000,000 wine gallons of industrial alcohol were diverted for beverage purposes. A staggering figure, is it not? But, after all, there is a rather considerable difference between fifteen millions and one hundred and three millions, and it is hardly to be supposed that that difference is being supplied by the moonshiner and the bootlegger. When all is said, is it reasonable to suppose that as much liquor is being bought in speakeasies where one must present a card of admission as used to be bought in open saloons where all that one needed to do was to step up to a bar and order a drink? Is it reasonable to suppose that the unlicensed bootlegger is doing as flourishing a business as the licensed bartender ever did? Has the passing of the saloon, with its open doors, bright lights, free lunches, convivial company, and odoriferous invitation made no difference? Has the increased cost of liquor and the increased chance of poisoning from liquor made no difference? And the abolition of the ancient practice of treating, round after round of increasingly reckless treating—has that made no difference?

It may be true that some people who used to drink wine

and beer are now drinking whiskey. It may be true that some people are drinking more today than they did nine years ago. It may even be true that some people who did not drink nine years ago are drinking now. But an economist of such distinction as Professor Irving Fisher of Yale, basing his statement on a careful survey, has not hesitated to affirm that "the amount of liquor now being poured down human throats in the United States is certainly less than 16 per cent of pre-prohibition consumption." [3] And although it is probably true that, in a case of this sort, even a conscientious and painstaking economist may arrive at a conclusion that is sadly inaccurate, is it not also probably true that his judgment is at least more reliable than is the snap judgment of the man on the street?

The situation is not as bad as it is sometimes painted, but it is bad enough. The driest of drys can hardly refuse to acknowledge that a vast deal of liquor is being illegally manufactured and sold. Nor can he refuse to acknowledge that the present unholy alliance between the criminal boot-legger and the criminal politician has become an awful menace in a city like Chicago.

But even here must we not acknowledge that it is no new situation with which we are confronted? When was liquor not illegally manufactured and sold in these United States? Did not dry counties have liquor shipped into them from wet counties contrary to law? Were not dry states invaded by the liquor interests of wet states contrary to law? Even

[3] See his "Prohibition At Its Worst," and "Prohibition Still At Its Worst."

in wet states, was not liquor illegally sold to drunkards and to minors; and times without number was it not sold in speakeasies without a license? When has the liquor traffic observed the law? When has it showed any regard for the welfare of the people? And as regards the alliance between criminal liquor dealers and criminal politicians, when did it not exist, and when was it not a menace? When it comes to law defiance, what we are now witnessing is nothing new under the sun and nothing worse in its social effects than what we have had before. Undoubtedly, more people today are defying law than ever defied it before. But is it, after all, perfectly clear that the social effect of their law defiance is anything worse than was the social effect of the kind of law defiance which we had in pre-prohibition days? The assertion so frequently made that disregard for prohibition law is breaking down regard for all laws is, in my judgment, open to challenge. There are many persons whose regard for the Eighteenth Amendment leaves at least a little to be desired, but whose respect for other laws is just as profound as it ever was. In their case, certainly, disregard for the Volstead Law is not breaking down regard for all law. In saying this, I am not condoning disrespect for law. I am merely suggesting that the law defiance which we are now witnessing, bad though it undoubtedly is, is probably no worse in its social effects than was the law defiance which characterized the licensed saloon business.

The claim is made that the Eighteenth Amendment is a serious infringement of personal liberty. Of course it is.

So is the law which forbids me to drive my car more than ten miles an hour on —— Street during business hours. So is the law which compels me to send my children to school, and to have them vaccinated whenever the health authorities say that they shall be. All sanitation laws, all pure food laws, all laws of any kind whatsoever represent an infringement of personal liberty. And yet, as everybody who is still clothed and in his right mind knows perfectly well, there would be even less liberty were there no law. One of the greatest guarantors of liberty is law. Because I cannot drive my car more than ten miles an hour on —— Street during business hours I have more liberty to shop on —— Street than I would have if there were no limit to the speed of motor cars.

There is, however, an important difference between traffic laws and prohibition laws. The need of laws governing motor traffic is universally recognized. Pedestrians recognize it, drivers of cars recognize it. The need of an Eighteenth Amendment is by no means universally recognized. There is, certainly, at this present time a very large minority of the people of the United States who, if one may judge from their practices, are vigorously opposed to the Eighteenth Amendment and to the laws which have been framed to enforce it.

Beyond dispute we are, as a nation, historically committed to the principle of majority rule. Once and again we have said that in this country the will of the majority must prevail, that after a free discussion and a fair vote the minority should be "good sports" and give in. But in

the Eighteenth Amendment we have for the first time in
our history a constitutional law which calls for drastic alterations in the daily lives of millions of people, and it is, in
my judgment, a perfectly proper and very important question just how far a political majority has the right to go in
imposing upon a large minority a law which vitally affects
their daily lives and which they consider harsh and unwarranted. There are literally millions of individuals in
this country who sincerely believe that a moderate use of
wine and beer is neither physically harmful nor morally
wrong. Some of them are under the influence of Old
World traditions. Many of them belong to a church by
which the Puritan position with respect to intoxicants has
never been taken. Neither their cultural background nor
their religious background inclines them to be sympathetic
toward the Eighteenth Amendment. Even among Protestants and persons of North European extraction there is
a very considerable number who are honestly of the opinion
that the Eighteenth Amendment is a mistake. Just how
far, then, has a majority the right to go in the imposition
of a law which to millions of individuals appears unjust
and unwise?

There is small likelihood that the Eighteenth Amendment will ever be repealed. Just thirteen states could prevent its repeal. Indeed, as Professor McBain has discovered, it would be politically possible for not more than 5
per cent of the people of the United States to prevent the
repeal of the Eighteenth Amendment. And unless and

until it is repealed no drastic modification of the Volstead Act appears to be possible.

What our so-called "wet" friends want is, undoubtedly, real wine and real beer. Just as undoubtedly, real wine and real beer are intoxicating. That is to say, if you drink enough of them you will find it a bit difficult to distinguish between a red light and a green light on your way home! But any act that would legalize real wine and real beer would be in contravention of the constitutional law of the United States which now prohibits the manufacture and sale of intoxicating liquors.

Nor could any substantial modification of the Volstead Act be secured by giving to the several states the right to determine for themselves the legal amount of alcohol which may be used in beverages. That amount, as everybody knows, is now one-half of one per cent. What everybody does not know is that, long before the Volstead Act was even contemplated, one-half of one per cent was suggested by the brewers themselves, who said that it would be a fair way of drawing the line, for purposes of taxation, between intoxicating and non-intoxicating beverages. Suppose now that the power to determine the amount of alcohol which may be legally used in popular beverages should be taken away from our national Congress and given to the legislatures of our several states. What in that case could legally be done? Kansas might reduce the amount to zero. Illinois might increase it to two and three-quarters per cent. But to persons who desire a more kick-producing beverage than Bevo or Coco Cola, not even two and three-quarters per cent would be acceptable; and any state act which would aim to give to such persons a beverage that would be acceptable would be in contravention of the constitutional law of the land.

The one legal way of securing a drastic modification of the Volstead Act has been pointed out by a professor of constitutional law in Columbia University,[4] who suggests that the Supreme Court of the United States might conceivably decree that the question, What constitutes an intoxicating beverage? may be regarded, not as a scientific question, but as a purely political question to be settled by Congress by a majority vote. In that event, Congress might declare that liquors which, from the standpoint of science and of human experience, are undoubtedly intoxicating, are nevertheless not intoxicating from the standpoint of the law. A prohibition officer might say to the court, "Plainly, your Honor, this man is drunk." And the court might reply, "There is no doubt about that; but Congress has declared that the liquor he drank is not intoxicating, and so, although he is actually drunk, he is legally sober!" Does anyone seriously suppose that the Supreme Court of the United States will ever give its consent to any such legal hocus-pocus as that, or that the people of the United States would long tolerate it if the Court did?

Looked at from any point of view, national prohibition at this present time presents a pretty problem, and let me hasten to add that I for my part do not claim to possess the

[4] Howard Lee McBain. See his important book, "Prohibition, Legal and Illegal."

secret of its solution. I have, however, two convictions which I am going to state for whatever they may be worth. The first is that national prohibition ought to be given a sporting chance to show what it can do. As I have already indicated, the Eighteenth Amendment was adopted after fifty years of earnest but futile attempt to regulate a lawless institution and in the face of conditions which literally smelled to heaven. In view of all that we once suffered at the hands of a conscienceless and uncontrollable liquor traffic, ought we not now to be willing to give prohibition a fighting chance?

In spite of all the obstacles thus far encountered, national prohibition has produced a vast deal of good. It will, I think, be generally conceded that the United States today is more prosperous than it has ever been, and more prosperous than any nation in history has ever been. Is prohibition alone responsible for this unprecedented prosperity? Of course not. Has prohibition had absolutely nothing whatever to do with it? Is it not a bit strange that some people have been able to persuade themselves that prohibition is responsible for all the crime in this country, but not at all responsible for some of the prosperity in this country?

How is one to account for the fact that postal savings in 1914 averaged a little less than $112 per depositor, and that postal savings in 1926 averaged a little more than $336 per depositor? [5] How is one to account for the fact that during the period covered by national prohibition the number

[5] See "Prohibition, Its Economic and Industrial Aspects," by Herman Feldman, Assistant Professor of Industrial Relations in Dartmouth Col-

of depositors in savings banks has risen from less than thirteen millions to more than fifty millions? One-fourth of this increase is due to the fact that in recent years school children have been encouraged to open savings accounts. But how is one to account for the remaining three-fourths?

How is one to account for the fact that the amount of industrial insurance written in 1925, as compared with the amount written in 1914, represented an increase of 208 per cent? Or for the fact that in 1925 twice as many homes were in process of construction as were being built in 1915? Or for the fact that in 1926 the number of licensed passenger automobiles was nearly three and one-half times greater than was the number of such automobiles in 1918?

It would be manifestly absurd to say that prohibition alone has brought about this increased prosperity, but would it not be equally absurd to say that prohibition has had nothing whatever to do with it?

The years since the Eighteenth Amendment was adopted have witnessed a truly marvelous increase in industrial efficiency. One great industry after another has reported gains in output per person ranging all the way from thirty-six to one hundred and thirty-nine per cent. Indeed, in the opinion of the United States Bureau of Labor Statistics, this remarkable increase of productivity constitutes "a new industrial revolution which may far exceed in its economic importance the older industrial revolution" brought about by the introduction of labor-saving machines. Is all this in-

lege. To this book I am indebted for many of the statistics cited in the following paragraphs.

crease of productivity due to prohibition? Manifestly not; but some of it undoubtedly is.

These prohibition years have witnessed, also, a notable increase in consumption. Many persons have observed workingmen drinking milk at their noon-day lunch. Statistics actually show that 50 per cent more milk is now being used in this country for household and beverage purposes than was used before the adoption of the Eighteenth Amendment. Remarkable increases have been reported also by the manufacturers of candy, ice cream, ginger ale, root beer, and other soft drinks. It does look as if certain substitutes for intoxicating liquors were being found by the American people.

Nor is even this the whole story. Remarkable also has been the increase in the number of eating places, especially cafeterias, sandwich shops, and small restaurants. And in the number of persons using hotels, frequenting motion picture theatres and other forms of amusement, and buying automobiles and radios. Here, again, factors other than prohibition must undoubtedly be taken into account, but must not some account be taken of prohibition? The President of the Illinois State Federation of Labor says: "I know perfectly well what the economic effect (of prohibition) has been on our people. The trade union dues are paid up better than before prohibition. There are fewer men who have to receive union benefits. In addition, these men are spending their wages on their wives and babies. Working people have automobiles and radios which they did not have before prohibition." Professor

Feldman states that economists are agreed that the most astonishing increases in production and consumption have occurred in the two fields of recreation and household conveniences. Is it not reasonable to suppose that for these increases prohibition is at least partly, if not largely, responsible?

Consider, also, the indisputable increase in school attendance throughout the United States, and in the amount of money that is being devoted to education. Consider the equally indisputable decrease in the number of cases being handled by societies for the prevention of cruelty to children, and of charity cases due to liquor. Consider a decreased death rate which in no year since prohibition has been as high as was the lowest annual rate before prohibition. Contemplate the number of automobile accidents that are now occurring as the result of careless driving; and then contemplate the number which would be likely to occur under an open saloon régime!

Do we want the saloon to come back? No! Nobody wants it to come back. Can anybody be sure that in the event of the legalization of light wines and beer, the saloon would not come back? No! Nobody can be sure of that. Why not give prohibition a sporting chance? If it has not accomplished all that its most ardent supporters claim for it, it has, in my judgment, accomplished enough to justify the continuation of a great experiment. It is not only possible but highly probable that at least a part of our present prosperity is due to the fact that, the awful temptation of the open saloon having been removed, thousands

upon thousands of men have either stopped drinking, or
are drinking less, and are in consequence able both to produce more, and to consume more, of the undoubted goods
of life. And is it not at least conceivable that, given a
longer period and a fairer chance to show what it can do,
national prohibition may pave the way for such indisputable moral and economic gains as will convince the world
that this much derided American experiment has been a
success?

But I have also this further conviction, that the possible
success of national prohibition cannot be secured by ruthless coercive measures. I believe for one thing that you
simply cannot compel millions of individuals to obey a law
which they regard as harsh and unwarranted. I also believe
that if you could do so, it would be very dangerous to try.
Suppose a Government should make the discovery that
by the employment of ruthless police methods it was able
to compel a large and protesting minority to do its bidding.
Would not such a Government be terribly tempted, by the
employment of similar methods, to coerce all minorities into
doing its bidding, however just and wise the position of
some of them might be?

Already, in the attempt to enforce national prohibition,
certain basic human rights have been dangerously jeopard-
ized. Private telephone wires have been tapped. Private
homes have been invaded and searched without a warrant.
At least a few persons have been punished more than once
for the same offense, once by a State court and again by a
Federal court. At least a few innocent persons have been

killed! [6] Is that the way to carry on a great social experiment? In my judgment, a far better and more effective way would be for our Federal Government to carry on a campaign of education, using the public school, the press, the motion picture theater, and any other suitable agency, as a means of acquainting people with the demonstrated value of prohibition not only to the moral but to the economic life of the nation.

There is one effective way of putting an end to bootlegging. What is it? Stopping the demand for what the bootlegger has to sell! Up until now we have been going after the disreputable bootlegger—more or less. My own belief is that from now on, without neglecting him, we ought to go after his respectable patron. Not with cold steel but with cold facts—facts which would convince him that so great is the amount of good, not only for his generation but for succeeding generations, which might be derived from a continuation of the prohibition experiment that he cannot afford to let his own appetite stand in the way of it, and that he certainly cannot regard himself as a patriotic citizen if he does.

We have had enough of the saloon. God forbid that like a dog to its vomit the American people shall ever go back to the old saloon! By overwhelming majorities, both in our national Congress and in our state legislatures, we have committed ourselves to this great, new experiment. Now let us see it through. Not only for our own sake, but for the world's sake, and for the sake of generations yet un-

[6] See cases cited by Professor McBain in "Prohibition, Legal and Illegal."

born, let us see what can be done by the prohibition of intoxicating liquors which have, undeniably, stolen away the
brains of men, made unhappy the homes of men, and reduced at once men's power to produce and their ability to
enjoy the undoubted goods of life.

XIII

THE MODERN JONAH

THE book of Jonah is the first great missionary tract ever written. It is one of the greatest books in the Old Testament. Its unknown author appears to have possessed the vision of a Saint Paul, the satiric power of a George Bernard Shaw, and the delicious humor of a Gilbert Chesterton. Is this great little book a true story? As well ask, Is the parable of the prodigal son a true story? Neither the one nor the other represents an actual occurrence; yet how persistently true they are, how utterly accurate as portraits of a multitude of human hearts! In that prodigal son who gathered all together and went into a far country and wasted his substance in riotous living and began to be in want, how many a man has recognized himself! And if in that disobedient prophet whose racial prejudices led him to refuse a divinely appointed task many another man does not recognize himself, it is only because the everlasting meaning of the book of Jonah has been lost sight of in the dust of a foolish, futile controversy over the ability of a fish to swallow a man and the ability of a man to live three days and three nights in the belly of a fish. It is, indeed, a curious fact that many persons who have insisted upon the historicity of the book of Jonah have revealed in their own lives much the same sort of racial prejudice which the author of the book was trying to smite.

Recall the story. Once upon a time a Hebrew prophet was commanded by God to go to the city of Nineveh with a message. Nineveh was the capital of the Assyrian empire. It was a large city, a wicked city, a pagan city. Jonah was bidden to say to the people of Nineveh that the reputation of their city smelled to heaven and that Jehovah could endure it no longer. But Jonah felt no interest in the people of Nineveh. If their city was doomed—well, let it be doomed. Why should a one hundred per cent Israelite give himself any concern about it? Mere foreigners, these Ninevites, whose ways were not the ways of Israel, who knew not the law, and were, therefore, accursed! Nineveh was east. Jonah went west in order to get away from Nineveh; in order, also, to get away from Jehovah, for, in the thought of Jonah, Jehovah was a tribal god whose jurisdiction stopped at the frontier.

The unwilling prophet secured passage on a ship sailing for Tarshish, a point on the coast of Spain. Once on board he felt very much relieved and, lying down, he fell asleep. But suddenly a terrible storm arose and the ship was in danger of sinking. The brave though superstitious sailors cast lots to discover who it was that had angered the gods. The lot fell upon Jonah. Then the faithless prophet confessed that he it was who was responsible for the danger in which the ship's company found themselves, and gallantly suggested that they throw him overboard and so save the ship. This, however, the rough sailors were not willing to do. Pagans though they were, they were not without bowels of compassion. A lively consciousness of their own failings had made them charitable toward human frailty, and they had no desire to sacrifice a man who, once in his life, had side-stepped the rugged path of duty. They made every effort possible to save the ship and Jonah. But when, in spite of all their efforts, it became evident that the ship was about to capsize or go to pieces, they reluctantly took the prophet's own advice and cast him overboard. Immediately the storm subsided.

For Jonah, however, the situation was still critical. But, at just the right time, a huge fish appeared and swallowed him. Then, for three days and three nights, Jonah lived in the belly of the big fish, and wrote a psalm of thanksgiving. At the end of the seventy-two hours, he was vomited out upon the dry land.

Cured of his disobedience though not of his bigotry, Jonah proceeded forthwith to Nineveh and on the streets of the city delivered his message. "Within forty days," cried he, "your great, wealthy, wicked city will be destroyed." Then, to his surprise—and disappointment—this great pagan city repented. The king arose from his throne, laid aside his royal robes, and put on sackcloth smeared with ashes. All the people, likewise, put on sackcloth and denied themselves both food and drink. Even the horses and cows were covered with sackcloth to show how thoroughgoing was the repentance of the city. The king and all the people put away their evil doings and cried aloud unto Jehovah for mercy. Their petition was granted. The city was saved.

Jonah was very angry! Had he not been commanded to prophesy the destruction of Nineveh? Had he not—after a little delay—fulfilled his mission? Why, then, was the city spared? What would people say about him, a man whose confident, and secretly enthusiastic, predictions had been falsified by the event? Jonah felt that he had a right to be angry. So he turned his back upon a city that Jehovah had spared after he had said that it was doomed and, leaving by the nearest gate, started to return home. But the road was long and the sun was hot, so he stopped and erected a rude canopy to protect himself from the burning heat. Beneath this canopy he lay down and slept. In the morning, when he awoke, he discovered that during the night a gourd had sprung up and completely covered his little hut, affording him a most welcome shade. But, presently, a worm appeared and destroyed the gourd.

When Jonah expressed pity for the gourd—and, incidentally, for himself—Jehovah said to him, "Thou hast had regard for the gourd, for which thou hast not labored, neither madest it grow; which came up in a night and perished in a night; and should not I have regard for Nineveh, that great city, wherein are more than six score thousand persons that cannot discern between their right and their left hand?" The story ends with the sulky prophet sitting beneath his canopy considering the searching question of Jehovah.

God cares for the Jew, but also for the Ninevite. He cares for the native-born, but also for the foreign-born. He cares for the white man, but also for the yellow man, and the brown, and the black. The love of God is broader than the measure of prejudiced people's minds. The concern of God reaches farther than hooded klansmen suppose. That is the abiding message of the book of Jonah.

Let no one suppose that Jonah is dead. He is as much alive as are people who call black men "niggers." He is the man who, in his attitude toward persons belonging to other racial groups, is governed by his prejudices rather than by the findings of science or by the solicitude of God.

It is worthy of note that Jonah is not born with racial prejudices. A normal white boy reveals no feeling of repugnance toward a normal colored boy until his mother informs him that with little colored children little white children ought not to play. Race antipathy is not instinctive; it is acquired. It is not God-given; it is society-given. In generation after generation, an adult world imposes upon a juvenile world its own antipathies. Jonah is not born prejudiced; he achieves prejudice, has prejudice thrust upon him.

It was probably true of the ancient Jonah that he felt no need of rationalizing his racial antipathies; but the modern Jonah has attempted to secure for his a scientific justification—a fact which may indicate that the spirit of Jesus has been brooding over the hearts of men with such effectiveness that, whereas nineteen hundred years ago one might not only without shame acknowledge a feeling of race antipathy but even boast of it and glory in it, today one feels the need of discovering some sanction for it, if not in Christianity at least in science.

A few years ago Jonah was busily engaged in weighing human brains. He discovered, much to his delight, that the brain of the average white man weighs something more than the brain of the average negro; and if only he had stopped there, all would have been well for his prejudices. But he proceeded to weigh the brains of a certain number of Orientals and discovered to his dismay that the brain of the average yellow man weighs something more than the brain of the average white man. That, of course, was a jolt; and he was destined to experience an even bigger jolt, for when he still further proceeded to weigh the brains of some of the most gifted and distinguished men belonging to his own race, he discovered that the brain of a certain eminent statesman weighed considerably less than that of the average negro in the African forest. Today, therefore, Jonah is reflecting upon a well-known nursery rhyme which says:

> Little head, little wit;
> Big head, not a bit—

and looking elsewhere for a scientific confirmation of his racial prejudices.

He inclines to believe that he has found it in the shape of the human head. He has noted the fact that many Anglo-Saxons have long heads and that many Latins and Slavs have broad, or flat, heads. Being himself an Anglo-Saxon, with a head undeniably long, and being fully persuaded of the inherent superiority of Anglo-Saxons to all other peoples whatsoever, he has concluded that the presence of a long head is Nature's own assertion of the scientific right of every Anglo-Saxon to consider himself the lawful lord and bully of the planet. There are times, to be sure, when

Jonah's complacency is somewhat disturbed. He finds it a bit awkward to account for the greatness of such broad-headed Latins as Dante, Michelangelo, and Raphael, not to mention the greatness of certain Englishmen whose portraits suggest that their heads were not long, but flat. Nor is he easily able to give a reason for the faith that is in him when his wife calls his attention to the indisputable fact that one of his own sons has a long head, the other a head that rather curiously suggests a bullet flattened a bit on top.

But, although Jonah has moments of horrid doubt, he has not yet acknowledged that his own head, metaphorically speaking, is a trifle thick. He turns most hopefully to certain intelligence tests which seem to show that the children of white folk possess a much greater degree of native ability than do the children of black folk. But these far-famed intelligence tests only seem to show what he wants them to show. If they suggest that certain white children are more highly gifted than certain black children, they also suggest that at least a few black children possess a larger native endowment than do many white children. Moreover, whether or no any child is able to answer the questions that are put to him depends, in part at least, upon the cultural environment in which he has been brought up. A colored boy whose parents are college graduates finds it a good deal easier to pass almost any kind of examination than does the white boy whose parents are illiterate and who has grown up in the slums. The question not unnaturally presents itself whether environment must not be taken seriously into account in the application of intelligence tests. Human beings do, undeniably, reveal marked differences of native capacity. As Jesus suggested, to some of us are given five talents, to some two, to others only one. But are all the five-talent individuals to be found in the white race, all the two-talent individuals in the yellow race, and all the one-talent individuals in the black race? Is it not, rather, true that when it comes to sheer native capacity the differences between human beings are not racial but personal?

Jonah, however, is still unconvinced. Only the other day I met him on a Pullman in which we both happened to be traveling, and the conversation drifted into a discussion of the potential ability of the negro race. I held to the opinion that the negro's potential ability is very great; that, in view of what the negroes in America have accomplished in the sixty years of their enfranchisement, we are entitled to suppose that, given fair opportunity for self-development, the black man will one day astonish the world. I ventured to refer to the work of such negroes as McCoy, the inventor; Scott, the mural painter; Tanner, the painter of religious subjects; Chestnut, the novelist; Roland Hayes, the tenor; William Stanley Braithwaite, the literary critic; W. E. Burghardt Dubois, the brilliant savant; and Paul Laurence Dunbar, the poet, whose

> Lay me down beneaf de willers in de grass,
> Whar the branch'll go a-singin' as it pass,
> An' w'en I'se a-layin' low,
> I kin hyeah it as it go
> Singin', Sleep, my honey, tek your res' at las'

has made the whole world of sensitive spirits his debtor. I did not know at that time what I have since discovered, that Lord Bryce once expressed the conviction that in sixty years the American negro has developed more than did the Anglo-Saxon in six centuries.

But Jonah, although he admitted the possibility of brilliant exceptions, held solemnly to the opinion that the black race as a whole will never rise very high. "Why," said he, "is it not an undeniable historic fact that for thousands of years and, indeed, until the coming of the white man, black Africa never invented an alphabet, nor produced a single significant invention, or a single work of enduring art? How, then, can you cherish the hope that the black man has a brilliant future?"

But consider another undeniable historic fact. When Julius Cæsar landed on that little island which has since given to the world a Shakespeare, a Ruskin, a Turner, and a Gladstone, what did he find? He found men who possessed the power of life and death over their wives and children and who offered human beings as sacrifices to their gods. Some of them, he discovered, had "huge wickerwork images which they stuffed full of living men and women and then set on fire." Two thousand years ago, when the ancestors of those Italian laborers who build our railroads for us were building

> . . . the glory that was Greece
> And the grandeur that was Rome,

the ancestors of some of us were living at a stage of civilization not very much, if any, higher than that now occupied by many of the tribes of the African forests. And not until the Roman came did our ancestors produce anything of enduring worth to mankind. The fact of the matter is that even the marvelous culture of the Anglo-Saxon was developed under the stimulus of an imported culture. And if, two thousand years ago, that brilliant civilization along the Mediterranean coast had moved eastward instead of westward, who knows but that today white England would present much the same sort of arrested development as does black Madagascar? From the present vantage ground of the cultivated Anglo-Saxon, the negro is undeniably a backward race; just as twenty centuries ago, from the vantage ground of the cultivated Roman, the Anglo-Saxon was a backward race. But in the long view which the story of evolution necessitates, a few thousand years are but as yesterday when it is past, and who knows what the year four thousand will reveal?

If some day, in a gush of genuine scientific enthusiasm, Jonah should turn aside from those clever popularizations of pseudo-science which undertake to rationalize his prejudices and begin to read some such volume as Professor Conklin's "The Direction of Human Evolution," he would presently come upon a clean-cut statement of this sort: "Biology and the Bible agree that God hath made of one blood all nations of men"; and an equally clean-cut statement to this effect: "The resemblances between all types of men are vastly more numerous and important than the differences." Differences there are between the present political and cultural achievements of men, but does impartial scientific investigation furnish any justification for the belief that the human race may and must be divided into groups some of which are inherently superior to the rest? None whatever.

Jonah today has not a single scientific leg to stand on. What, then, will he do? In many cases, no doubt, he will hobble through life under the handicap of his prejudices, getting in the way of human progress, and missing all the fun of a great and thrilling adventure. But at the close of the Biblical story, we find him sitting under his canopy considering the searching question of Jehovah; and at the close of this present discussion, let us suppose that he is giving thoughtful attention to such considerations as these:

What is pictured in Hollywood is seen in Tokio, not always to the moral advantage of the Japanese. What is spoken in Chicago is heard in Shanghai. What is done in London is felt in Calcutta. What is whispered in the ear in the chancelleries of Europe and of America becomes a topic of conversation for the educated portion of the Orient and, after a little, even for the coolie and the jinrikisha man. The day of isolation is forever past; the day of world-wide contact has arrived. More and more the peoples of the world are going to mingle. Old King Canute, standing on the beach and commanding the tide to stand still, is a no more ludicrous or pathetic figure than the man who supposes that by any number or kinds of exclusion acts the intermingling of racial groups can be permanently checked.

The greatest, then, of all the political and social problems which now confront us would appear to be this: How may the various nations and races of mankind live together in prosperity and peace? Never was it as true as it is today that united we stand, divided we fall. United, capital and labor could produce enough to make it possible for every man, woman, and child all over the world to possess at least the physical equipment for a healthy, happy life; divided, they can but keep the world in perpetual turmoil and discontent. United, in some great and powerful association of nations, what could modern states not accomplish in fighting disease, and such moral plagues as the traffic in women and children and the traffic in drugs; what could they not accomplish in the diffusion of knowledge, the development of science, the enrichment of life? Is it not true, as Professor William MacDougall suggests, that "only through the further development of the collective life of nations can man rise to higher levels than he has yet known"? But divided, modern states now possess the power to destroy civilization. United, not by marriage but by a common faith in the possibility of world progress and a common devotion to great world interests, what could not the races of mankind accomplish in the liberation of the human spirit from ignorance and superstition and fear, and in the creation of a great world civilization in whose manifold blessings every people would have a share? But divided as they now are, will they not, late or soon, bring on a death struggle compared with which the war of 1914 would appear to be but a small and localized disturbance?

One detects today in the minds of far-seeing Englishmen

a kind of glow at the thought that they belong to a far-flung commonwealth which includes in its membership a great variety of peoples representing differing cultures and temperaments and tastes. Is it not possible to conceive of an even more wonderful commonwealth, a far-flung commonwealth of mankind that would embrace a still greater variety of peoples, each with its own distinctive culture, its own mentality, and artistic taste? And is it not reasonable to suppose that in such a commonwealth the race as a whole would climb to more splendid heights than it has yet reached or, under present conditions, is likely to reach? The genius for government that is Britain, the beauty that is France, the scientific thoroughness that is Germany, the practical idealism that is America, the laughter that is Africa, the courage that is Japan, the spirituality that is India—suppose all these should unite to form one great world-wide civilization. Would there not presently appear a new glory in the face of mankind?

XIV

PATRIOTISM

THAT oft-quoted saying of Samuel Johnson that patriotism is the last refuge of a scoundrel is often misquoted. It is quoted in support of the suggestion that there is in patriotism itself something that is ignoble, whereas all that the author of it really meant was that in the name of patriotism ignoble men may do ignoble things. And he might, of course, have made a similar observation concerning religion. He might have said that religion is the last refuge of a scoundrel, intending no disrespect to religion.

But even among persons who are entirely agreed as to the value and nobility of patriotism there appears to be no little disagreement as to what patriotism is. Today, the question, Who is a patriot? would probably evoke as much discussion as the question, Who is a Christian? The assertion that a Unitarian may be a Christian would certainly occasion heated debate in many sections of our country; and so would the assertion that a pacifist may be a patriot, or even the suggestion that there is no incompatibility between a thoroughgoing patriotism and a proposal to effect some change in the Constitution of the United States. Not long ago, in California, the Better America Federation attempted to secure the passage of a bill to prohibit a teacher in the public schools from advocating any change whatsoever in the Constitution of the United States! In view, therefore, of the confusion that appears to exist in the minds of many people as to the meaning of patriotism, surely it is incumbent upon us at this point to do some clear thinking.

Open almost any dictionary you please at the word "patriotism" and what do you find? You find it stated that patriotism is love of one's country. According, then, to a generally accepted definition it might be said quite simply that a patriot is a man who loves his country.

Why does a man love his country? This question is not irrelevant to the matter which we have in mind because it points to the soil from which patriotism springs. A man loves his country because, for one reason, it is the place where his home is. During the War, a young American soldier wrote in France:

> My native land! What does that mean,
> That phrase to me?
> Not power most of all,
> Nor even liberty,
> Nor wealth, nor fame
> Of honor brightly kept;
> Not the high title of democracy,
> Of refuge, haven,
> The land of even chance.
> All this may mean America, my native land,
> To others.
> But just to me it means
> The little house beneath the elms
> Where I was born.

Is not that what native land means first of all, if not most
of all, to any man? The place where he was born. The
dear, familiar scenes of his childhood. The old farm, if
he was brought up in the country. The old—what, if he
was brought up in the city? Tender memories. Hallowed
associations. "Patriotism," "pater"—the very word suggests
that natural and altogether proper love which a man has
for his home.

But, now, must we not think also of many persons who
love America, for instance, as they love no other country
on the face of the earth, notwithstanding the fact that
they were not born here; who today are Americans, and
proud to be, not by the accident of birth, but by deliberate
choice? Such persons compel us to recognize the fact that
patriotism may have its roots in something other than the
dear associations of childhood. A man's love for his
country may spring from gratitude for what his country
has done for him, for all the opportunities it has given to
him. It may spring from respect and admiration for certain ideals for which his country stands. It may spring
from a profound appreciation of certain contributions
which his country has made to the culture of mankind. It
would be very difficult to mention the name of any country which has not given birth to at least a few individuals
of world importance; or which has not in literature, or art,
or music, or science, or invention, made at least some contribution to the higher wealth of the race. Here, then, is
another reason for love of country. A man may love his
country, not only because it is the place where his home is,

but also and even more so because it is the place where his heart is—the place which his heart applauds and for which it is unspeakably grateful.

Patriotism is, essentially, love of country. To that statement, I venture to think, no exception will be taken; nor to the further statement that just as faith without works is dead, so love without devotion is mere pretense. Any man who says that he loves his country and who, on national holidays, somewhat conspicuously displays his country's flag, but who is never seen under any circumstances devoting himself to the welfare of his country, is a pseudo-patriot and (to speak plainly) a liar. To that statement, likewise, no exception is likely to be taken—not at least aloud. But the moment one puts the question, How should devotion to country express itself? the stage is all set for a lively, if not a deadly, debate.

By many persons, today, devotion to country is identified with allegiance to government. Such persons sincerely believe that the only way in which a man may prove his love for his country is loyally to support his country's government in whatever it proposes to do. Now, to some minds, that position may appear to be totally incomprehensible. In what other field of endeavor have human beings been so little successful as they have in the field of government? Theocracy, which in practice has meant government by a priestly caste; oligarchy; monarchy, both absolute and limited; democracy—man has tried them all. And which one of them has proved to be a completely, or even nearly, perfect solution of the great problem of political organization? Is not political history the least inspiring and most depressing part of the whole human story? In literature and law, in art and science, in business and industry, has not man achieved a far greater success than he has been able ever to achieve in government? How strange, then, to identify devotion to country with allegiance to government, when government is admittedly the least successful and admirable of all human undertakings. Strange, no doubt, but not incomprehensible; because any existing government, however imperfect, does stand for order as opposed to anarchy. It stands for security, stability, and a measure at least of opportunity. Many persons, therefore, are firmly convinced that the only way to maintain security, stability, and prosperity is loyally to support government in whatever it proposes to do.

But because this position is comprehensible it does not follow that it is true and righteous altogether. Here is a man who loves, say, the Methodist Episcopal Church. He rejoices in the fact that Methodism was built upon a rock, an unyielding foundation of spiritual experience; so that when the rains of "higher criticism" descended, and the flood of "evolution" came, Methodism stood unshaken, having been builded upon a foundation of spiritual experience that neither Biblical criticism nor biological theory could destroy. He rejoices also in the further fact that Methodism was born, not only of religious experience, but of social passion, not only of an immediate awareness of the presence of God but of a sympathetic awareness of the needs of men; so that, historically speaking, Methodism has played a fairly creditable part in the rectification of social wrongs. He feels, therefore, a good deal of affection for the Methodist Episcopal Church. But does it follow that in order to prove his love for Methodism he must be prepared to support its ecclesiastical leaders in whatever they may propose to do? For the sake of the illustration, let us imagine a contingency which is not likely ever to become a fact, namely, that the governing body of the Methodist Episcopal Church should seriously propose to bar from the membership of the church all persons of whatsoever character whose skin was not white. In that case, would love for Methodism truly express itself in loyal support of what its governing body was proposing to do? Would it not rather express itself truly in utter repudiation of what the governing body was proposing to do?

I have cited this analogous case of love for a church because, at the present moment, it appears to be a bit easier to think dispassionately about the church than about the state. But this distinction which we have just recognized between love for a church and uncritical support of whatever its ecclesiastical leaders propose to do is no more valid nor vital than is the distinction between devotion to a country and uncritical support of whatever its political leaders may propose to do; as almost anybody will see clearly enough if he examines the recent history of other countries, or goes far enough back into the history of his own country.

In Germany, for instance, in August, 1914, did Karl Liebknecht cease to be a patriot when he refused to support his government in what it was proposing to do? Did he not truly and grandly display his love for Germany when he publicly repudiated the suicidal program of her military leaders? In England, in the year 1899, did John Morley and Lloyd George cease to be patriots when they refused to endorse what the government of their country was doing in South Africa? Did they not splendidly prove their love for England by protesting against a war which, today, very few Englishmen recall with pride and many recall with profound regret? In the United States of America, in the year 1848, did Abraham Lincoln cease to be a patriot when he protested in the halls of Congress against our war with Mexico, and voted an appropriation for supplies for soldiers but refused to vote approval of any other measure proposed by the Administration?

When he examines the recent history of other countries, or even the somewhat more remote history of his own country, who can fail to see that there is a profoundly important distinction between devotion to country and allegiance to government? Yet when it comes to the contemporaneous situation, many persons do fail to see that such a distinction exists—except, of course, in relation to an Eighteenth Amendment. How uproariously inconsistent the way in which certain Americans brand unpatriotic, and even treasonable, anybody who refuses to support Government when it asks for additional cruisers, yet who themselves refuse to support Government when it asks that a decent regard shall be shown for the Volstead Act so long as it remains the law of the land. Such persons appear to be taking the interesting position that you may refuse to endorse any governmental measure which they themselves do not approve and still be considered a thoroughgoing patriot; but if you refuse to endorse any governmental measure which they themselves do approve, you belong to the company of such national dangers as Miss Jane Addams, Professor John Dewey, Rabbi Stephen S. Wise, and the Federal Council of Churches!

Said Jesus, in one of the noblest and most significant utterances ever delivered in this world, "The Sabbath was made for man, not man for the Sabbath." The principle enunciated in that immortal declaration applies to any and every human institution. And how enormously important it is that people everywhere should see that it applies to the state. The state was made for man, not man for the state. Governments are created for peoples, not peoples for governments. "This country with its institutions belongs to the people who inhabit it. Whenever they shall grow weary of existing government, they can exercise their constitutional right of amending it or their revolutionary right to overthrow it." That sentiment was not expressed by Lenin or Trotsky, by Eugene Debs or William Z. Foster. It was expressed by Abraham Lincoln; and it is, of course, but an application to government of the principle enunciated by Jesus when he said, "The Sabbath was made for man, not man for the Sabbath."

Once it is clearly seen that this principle does apply to government, something far truer and nobler than the popular conception of patriotism begins to appear; for then patriotism can be divorced from an uncritical, unconditional allegiance to government, no matter what it proposes to do, and can be associated with an intelligent devotion to the highest welfare of one's country. And note some of the advantages of that association.

Patriotism is then enabled to walk hand in hand with intelligence. Loyalty to government is blind. It believes whatever it is told. It approves whatever it is bidden to approve. It goes wherever it is led—no matter what happens to the country. In the Junior R.O.T.C. Manual, the manual used by high school students taking military training, a parent is made to say: "I want my boy to do his bit. I want him to willingly submit to all sacrifices. I place no limit. I want him to obey orders, all orders. That means wrong orders as well as right orders." Well, when it comes to a soldier, on duty, an unquestioning obedience to orders, wrong orders as well as right orders, is absolutely essential. But when it comes to a civilian, it is not only non-essential, it is disastrous. Of soldiers it may properly be said:

> "Theirs not to make reply,
> Theirs not to reason why,
> Theirs but to do and die."

But when civilians do not "reason why," and do not on proper occasion "make reply" to their government, there is likely to be the devil to pay in corrupt municipal politics and dangerous national policies. A patriotism which pledges an unconditional allegiance to government is cer-

tain to be a blind patriotism; and when blind patriots follow a blind government, the country may fall into the ditch
—as many an European country has done during recent
years.

Loyalty to country is not blind. It cannot afford to be
blind. Loyalty to country *requires* patriotism to walk hand
in hand with intelligence.

And it makes of patriotism a further demand, namely,
that it shall give attention to the spiritual life of the nation.
It is, I am very sure, entirely possible to underestimate
the importance of material prosperity. It is also possible to
lose sight of the fact that what makes any nation truly
great is the number and character of its spiritual achievements. Vast land areas, immense populations, huge trade
returns—when have these alone made any nation truly
great or permanently significant? How much in the way
of land area had Elizabethan England? How much in the
way of population had medieval Florence or ancient
Athens? How much in the way of trade returns had
ancient Israel? Yet the England of Shakespeare and Ben
Jonson, the Florence of Michelangelo and Leonardo da
Vinci, the Athens of Socrates and Plato, the Israel of Isaiah
and Jesus, placed all mankind and all future generations in-
calculably in their debt. And if ever the United States of
America shall occupy a place in history alongside of these
as an unforgettable contributor to the imperishable wealth
of the race, it will be not because of our territorial acquisi-
tions, or because of our population statistics, or because
of our trade returns and our material prosperity. It will be

rather because the United States of America has been indeed a "sweet land of liberty" and of opportunity; because it has given to all sorts and conditions of men a real chance to climb to the best that is in them; and because it has, in some way, enriched forever the human spirit.

Once patriotism becomes identified with devotion to the highest welfare of a nation it becomes profoundly concerned about those spiritual achievements without which no nation ever becomes truly great. The aims and interests of a true patriotism were seen and expressed by William Blake in words which have secured the applause of the best minds in present-day England:

> Bring me my bow of burning gold!
> Bring me my arrows of desire!
> Bring me my spear: O clouds unfold!
> Bring me my chariots of fire!
>
> I will not cease my mental fight
> Nor shall my sword sleep in my hand,
> Till we have built Jerusalem
> In England's green and pleasant land.

Furthermore, devotion to the highest welfare of a nation never becomes an exclusive passion, a chauvinistic, jingoistic passion. When it comes to "spheres of influence" and "economic concessions" and armies and navies and "balances of power," the interests of nations sometimes clash. And, let it be noted, it is precisely concerning such matters as these that governments, ordinarily, are chiefly concerned; so that an uncritical support of the proposals of government is almost certain to make of patriotism an exclusive passion, crying down the merits of other nations; a chauvinistic passion, exaggerating the merits of one's own nation; a jingoistic passion, jealous, suspicious, combative, boasting:

"We don't want to fight, but by jingo if we do,
   We've got the men, we've got the ships, and we've got the
      money too."

But when it comes to education or health; when it comes to art, or literature, or music, or science; even when it comes to material prosperity—the prosperity of all the people, not merely of a favored few of the people—the interests of nations today do not clash. Who today is disturbed by the fact that Shakespeare was an Englishman, or that Pasteur was a Frenchman, or that Dante was an Italian, or that Goethe was a German, or that Tolstoi was a Russian? Who today even recalls the fact that Jesus was a Jew? Such men do not belong to any one nation. They belong to all nations. All that they represent, all of imperishable worth and glory and inspiration, is today the common heritage of mankind. The patriot who is concerned about the highest welfare of his country is by very virtue of that fact concerned about the highest welfare of all other countries, because he sees that in all its higher interests the world is one.

A true and noble patriotism may, therefore, walk hand in hand with religion. It is the only kind of patriotism which can. A patriotism which pledges an uncritical allegiance to any government on the face of this earth may some day discover that it is standing in opposition to Almighty God. In our modern world there has developed an idea which the medieval world would not have sanctioned for a moment—the idea that the state owes no allegiance to any authority beyond it or above it. Dean Inge has truly declared that this notion that the state is above law, all law, that it is indeed a law unto itself, would not have been tolerated by those Middle Ages which many persons today feel disposed to despise. It was introduced by Machiavelli, sponsored by Francis Bacon, applauded by James I and Louis XIV, and is today endorsed by thousands of people who know nothing about its history, but who find it convenient when it comes, for instance, to the industrial exploitation of backward, undeveloped countries. In consequence, international conduct has been shockingly bad. It has been characterized by a cynical disregard, not only of international law, but of elemental human rights. What honorable human individual would think of behaving toward other human individuals as countries who are extraordinarily sensitive about their "national honor" have behaved toward other countries? What would certainly not be tolerated among gentlemen has been condoned and applauded among nations. Someone has said with not very much exaggeration that governments have "lied and called it diplomacy, stolen and called it annexation, borne false witness and called it a state paper, coveted and called it manifest destiny, killed and called it war."

To any man who is able to take a long view of the human situation it must be evident that this notion that the state is above law will have to be repudiated if civilization is to endure. The time has come when even the state must recognize the existence of a higher sovereignty than that which any human institution may be said to possess. In principle, this higher sovereignty is recognized each Sunday morning when, on every battleship of the United States Navy, above even that dear flag which stands for native land, there is hoisted that white flag which stands for the all-inclusive kingdom of God. But the time has come when this higher sovereignty must be recognized, not only in principle and in ritual, but in actual fact, in all governmental policies and procedures. The state must seek first, not its own selfish interests and aggrandizement, but the universal good and glory of mankind. And this it will do if ever there shall be established in human hearts that true and noble patriotism which, because it is concerned about the welfare of all peoples, is able to walk hand in hand with religion in loyal devotion to the will of God.

XV

AN ADEQUATE NATIONAL DEFENSE

THERE is, I take it, an all but universal agreement as
to the imperative need of national defense. "He who loves
not his home and country which he hath seen, how can
he love humanity in general which he hath not seen?"
So asks Dean Inge; and he adds, "There are, after all, few
emotions of which one has less reason to be ashamed than
the little lump in the throat which the Englishman feels
when he first catches sight of the white cliffs of Dover."
There are a few persons among us who say that they have
no fatherland, that humanity is their fatherland. But there
seems to be some ground for the widespread belief that
there is something wrong with that vague sort of humani-
tarianism which loves everybody in general and nobody in
particular.

As a matter of fact, most men do love their home and
their country, and profoundly desire that their home shall
be protected, that their country shall be defended. When
a man thinks of his home, he thinks of his mother, or of his
wife and his children. When a man thinks of his country,
he thinks of a good deal that has made life good and sweet
under the sun.

A nation is not merely a physical entity, it is a spiritual
214

entity. To any Englishman, what is England? An island? How much more than an island! England is the English Bible; it is Shakespeare, and Milton, and Wordsworth, and Charles Dickens; it is York, and Canterbury, and Westminster Abbey; it is Oxford, and Cambridge, and the cricket fields of Eton. To any German, what is Germany? Merely a place on the map? No, Germany is Goethe, and Schiller, and Heine; it is Kant, and Hegel, and Schleiermacher; it is Beethoven, and Bach, and Händel, and Hayden, and Brahms. And what is America? Is America merely a geographical location bounded on the north by Canada, on the south by the Gulf of Mexico, on the east by the Atlantic, and on the west by the Pacific? No, America is the Pilgrim fathers, and the public school. America is democracy and opportunity. It is Washington, and Jefferson, and Abraham Lincoln. It is a vast melting pot in which is being produced a richer and more varied culture than the world has hitherto known. It is Horace Mann, and Carl Schurz, and Jacob Riis. America is a mighty faith, a daring experiment, a sustaining hope.

Inasmuch as a nation is not merely a physical entity but a spiritual achievement which for millions of people has made life more worth the living, should it be defended? Let young Nathan Hale answer, not only for every American, but for every patriot of whatever nation: "My only regret is that I have but one life to give for my country."

We are all agreed as to the need of an adequate national defense. Where we begin to differ is at the point of the question, "What constitutes a really adequate national defense?" In this connection I should like to suggest that two words, now in common use, ought either to be disused or more carefully and intelligently used than they are today. I refer to the word "militarist" and the word "pacifist." As now used, these words do not serve to define thought, they merely serve to express emotion. They are not words to think with, they are merely words to swear with. With the connotations which they now have, they describe nothing, they fit nobody.

When a so-called pacifist pronounces the word "militarist," what is the mental picture which appears in his mind? In most cases is it not that of a fierce-hearted individual who for some unaccountable reason wants another war? And when a so-called militarist pronounces the word "pacifist" (and qualifies it with a certain adjective), what is the mental picture that rises in his mind? Is it not that of a weak-kneed individual who wants to leave his home unprotected, his country undefended? But where is the man of whom either of these pictures is an authentic likeness? Where is the man who wants another war—blood, mud, vermin? If you have ever had a cootie, you never want another one, and I am not ashamed to say that I speak from experience. Where is the man who wants another war? Who can give his street address? Who has ever talked to him? And where is this man who wants to leave his mother and his wife and children unprotected, his country undefended? The fact of the matter is that the so-called militarist is just as eager to secure

peace as is the so-called pacifist, and that the so-called
pacifist is just as eager as is the so-called militarist to protect his home and to defend his country.

What, then, is the difference between them? Is not the
real difference just a different notion as to the way to get
peace and to defend a nation? The militarist believes that
the way to get peace is to become so physically strong that
nobody will dare to attack you. The pacifist believes that
the way to get peace is to become so just and so friendly
that nobody will desire to attack you. The militarist believes that an adequate national defense calls for a great
army or a big navy and an adequate air force. The pacifist
believes that the only really adequate national defense lies
in national policies that inspire confidence in the governments of the world and good will and friendliness in
the peoples of the world. That is the real difference between the "militarist" and the "pacifist," and if these two
words could be used to make this difference clear, they
would serve a useful purpose. As they are now used, they
merely give vent to prejudice and ¬assion and obscure the
issue.

As for myself, if I really believed that huge military
establishments could defend all that I hold dear in this
world, and if I believed that goodwill was too weak to
defend it, then I would be for a big army and a big navy.
But because I believe that, under modern conditions, huge
military establishments cannot defend, and goodwill could
defend, all that I hold dear in the world, I am for goodwill.

Nobody can say that twentieth century Europe was not prepared for peace in accordance with the militaristic notion of what preparation for peace involves. Never before in human history was military preparedness brought to the degree of perfection which it had reached in the Europe of 1913. What an adequate national defense Germany had in her army, and England in her navy, according to the militaristic point of view! But did all these huge armaments secure peace for Europe? Did they purchase security for the peoples of Europe? On the contrary, they created a situation so tense and trying that an explosion was bound to occur. Far from maintaining peace, they incited war. Far from achieving security for the peoples who so heavily paid for them, they made them horribly insecure. Far from defending them, they left them in the end bleeding and bankrupt. Ten million soldiers dead, thirteen million civilians dead, five million widows, from seven to nine million orphans, ten million refugees, debts so huge that coming generations will still be paying on them—does all this look as though military defenses really defended?

Under modern conditions, military defenses no longer defend. And the reason is not far to seek. "The increase of armaments that is intended in each nation to produce a consciousness of strength and a sense of security does not produce these effects. On the contrary it produces a consciousness of the strength of other nations and a sense of fear." So writes Lord Grey, who adds: "The enormous growth of armaments in Europe, the sense of insecurity and fear caused by them—it was these that made war inevitable."

Pacifists are not people who want to leave their homes unprotected, their country undefended. They are people who want to secure for their homes and their country a kind of defense that really defends, and who, in the light of what happened in 1914, have come to the conclusion that huge military establishments do not, and indeed cannot, really defend for the reason that they tend to stir up the very trouble which they are expected to avoid.

Now, I think it may be said without any fear of contradiction that the world is passing from the militaristic viewpoint to the pacifist viewpoint. Slowly, of course, for it is too much to expect that men should pass easily and quickly from reliance upon one set of forces to reliance upon an entirely different set of forces. It is well for pacifists to remember that they themselves, in most instances, came but slowly to the point of view which they now occupy. The habit of depending upon physical force is so old and so powerful that it cannot be broken over night. It has been bred into the very bones of men. They have imbibed it with their mother's milk. Swords and guns and uniforms have become so familiar a part of the world we live in that a world without them is almost unimaginable. Human nature being what it is, war is not inevitable; but human history being what it is, a war-made mentality cannot be immediately discarded. Nevertheless, slowly but surely the world is passing from the point of view represented by an American secretary of war when he said,

"There is nothing so cooling to hot temper as a piece of cold steel," to the point of view represented by Calvin Coolidge when he said, "Peace and security are more likely to result from fair and honorable dealings and mutual agreements for the limitation of armaments than by an attempt at competition in squadrons and battalions."

There is the story of a king who, in the midst of a bitter war, declared that if he won that war he would see to it that his enemy never troubled him again. He did win the war and imposed on his defeated foe terms of peace incredibly mild! Whereupon, one of his generals rebuked him, saying, "Did you not vow that if you won this war you would see to it that this our enemy would never trouble us again?" To which the king replied, "And haven't I kept my vow, for this, our enemy, has become our friend?" Probably a legend; but what a significant legend!

And this is not a legend: For considerably more than a hundred years there has been between Canada and the United States an unbroken peace. During all that time, an exposed frontier of three thousand miles has been successfully defended by what? Forts? No. Gunboats? No. What, then? Goodwill; just and friendly relations. Today it is unthinkable that we and our Canadian neighbors should go to war. We have seen to it that they will never trouble us again. We have made them our friends.

What has happened in the case of Canada and the United States might happen in the case of Germany and France. Let those two nations stop depending for security upon guns and gas and begin to develop the same sort of friendly relations that now exist between ourselves and the people of Canada, and the security which they long for they will one day achieve.

When it comes to a really adequate national defense, one man like our present (1928) ambassador to Mexico is worth more than a dozen battleships costing forty-five million dollars apiece. At a time when, in spite of all our battleships and cruisers and submarines, our relations with our southern neighbor were considerably strained, Mr. Dwight W. Morrow went down to Mexico with an open mind and a friendly heart, inspired confidence in the Mexican government, established friendly connections with the Mexican people, and in a few months the whole situation was changed! Place a few men like Ambassador Morrow in strategic positions throughout the world, and every country which they represent will achieve a kind and degree of security which no nation in history has ever achieved by competitive armaments.

August 27th, 1928, may become one of the most significant of all dates in the history of mankind. On that day representatives of fifteen nations, including all the great powers, signed a pact which condemns recourse to war for the settlement of international controversies, renounces war as an instrument of national policy, and pledges the contracting parties to settle by pacific measures all disputes of whatever character or origin which may ever arise between them.

Not in the pact itself, but in the correspondence which

led up to it and which interprets it, there are, to be sure, certain reservations. It is understood, for instance, that "defensive wars" are not prohibited; and, of course, in the event of a crisis, it would be perfectly possible for a militant government to declare, and for a frightened people sincerely to believe, that it was in imminent danger of an unprovoked attack, even though the government making this declaration was itself at least partly to blame for the situation which had developed. It is also understood that if any nation which has signed the pact violates it, all the other nations which have signed it automatically recover their freedom of action, and that every nation may decide for itself whether or no the pact has been violated. These resolutions were, of course, dictated by fears and distrusts which history has produced and which men are not able immediately to overcome. And it is probably true that they leave the world very much in the condition of a man who is trying to break a long-standing and exceedingly costly liquor habit, and who publicly renounces his right to drink whiskey except in case of snake bite, toothache, malaria, and abdominal cramp. The number of stomach aches with which such a man may appear to be threatened is likely to prove astonishing to his friends!

Nevertheless, the Pact of Paris is at least a step in the direction of a new and more adequate kind of national defense. The governments which have signed it have renounced aggressive war for selfish ends. They have solemnly, before the whole world, pledged themselves to do this. They have likewise promised, in the face of the entire world, to settle by pacific means all disputes of whatever character or origin which may ever arise between them. Whether or no they will keep their word remains to be seen; but let not the fact be overlooked that it is possible to make them keep it. Civilization has now arrived at a point where an aroused and determined public opinion can get anything it wants. Governments can be compelled to keep such pledges as were entered into on the 27th day of August. And if they do keep them, international war will be no more. If aggressive war for selfish aims is really renounced, there will be no need of defensive war; and with the removal of any possible pretext for a defensive war, what excuses could governments give for not beating their swords into plowshares, their spears into pruning hooks, and learning war no more?

For the first time in history, war has been officially condemned as an instrument of national policy and as a means of settling international disputes. Whether or no this official condemnation shall turn out to be anything more than a scrap of paper it lies with the peoples of the world to say. But they have at least a chance to say that the Pact of Paris shall be taken seriously, and if they do say it, international war will be done away.

If, however, war is renounced as a means of settling international disputes, some other means of settling them must be provided. Disputes between nations are, for one cause or another, bound to arise. (Even in the sacred bonds of matrimony they sometimes arise.) When they do arise between nations, how are they to be settled? If there is to be no recourse to war, then so far as anybody is now able to see there are just two other ways of arriving at a settlement. They are new with respect to nations, but not new with respect to individuals. For a long time now the vast majority of human individuals have not undertaken to settle personal disputes by sword or pistol. They have undertaken, first, to settle them out of court by conference; and when conference has failed, they have undertaken to settle them in court by judicial processes. Are there any other ways in which, without resorting to arms, nations may hope to settle their disputes?

Now the first way, conference out of court, does not, I suppose, inevitably call for a League of Nations. But is it not becoming increasingly clear that a League of Nations does, or at least might, provide an exceedingly helpful agency for the securing of conference out of court? In 1914 an international explosion occurred at Serajevo. An Austrian archduke was murdered, presumably by a Serbian. When the situation became critical, Sir Edward Grey proposed a conference of the governments involved. But he himself says that he hesitated to do so, fearing lest he might appear to be trying to play too prominent a part in Continental affairs. His proposal was not, as a matter of fact, resented; but nothing came of it. No conference was held, and early in August the cables were cut, the war began. In 1923 an international explosion occurred at Corfu, when that island was occupied by Italians after a bombardment in which several persons, including children, had been killed. On the following morning, the Greek government appealed to the Council of the League of Nations, and before the day was over representatives of both Greece and Italy were in conference with representatives of nine other nations concerning a way out of the dispute. In any international crisis, when conference is desperately needed, a League of Nations provides an agency for bringing it about. More than that, it provides a permanent agency for continuous conference upon matters of interest and concern to any section of the world. And given a natural and easy opportunity for continuous conference on matters of moment, will not international crises be less likely to occur?

But what if conference fails? We are assuming now that war has been renounced as a means of settling disputes between nations, just as the dual has been renounced as a means of settling disputes between individuals, and we are demanding to know what disputing nations are to do when they discover that through conference no agreement appears to be possible. In that case, must not nations do what individuals do under similar circumstances? Must they not go into court and allow an impartial tribunal to settle their affair in accordance with law and justice? And must not nations, like individuals, become willing to abide by the decisions of the court?

The time has passed when, with any slightest degree of propriety, a man might stand up and sneer at all this and pronounce it hopelessly Utopian. For what is the alternative? Since the signing of the Armistice we have doubled the range of guns. We are now able to maneuver bombing planes by radio. We have developed gases a thousand times more destructive than any gas which was in use in 1918. And a distinguished soldier of the British Army has declared that the final form of human strife will be disease warfare. What is the alternative? Not a few men in high position, who simply cannot be dismissed with a sneer, have not hesitated to say that the alternative is the destruction of white civilization. "The world," says General Pershing, "does not seem to learn from experience. It would appear that the lessons of the last six years should be enough to convince everybody of the danger of nations striding up and down the earth armed to the teeth. But no one nation can reduce armaments unless all do. Unless some such move be made, we may well ask ourselves whether civilization does not really reach a point where it begins to destroy itself and whether we are thus doomed to go headlong down through destructive war and darkness to barbarism."

There is, then, this choice before us. We may go on clamoring for a kind of national defense that doesn't defend, that provokes the very thing which it was intended to avoid and thus imperils all that we hold dear and sweet under the sun; or we may begin to develop a new kind of defense which will really protect our homes and our country.

XVI

THE UNFINISHED TASK

EIGHTEEN hundred years ago an unknown Jew wrote a chapter which might fittingly be called "The Hall of Fame" of the Bible. He recorded in it the names of the heroes of his race, men who in war and in peace had striven valiantly for the common good; and concerning them not only, but others whose names he did not mention, he made this very significant statement: "These all having had witness born to them through their faith received not the promise, God having provided some better thing concerning us that apart from us they should not be made perfect." "Therefore," he added, "let us also, seeing we are compassed about with so great a cloud of witnesses, . . . run with patience the race that is set before us."

In the year 1863, a great American stood on the battlefield of Gettysburg and, referring to the thousands of men who there had yielded up their lives, said this: "It is for us, the living, to be dedicated here to the unfinished work which they who fought here have thus far so nobly advanced. It is for us to be here dedicated to the great task remaining before us, that from these honored dead we take increased devotion to that cause for which they gave the last full measure of devotion; that we here highly resolve that these dead shall not have died in vain; that this nation under God shall have a new birth of freedom; and that government of the people, by the people, and for the people shall not perish from the earth."

In these two deliverances, separated in time by eighteen stormful centuries, the words are somewhat different, but the thought is essentially the same. Men have lived unselfish lives and died heroic deaths; yet the causes for which they lived and died have not fully triumphed. They cannot triumph apart from us. Let us, therefore, highly resolve that these noble dead shall see through us the fulfillment of their hopes.

It is surely important for us to recognize the fact that progress is not inevitable. A generation ago, Herbert Spencer was saying that "progress is not an accident, not anything under human control, but a beneficent necessity." How does that statement look today in the light of what happened in Europe only eleven years after Herbert Spencer died? Gilbert Chesterton is sometimes wittier than wise, but is there not wisdom as well as wit in his famous observation concerning some of the early deductions from the theory of evolution? Some persons leaped to the conclusion that because they were passing from the ape they were going to the angel. "But," said Mr. Chesterton, "you may pass from the ape and go to the devil." Today, not a few more or less distinguished persons appear to think that we *are* going to the devil. Mr. Lothrop Stoddard is afraid that the white race will go down in a sea of blood, that "the East will put the West to bed." Santayana is afraid that civilization is "entering upon one of those long winters which overtake it from time to time." And Dean Inge is inclined to believe that civilization is a disease which is likely to prove fatal unless its course is checked.

Well, we need not perhaps take too seriously such jeremiads. Some of our contemporaries appear to be in a blue funk, the result no doubt of post-war disillusionment. Some of them appear to be under the influence of certain obsessions, as, for instance, Lothrop Stoddard's fear that the political supremacy of the Nordic peoples may suffer a decline, and Dean Inge's fear that political and industrial democracy will not suffer a decline. Some, also, have made the discovery that as a literary motif the faults and follies of human nature offer certain not to be neglected advantages, of which one is a very considerable profit in the way of royalties. They have discovered that a novel which spends three hundred and seventy-five pages exclaiming, "What a mess is man!" is likely to run into at least twenty editions.

But all this being conceded, the fact remains that progress is not inevitable. History on the whole indicates advance, but no continuous or universal advance. In Mesopotamia not long ago, an archæologist talked with a native boy who could not read or write, who had never in his twelve years met anybody who could read or write; and yet within a hundred yards of the spot where they were standing was the site of one of the greatest universities in the ancient world. Plainly, progress is not inevitable. Light may become darkness. Gains may be lost. Advance may be followed by retreat. It has happened before. It may happen again.

Civilization, insofar as it has triumphed, represents a continuous struggle against inertia and ignorance and cupidity and fear. If civilization is to endure, that struggle must go on without any interruption. There must be no cessation of hostilities against human inertia, no truce with ignorance, no peace with cupidity, no capitulation to fear. Humanity's fighters may be granted an occasional furlough but never discharged from the war.

Now, the meaning of all this so far as the dead is concerned is clear enough. We have the dead at our mercy. All that they lived and labored to do, all that many of them gave their lives to accomplish, we, the living, may either advance or retard, conserve or destroy. The dead can do nothing now apart from us. If we choose to do so, we can leave unfinished the tasks which they nobly began.

In the interest of a larger degree of democracy, Mr. Chesterton is proposing an extension of the franchise. He suggests that we ought to extend the franchise to the dead. In one sense, of course, we have already done this. Insofar as we permit tradition to determine our present beliefs and practices, we *are* giving votes to the dead. That is what tradition really amounts to, the casting of votes by the dead. And I do not hesitate to say that when it comes to the dead I, for my part, do not favor a universal franchise. I should hate very much to have my present beliefs determined by the votes of men who believed, for instance, in the eternal damnation of unbaptized babies; and I should hate to have my practices governed by the votes of men who believed that you cannot be a gentleman and work with your hands. When it comes to the dead, what I would advocate is a limited franchise, granted only to those whose leadership the living could afford to follow. But the noble dead, the men and the women who started great enterprises which they were unable to finish, who gave their all to secure some great human advance—they, surely, have the right to vote. To disenfranchise them would be an act of treachery which no living generation could ever live down. Any living generation that should disenfranchise the noble dead would occupy a place in history comparable to that occupied by Benedict Arnold and Judas Iscariot.

There is also another direction in which the franchise might properly be extended. When it comes to some issues the unborn have a right to vote. What shall we do with our forests, our mineral deposits, our oil reserves? What shall we do with beautiful and fascinating forms of wild life, animals and birds? When it comes to such questions as these the right of the unborn to vote is incontestable. No living generation has any right to use up for itself all the natural wealth of the world, or to exterminate beautiful species of animal and bird life from which coming generations might derive enjoyment.

If the cure for democracy is more democracy, I respectfully suggest that more of democracy might be obtained, not by giving the right to vote to every moron who is twenty-one years of age, but by extending the franchise to the noble dead and the unborn. I am not at all sure that the interests of mankind will be greatly served by permitting every Tom, Dick, and Harry who has attained his majority to select the mayor of Chicago, but I have a conviction that the interests of mankind would be greatly advanced by giving the unborn a voice in determining the future development of Chicago's lake front, its park system and forest preserves, and by giving to Abraham Lincoln a voice in determining how its colored citizens shall be housed and treated. Civilization is inevitably a cooperative enterprise in which not only the living but the noble dead and the unborn must be given a share.

Consider a few unfinished tasks and see how true it is that the men who began them can never see the realization of their hopes apart from us.

Take for instance the missionary enterprise. It has passed through several phases. Its first phase was dictated by the belief that for men who die without Christ the future is hopeless. Its second phase was dictated by the far more credible belief that for people who live without Christ the present is hopeless. The first missionaries went out to rescue the heathen from hell hereafter. Later generations of missionaries went out to rescue people from hell here and now. Today, the missionary enterprise is beginning to enter a third phase. It was once assumed that the West was Christian and the East pagan. How naïve that assumption! How curiously blind to the best in the

East and the worst in the West! Today the conviction is gaining ground that paganism has no particular geographical location. If paganism is the worship of Mammon— the Almighty Dollar—then paganism exists in America, not only in Asia. If paganism is the type of human faith which puts its trust in battalions and battleships, then paganism is to be found not only among peoples who are reputedly pagan but among peoples who are professedly Christian. Now, therefore, the missionary enterprise is entering upon a third phase dictated by the belief that the West no less than the East needs to be brought under the influence of the personality of Christ; that unless the people of every nation and of every race can be induced to accept Jesus' faith as to the fundamental nature of life and exhibit at least a little more of his spirit in their relationships one with another, the whole world situation will become increasingly hopeless. The new type of missionary is going out with no superiority complex, no holier than thou attitude, but with the profound conviction that it is Christ or chaos for the East not only, but for all the world.

These three phases of the missionary enterprise have been somewhat different, each from the other, but they have had at least one great and glorious thing in common —a long-range concern for the highest welfare of other people. You may, perchance, feel disposed to quarrel with the theology of any man who believes that for people who die without Christ the future is everlastingly hopeless; but surely you cannot refuse to applaud the spirit of any man who, having that belief, is ready to go to the ends of the earth to prevent such a catastrophe. A long range concern for the highest welfare of the people of every nation and of every race—that has characterized every phase of the missionary enterprise. That, when all is said, is the greatest contribution which the foreign missionary enterprise has made to the world. Not the doctrines it has promoted, not the churches it has founded, not the schools it has established, not the hospitals it has operated, but the habit of thinking in world terms, the habit of giving consideration to the rights and needs of people who live on the other side of the globe—that is the great, distinctive, and all-important contribution with which the missionary enterprise ought to be credited. That is the way in which it has given Christ to the world, called the world's attention to what is essential in Christianity: the faith of Jesus in the Fatherhood of God and the Brotherhood of Man, and the spirit of Jesus in every human relationship.

The question now is, Shall this long-range concern for the highest welfare of other people be kept alive in the world? It will not keep itself alive. We, the living, must keep it alive. It can very easily be lost. Let the missionary enterprise be junked. Let the spirit which has promoted it die out. Let a greedy commercialism develop unchecked in the far corners of the earth. Let a ruthless industrialism begin to do in China what it did in England before Lord Shaftesbury fought the battle of defenseless and exploited children. Let a militaristic imperialism attempt to maintain its economic invasions by a display of military force, undeterred by any Christian conscience. Let such events as these occur, and in a single generation the great, distinctive contribution which the missionary enterprise has made to the world will have been lost. The missionary can never see the fulfillment of his hopes apart from us.

Consider also the fight for freedom. It does not always and everywhere go without saying that freedom is essential to human welfare and human progress, so once more let it be said that freedom is worth fighting for. Tolstoi once wrote a letter to a friend in which he complained of the Russian censorship and spoke of the effect which it had on his own mental activity. He wanted to write what he felt. But whenever he sat down to do so, he found himself considering what he would be permitted to publish or forbidden to publish; and with the awful spectre of the censorship before him, once and again, he found it impossible to write anything. Let any ex-soldier who saw service in France say whether it was easy to write even so much as a letter to his sweetheart under the invisible eyes of the inevitable censor. Suppose you had always to write under the invisible eyes of a suspicious and relentless censorship. Suppose you knew that some of your very deepest convictions you could not hope to have published. What effect would that have upon your mental activity?

Nor is it only the interest of the individual that is here at stake. What is finally at stake is the possibility of intellectual and social advance. Not long ago, in a New Jersey town, when the suggestion was made that a war memorial should bear the inscription, "The nations shall beat their swords into ploughshares," a veritable storm of protest was raised by zealous patriots who suspected that that inscription had been inspired by Moscow. Suppose that twenty-eight centuries ago zealous patriots had prevented the utterance of that inspiring prophecy! In the year 1915, when a group of Quakers expressed a desire in France to minister to the victims of the war, they were told by the French Government that they might do so provided only that they made no attempt to promulgate their own peculiar doctrines. Desiring to know how far they might go, they asked whether it would be permissible for them to read in public, without comment, the New Testament. They were told that portions of that book might be very objectionable! Suppose that in ancient Galilee a strong armed squad had prevented the delivery of the Sermon on the Mount. Thanks to the splendid scholarship and noble heroism of William Tyndale, the Old and New Testament scriptures were translated into English; for which service the translator was speedily translated to another world. Having been betrayed by a friend, he was cast into prison, kept there for more than a year, then strangled to death and his body burned. It is largely due to the literary taste of William Tyndale that the English Bible is characterized by a simplicity which has made it one of the great classics of the world. What if Tyndale had not claimed and exercised a freedom which he did not officially possess? Three hundred years ago, a little group of harassed Christians brought their wives and children across three thousand miles of threatening sea to a new continent, and then, in the face of terrific odds, established a foothold in a wilderness in order to secure for themselves and their children freedom to worship God in accordance with the dictates of their own conscience. What if neither they nor anyone else with that purpose had ever come? In respect of freedom what is finally at stake is the possibility of human advance.

And note this fact: the fight for freedom is never permanently won. It is always an unfinished task. The freedom that is won by one generation must be fought for again by succeeding generations. Freedom appears to be one of those acquired characteristics which are not socially inherited. It is not something that one generation can pass on to the next. It is something that the next generation must win for themselves. Freedom of speech, freedom of the press, the right of the people peaceably to assemble and petition the government for a redress of grievances—such rights as these we thought we had here in America. Had not our fathers sweat and shed blood to secure them? Were they not guaranteed to us by our constitution? Yet during the past ten years, in one part or another of these United States, every one of these constitutional rights has been denied. And the American Civil Liberties Union, organized and operated solely for the purpose of protecting American citizens in the exercise of their constitutional rights, has been branded unpatriotic and even treasonable by a considerable number of influential Americans. During recent months, an undergraduate Liberal Club has been ordered off an American campus and commanded to disband because it had arranged a meeting for the consideration of the notorious Mooney and Billings case, a post-war case in which justice so flagrantly miscarried that even the judge who presided at the trial has, after a re-examination of the evidence, pled for the pardon of its victims. And a successful teacher has been summarily dismissed from an American college for having written and published an article in which he protested against the outrageous methods being employed by the constabulary of the state in which he lives.

Unless the freedom that was won by one generation is fought for again by succeeding generations, it is lost. The valiant dead who gave their all in order to secure freedom for their children's children cannot see the fulfillment of their hopes apart from us.

Consider, likewise, the fight for peace. I find myself thinking of Professor Thomas Kettle of the National University in Dublin. "Tom" Kettle, as he was affectionately called by those who knew him well, was one of the brilliant and trusted leaders of the nationalist movement in Ireland. But when the War began, to the surprise and grief of his nationalist friends, he accepted a commission in the British Army, went to France with an Irish regiment, and fell at Ginchi while leading his men in a victorious charge. Here was a man who hated war with an intelligent and passionate hatred. He expressed the hope that he would live to use all his ability as a speaker and writer to push out of civilization this obscene thing called war and to put into its stead understanding and fellowship. "Unless you hate war," he said, "you do not hate Prussia. If you believe that war is an essential part of civilization, all that you hate is Prussian efficiency." But with all his hatred of war he went into the War in the hope that he might help to win a victory that would give peace to mankind. As he himself put it in a poem which he wrote in the trenches, and dedicated "To My Daughter, Betty, the Gift of God," he

> Died not for flag, nor king, nor emperor,
>   But for a dream, born in a herdsman's shed,
> And for the secret scriptures of the poor.

War is not only hellish, it is stupid. It settles nothing. It unsettles everything. Under modern conditions it benefits nobody, not even the military victors. Why, then, let war go on? Why not put an end to it? In the words of a recent British cartoon, "If war is hell, why not send it where it belongs?" But war will never go where it belongs unless it is sent. It will never go of its own volition; nor at the command of persons who think that it is inevitable, or who say such things as this: "I hate war as much as anybody does, but I believe that in order to protect ourselves we must have the biggest navy afloat." In spite of all the sacrifices, all the bitter loneliness and awful sufferings of the men who lie today where poppies grow in Flanders Fields, war will go on until it makes a cemetery of white civilization unless enough people can be found to say that it can and shall be ended.

We do well to bear in mind the fact that a new generation is growing up that knows nothing about the horrors of war, a generation that can be seduced as preceding generations have been by the glitter and glamour of military parades and by the specious arguments and lying promises of persons in high position to whom history has taught nothing and never will teach anything. Now, therefore, is the time to put an end to war. Now is the time to tell children the truth about war. Now is the time to prevent a reckless competition in armies and fleets. Now is the time to develop economic policies which are promotive of goodwill. Now is the time to create machinery by which international disputes may be judicially settled. Now is the time to keep faith with the dead. If we permit a new generation to grow up unacquainted with the fallacies that have supported the war system, and unprovided with any machinery for a peaceful settlement of international disputes, it will then be too late to keep faith with the dead. Now is the time highly to resolve that the dead shall not have died in vain, that this world under God shall have the peace which they gave their all to secure.

XVII

IN THE WILDERNESS

IT will, I think, be generally conceded that Jesus made of human life altogether the most splendid thing that has ever appeared in our world. Other men have achieved something which not only their own generation but succeeding generations have agreed to call greatness—Plato, Leonardo da Vinci, Shakespeare. But none of them affects us as does Jesus. Other men have achieved something which the moral sense of mankind has recognized as goodness—Socrates, Francis of Assisi, Abraham Lincoln. But none even of these inspires us as does Jesus. Who does not recognize the underlying truth of that oft-quoted statement of Charles Lamb, "If Shakespeare should come into this room, we should all rise up to greet him. But if Jesus should come into it, we should all fall and try to kiss the hem of his garment"?

It has been claimed for Napoleon Bonaparte that the very sight of him, sitting so coolly and confidently astride his white horse, was worth many a battalion to the morale of his soldiers. And it appears to have been true of every great captain of mankind that his very presence exerted an incalculable influence upon his followers, stimulating them to do deeds of heroism which apart from him they would not have done. But, ordinarily, for the exertion of such influence it seems to be necessary that the inspiring leader should be physically present or at least physically alive. Napoleon has been dead how long? A little more than one hundred years. And yet, today, would the very thought of him inspire men to do such deeds of valor as were done at Austerlitz?

Consider then the marvel of Jesus. The United States of America has been a nation but little more than one hundred and fifty years. The very existence of this western continent has been known to the rest of the world less than four hundred and fifty years. The conquest of England by William, Duke of Normandy, dates back less than nine hundred years. Even the downfall of the Roman Empire dates back less than fifteen hundred years. Nineteen hundred years have come and gone since Jesus of Nazareth yielded up his spirit, and yet what a grip he has upon the heartstrings of the race! Nor is this due solely to the fact that he has been apotheosized, that in the belief of a multitude of men he was and is very God of very God. There are men today, increasing numbers of them, who can hardly be regarded as orthodox Christians, but whose admiration for Jesus of Nazareth is simply boundless; who could, without any mental reservations whatsoever, say as did Robert Browning:

> That one face far from vanish rather grows,
> Or decomposes but to recompose,
> Becomes my universe that lives and knows.

Surely, then, it is worth our while to consider how Jesus met experiences which we ourselves may be called upon to meet and how, amid circumstances outwardly different from ours but essentially the same as ours, he managed to make of life so true and good and beautiful a thing that he has captured and held, through nineteen hundred years, the gratitude and reverence of mankind.

Goodness that has never been tempted is not goodness. It is merely innocence, the absence of evil: negative, not positive. The innocent man, as the word itself implies, is a man who will not hurt you; in which respect he bears a certain resemblance to a six months' old baby. But if the most that people can say of us is that we are harmless, we are not likely to play any of the leading rôles on the stage of life. To be an "innocent" is hardly to be a hero. Goodness, that is to say, involves temptation. No man knows, or can know, what manner of man he is until he has been tempted. That is at least one intelligible and morally satisfying statement which may be made in reply to the old question, Why evil? Take out of human life all temptation, let no man be tempted in any way whatsoever, and you will have a world in which there are no sinners—a world also in which there are no saints.

And, of course, the greater the man, the greater his temptations. Your mediocre individual will never be either a great sinner or a great saint. But your man of extraordinary capacity is likely to become either a great criminal like Lorenzo de Medici, or a great moral hero like Abraham Lincoln. Even though the New Testament writers had failed to say so, we would be compelled to believe that Jesus was tempted. The most stupendous personality that history knows anything about—was he tempted? He must have been, and his temptations must have been extraordinarily severe. As a matter of fact, however, concerning some of the temptations that came to Jesus, the New Testament writers do speak. He himself spoke of them and what he said they did not hesitate to report. As he came up out of the waters of the River Jordan, in which he had been baptized, he heard in his soul the voice of the Eternal, saying, "This is my beloved son in whom I am well pleased." And then, straightway, says Mark, "the spirit driveth him into the wilderness and he was in the wilderness forty days tempted by Satan."

After the Jordan, the wilderness. After a great spiritual experience, moral struggle. It is always so. When Luther entered the city of Worms, according to the testimony of a papal legate, "he looked about him with those demon eyes of his and said, 'God help me.'" A rather strange exclamation to fall from the lips of a man who had the eyes of a demon! Luther came out of Worms an excommunicated heretic, and the greatest moral power in Europe. But soon afterwards, from his retreat in the historic castle of Wartburg, he wrote a letter to his friend Melanchthon in which he said: "Now for a week I have not written, nor studied, nor prayed, vexed with temptations of the flesh and other ills." After Worms, Wartburg. After a great moral victory, a renewal of moral struggle.

On the night of the 24th day of May, 1783, in a little room of a house on Aldersgate Street in London, John Wesley felt his heart strangely warmed. He felt, to recall his own words, that he did trust Christ and Christ alone for his salvation and that Christ had given him a blessed assurance that his sins were forgiven. Lecky says that the movement which began in that little room on that night in May, 1783, was historically of far greater importance than were all the splendid victories by land and by sea won under Pitt. But Wesley tells us that later on, during that same night, he was much buffeted by temptations; and two days later he wrote that he was in great heaviness of spirit because of manifold temptations. After the light of the little room where he had felt his heart strangely warmed, the darkness of a London Street. After spiritual ecstasy, spiritual struggle.

Today, some young fellow comes to a great decision. Like the spiritually awakened Dwight L. Moody, he says to himself, "I am going to see what God can do with a fully surrendered life." And he means it, every word of it. He goes to his dormitory room with a hallelujah chorus in his heart; and the very next day, perhaps, he finds himself trembling like a leaf before some totally unexpected gust of temptation.

The explanation of this lies, I suppose, in the fact that in some high and luminous hour a man may advance to a position that he is not immediately able to maintain. The spiritual momentum that has lifted him far above his normal experience suddenly spends itself and, like the pendulum of a clock, he falls down and back. For one glorious hour he has stood on the summit of a great experience, but before he may permanently stand there he must master himself.

In Jesus' own case, the inevitable reaction from a great experience was accompanied by mental confusion. He had come under the influence of the fiery Baptist and had decided to make his own John's great concern, the kingdom of God. But how should such a concern express itself? What action should it dictate? He did not immediately know. He sweat blood before he found out. In his case "the wilderness" stood not only for moral struggle, but for mental confusion; and surely at that point we may feel spiritually akin to him. We, too, know the meaning of mental confusion. Thousands upon thousands of persons belonging to our generation are wandering in a mental wilderness where the trails are often far from clear.

For better or worse our generation has developed a state of mind that takes little if anything for granted. Did our fathers argue as we do about God, whether there is a God? They argued about baptism, the Lord's Supper, miracles, the authorship of Old Testament books; but they took God for granted! Did our fathers argue as we do about the possibility of life after death? They wondered oftentimes where heaven was and what it was like. They sang:

> Jerusalem, the golden,
>   With milk and honey blest,
> Beneath thy contemplation,
>   Sink heart and voice oppressed.
>
> I know not, oh, I know not,
>   What social joys are there,
> What radiancy of glory,
>   What light beyond compare.

But that there was a sweet and blessed country, the home of God's elect, it never occurred to them to question. Immortality, too, they took for granted.

They also took morality for granted. Most of them supposed that the moral code which had been handed down to them by their parents had been dictated by God. Even those among them who suspected that social customs have something to do with the making of moral codes felt no disposition to question the validity of the moral code which social customs had created for them. All that was suggested by the words "sex morality," "business ethics," "national honor," they took for granted. It would no sooner have occurred to them to question its eternal validity, its profound justification, than it would have occurred to them to question the multiplication table.

Today, we take neither our theology nor our morality for granted. Is there a God? We would like to know. Is there any possibility of life after death? We would like to know. Many of us are not at all sure that all that is connoted by "national honor" is really honorable, or that all that is permitted by "business ethics" is really permissible, or that all that is demanded by social conventions is really mandatory. We are indeed in a mental wilderness, reluctant to follow the old trails that have led to social swamps and quicksands, and yet unsure where new trails ought to be blazed. And our present situation is at once full of hope and full of danger.

It is hopeful because no existing order is ever a perfect order. The world in which we are living today is certainly not a perfect world. It contains a number of things which ought not to be taken for granted. International war, the sort of government we have in many of our cities, the tone of many of our theatres, a dual standard for men and women and for the rich and the poor, an educational system that seeks to standardize rather than to stimulate, religious superstitions that stand in the way of progress— none of these ought to be taken for granted. If we are not in revolt against them, we certainly ought to be. The hopeful element in our present situation lies just in the fact that so many people are in revolt against intellectual, moral and social absurdities.

Carlyle once declared that had it not been for the French Revolution he would have found it extremely difficult to believe in God. I venture to think that I speak for others besides myself when I say that were it not for an increasingly general and effective protest against established wrongs and imbecilities I, too, would find it rather difficult to believe in God.

But our present situation, although it is full of hope, is fraught also with danger. It can hardly be denied that the French Revolution went too far, that it developed excesses which nobody today would undertake to defend. The demand for liberty became a demand for license. The demand for equality resulted during the next generation in a leveling down rather than in a leveling up. The demand for fraternity, inasmuch as it fell short of being an all-inclusive demand, merely arrayed class against class, as it has done also in Russia during the past ten years.

How foolish it would be for us to suppose that we are in no such danger today. In our angry revolt against religious beliefs that have cramped the minds of men and narrowed the hearts of men, is there not some danger that we may lose sight of those supreme realities which the saints and the seers of the centuries have seen? In our contemptuous rebellion against social conventions that are unintelligent and sometimes cruel, are we not in some danger of ignoring those unimpeachable lessons which the race has learned in the long, hard school of life? We can very well afford to revise a lot of our theology; we cannot afford to lose our faith in God. We can very well afford to modify a number of our social conventions; we cannot afford to tamper with life's demand for purity and for integrity in men's and women's hearts.

In his wilderness of mental confusion, what did Jesus do? Remember that he, too, was in revolt against a great many things that were generally accepted and approved by the people among whom he lived. In one of those early Christian discourses reported in the Book of Acts, he is referred to as "the pioneer of life." This man who was in revolt, this blazer of new trails, this pioneer of life, when he was mentally confused, what did he do? He turned for guidance to the great prophetic spirits of the past, the men who before he came had seen farthest into the heart of reality. Question: Should he turn stones into bread, confine his ministry largely to the physical needs of men? Answer: It is written, Man shall not live by bread alone. Question: Should he leap from the pinnacle of the temple, gratify the desire of his contemporaries for a sign, a sensation? Answer: It is written, Thou shalt not make trial of the Lord, thy God. Question: Should he fall down and worship the devil in order to secure the kingdoms of the world and the glory of them? Should he, that is to say, compromise his principles in order to carry out his program? Answer: Get thee hence, Satan, for it is written, Thou shalt worship the Lord, thy God, and him only shalt thou serve. Notice: "It is written"; and, "Again it is written"; and, "Get thee hence, Satan, for it is written." That from the lips of a man who had the courage to stand up and say that a good deal which had been written was not true; who dared to say to his contemporaries, "Ye have heard that it was said to them of old time—thus and so; but I say unto you—something different." Jesus never considered himself bound by traditional views or social conventions. Once and again he broke with tradition and defied convention. On the other hand, he never considered himself free to disregard the moral intuitions, the spiritual insights of the noblest spirits of his race. In that case what had been written became for him a compass by which he steered his own adventurous steps.

We are beset, it appears, by two great dangers. One is the danger that we may keep something that we ought to throw away; the other is the danger that we may throw away something that we ought to keep. One is the danger that we may go on believing something that isn't true; the other is the danger that we may go on disbelieving something that is true and exceedingly important. One is the danger that we may become slaves to social conventions, even those that are cruel; the other is the danger that we may kick over the traces of all conventions, even those which in the long run minister to the happiness of men. One is the danger that we may become blind and timid conservatives; the other is the danger that we may become befogged and reckless radicals.

I do not shrink from confessing that my own temperament leads me to be very much more afraid of the first danger than of the second. I am much more afraid of becoming a conservative than I am of becoming a radical. But that the second danger is a very real one I have not the shadow of a doubt; and the longer I live, the more convinced I become that every man ought to have in his moral firmament at least a few fixed stars. In his wilderness of mental confusion, there are some things which a man ought not to permit himself to doubt. The moral intuitions, the spiritual insights of the noblest persons, not only of his own generation, but of many generations, he ought not to permit himself to doubt. Concerning some things a man ought to feel constrained to say with Jesus, "No, I simply cannot think that, I simply cannot do that, for it is written —otherwise."

We said a while back that the wilderness for Jesus stood for mental confusion. Now let us remind ourselves that it stood also for moral struggle. The Master was not only in doubt, he was actually tempted. It would have been so much easier for him to heal men's bodies than to change their minds. It would have been so much easier to tickle people with a sensation than to challenge them with an ideal. It would certainly have been easier to make a few concessions (calling them "adjustments") than it would have been to risk crucifixion. And he, no less than we ourselves, was tempted to take the line of least resistance. I myself believe that his mental confusion, as is the case with us, was due in part to a moral struggle. He could find such excellent reasons why he should take the line of least resistance. What harm was there in healing men's bodies? What harm was there in doing at least a few of the things that people wanted you to do? And if by making a few concessions, you could win the confidence and the good-will of certain influential persons whose support would matter much to the cause you had at heart, why should you not make them?

Men do not ordinarily do wrong deliberately with their eyes wide open to the fact that what they are doing is wrong. No, they first deceive themselves into thinking that what they are tempted to do is "all right." They indulge in a mental process which psychologists call "rationalizing" —a process which seeks to find, and eventually does find, perfectly plausible and respectable reasons for doing what one is tempted to do. No evil so long as it appears to be evil causes us any moral disturbance whatever. But the moment something that is evil manages to array itself in the garments of something that is good, the moment lust begins to look like love, or self-conceit begins to look like self-respect, or cowardice begins to look like prudence, or selfishness begins to look like service, the moment a man is able to persuade himself that the wrong which he is contemplating is all right, then is he really tempted. The wilderness in which he then finds himself is one not only of mental confusion but of awful moral struggle.

How did Jesus manage to get out of *that* wilderness with his soul unscarred? One answer to this question is, I believe, revealed in the words, "Get thee hence, Satan." Evil had appeared to him as it does to us in the guise of good; but he was able at last to strip off the disguise. He was able to see what it actually was that was making its subtle, insidious appeal to him. In a word, he compelled himself to stop "rationalizing." He gave up all attempt to find acceptable reasons for unacceptable motives and methods. He compelled himself to recognize evil for what it was and said, "Get thee hence."

Until a man does that there is no hope for him. Of all the forms of deception of which men and women are capable, the very worst, as has been so often said, is self-deception. The man who deceives himself is in a bad way; and if he goes on deceiving himself his way gets worse and worse. Even in your twenties, if you begin to deceive yourself, you are in danger; and if in your forties, you are still deceiving yourself, still seeking and, of course, finding acceptable reasons for doing unacceptable things, your situation is really tragic.

The way out of the wilderness of moral struggle begins in utter honesty. A man must stop rationalizing. He must stop lying to himself. He must stop calling bad things by good names. He must begin to call a spade a spade. If he is being tempted by lust, it is time for him to say to himself, "This *is* lust, sheer, naked brutal lust, and the question for you to consider is, Are you going to be a beast?" If he is tempted by cowardice, the thing for him to say is, "This *is* cowardice, nothing else, and the one question before you now is, Are you going to be a coward?" And if he is tempted by selfishness, it is time for him to say to himself, "This is not a question of making a decent provision for your wife and children. It is not a question of laying up enough in store so that in your old age it will not be necessary for you to go over the hill to the poor house. It is just the question, Are you going to have some thought and regard for the rest of the world, or are you going to think only of your own sweet self?"

The moment a man begins to talk honestly to himself, the moment he begins to call things by their right names, his feet are on a path which, if he will follow it, will take him out of the wilderness. But the question remains, Will he follow it?

He will, I believe, provided he does another thing which Jesus did. "Get thee hence, Satan, for it is written, Thou shalt worship the Lord, thy God, and him only shalt thou serve." *Him only shalt thou serve.* The last and greatest of our needs is what? A master! Not something to serve us, but something which we ourselves may properly serve. Something that is great enough and good enough to command us, organize us, unify us, keep us from being a house divided against itself, and so call forth all the latent energies of our lives and enable us to concentrate upon the great task which lies before us.

In the course of his Inaugural Address, delivered on the occasion of his admission into the French Academy, the greatest of all Frenchmen, Louis Pasteur, said this: "Blessed is the man who has in himself a God, an ideal, and who obeys it; ideal of art, ideal of science, ideal of gospel virtues; therein lie the springs of great thoughts and great actions." A man is never at his best when he is being served, when some valet is laying out his clothes for him, or some chauffeur is opening the door for him. Only when he is being lifted out of himself by something that is greater than himself to which he is devoting himself, is a man at his best; only then does he become capable of thinking great thoughts and doing great deeds. Let a man say, as Jesus said, and say it as Jesus said it, "Lo, I am come to do thy will, O God," and not only will he find the trail that leads out of the wilderness, but he will discover that he has the strength and the courage to walk in that trail.

XVIII

ON THE MOUNTAIN

NAZARETH lies in a pocket of the Galilean hills, and of course you cannot see very much from the inside of a pocket; but the moment you climb up and out of this particular pocket you can see thirty miles in any one of three directions. Below you on the west lies the Plain of Esdraelon, and beyond that the Mediterranean Sea. Northward, you may catch a glimpse of the Lebanons, with their unforgettable cedars, and a little to the right of them the snow-capped summit of Mount Hermon. On the east lies the Valley of Jordan, running between the Dead Sea and the Sea of Galilee; and toward the south winds a road which becomes lost to view amid the mountains round about Jerusalem. Indeed, from a point easily reached from Nazareth it is possible to see almost all of that land which, because of its associations with the mightiest insights and greatest spiritual achievements of our race, has been known for centuries as the Holy Land.

Did Jesus ever climb those inviting hills which sheltered the little village in which he was born? We may be very sure that he often did. We may even suspect that it was from those hill-tops that he got his first glimpse of the kingdoms of the world and the glory of them. We would not, I think, be very far wrong were we to suppose that much of that amazing insight which characterized his words and deeds was born of those clarifying hours which he spent alone on the hill-tops of Galilee.

That Jesus did spend many hours in the solitude of mountains every one of his biographers intimates. In his life, as it is reported to us in the New Testament, some of the most significant of all chapters are associated with mountains. On a mountain he chose his first disciples. On a mountain he delivered his most wonderful sermon. On a mountain, as he labored to adjust himself to the thought of a violent and brutal death, he became transfigured. When he was lonely or discouraged, when he was mentally confused or morally disquieted, he betook himself to the hills and remained there until his vision had become clear and his soul had become fortified. The mountain, therefore, may stand for certain experiences which Jesus had and which we, too, may have.

I suggest that we let it stand first for vision. From the top of any high mountain on a clear day what a marvelous view may be had! I have stood on the top of Long's Peak and seen the Arapahoes; and beyond them, the Moffat Pass; and beyond that, Mount Evans, glistening white; and beyond that, in dim outline, more than one hundred miles away, the Peak that bears the name of Brigadier General Pike. I have stood on the top of Ranier, which ought of course to be called Tacoma, and seen the silvery cones of Mount Hood, Mount St. Helena, and Mount Adams. Some day I should like to stand on the top of the Matterhorn and see almost the whole range of the Alps. Who can ever forget his first glimpse of high mountains? And the experience that was his when he first reached the top of a high mountain? One enthusiastic mountaineer has not hesitated to say that "even to stroll up a hill is very often to get from the summit a new vision of life and of its possibilities." Let the mountain, therefore, first stand for vision.

How very amazing the vision of Jesus! He was, in some respects, and of course inevitably so, a child of his time; yet he saw beyond his time. He thought and lived ahead of his time. He is still ahead of our time. The race has never advanced beyond him. It has not yet caught up with him. He is not behind us; he is still ahead of us. And in our own most lucid moments we know perfectly well that he is the Way, the Truth, and the Life. He once declared that his words would never pass away. They have not. Imperial Rome has passed away. Feudalism has gone. Medieval theology is, if not wholly gone, at least destined to go. Many also of our most confidently held modern beliefs may be compelled to go, along with some of our most thoroughly entrenched institutions. But the words of Jesus, the words that he spoke on the mountain—"Blessed are the meek; blessed are the merciful; blessed are the pure in heart; blessed are the peace-makers. Whatsoever ye would that men should do to you, do ye also unto them. I say unto you, Love your enemies; do good to them that hate you"—is there not reason to believe that such words as these will remain unrefuted and, indeed, irrefutable?

I sometimes wonder whether we have today any greater

need than the need of vision. When he was inducted into what is probably the highest office in the world, the hand of Herbert Hoover rested on a Bible opened, at his own request, at the place where it is written, "Where there is no vision, the people perish." How very comforting it is to know that there is in the Presidency of the United States a man who appears to recognize the imperative need of vision. *For where there is no vision the people do perish.*

Not long ago, a widely read newspaper published on its first page one of those political cartoons which are intended, we are told, to furnish "a check upon government such as no constitution has ever been able to provide." This cartoon was captioned, "Will Future Generations Look Upon This Art Exhibit?" And beneath the caption there was presented two statues. One was entitled "The Victory of Samothrace" and was, of course, a reproduction of the famous statue of that name which presents, as you will recall, a graceful female figure having wings, but minus arms and minus a head. The other statue was entitled "The Victory of Sam," and presented a figure of Uncle Sam having wings but minus arms and a head. Now, of course, the only real association between Samothrace and Sam is a purely phonetic one; the two words sound somewhat alike. But the association obviously intended by the cartoonist was in the thought that ancient Greece lost her position as a world power because she did not go in for a sufficiently big army and a sufficiently big navy; and that the United States of America is destined to lose its place as a world power if it makes a similar mistake. For the

Baedeker which is being consulted by those future generations whom the cartoon contemplates, informs them concerning this headless, armless figure of Uncle Sam, "He
was once the richest and most powerful nation in the
world until he lost his head and disarmed himself. It is
believed that he lost his arms chasing butterflies."

Well, it is really too bad that the producers of political
cartoons, aimed to furnish a check upon government, are
in some cases unacquainted with the history of mankind.
Just a little acquaintance with ancient history would have
made impossible the drawing of this particular cartoon; for
the testimony of history is exactly the opposite of the
thought of the cartoonist. History affirms that ancient
Greece lost her position as a world power because, quite
literally, she fought herself to death. She exhausted herself in petty tribal wars. She diverted her energy from
the production of great art to the fighting of battles in
which her embryonic artists were killed off. She lost her
arms because she used them destructively. She lost her
head because she failed to see that her real glory was not
in her armies but in her art. The glory that was Greece
perished through lack of vision.

Marmont said of Napoleon, "There is so much future
in his mind." Personally I do not believe that of Napoleon
this was notably true; except at times as when, for instance,
he said: "There are only two powers in the world, the spirit
and the sword. In the long run the sword will always be
conquered by the spirit." Or when he said: "Alexander,
Cæsar, Charlemagne, and myself founded great empires.

But upon what did the creations of our genius depend? Upon force. Jesus alone built his empire upon love and to this day millions of men would die for him." There was occasionally a good deal of future in the mind of Napoleon, and had there been more of it, he would not have died as he did, an exile on St. Helena. Napoleon perished, the Napoleonic ideal is destined to perish, through lack of vision.

The trouble today with many a man lies just in the fact that there is so little future in his mind. He does not see beyond the present. The yellow journal, the salacious play, the cheap song hit, the sensational sermon—it "gets over," we are told; it "goes big." So it does today, but how will it do tomorrow and the day after that? What place will be occupied in history by William Randolph Hearst? How many of the plays that are now being offered to the American public will be performed three hundred years hence, or even thirty? How many of the present popular song hits will find any permanent place among the haunting melodies of the race? How many of the preachers who are now packing their churches by the employment of sensational methods will stand before the eyes of a future generation alongside of Horace Bushnell and Phillips Brooks? How many of them will be able to maintain their present popularity a score of years?

In the long run, it doesn't "get over," it doesn't "go big," this deliberate appeal to the galleries, this conscienceless sacrifice of high professional aims for the sake of immediate popular applause. Had Jesus consented to play to the galleries, he would no doubt have achieved an immediate popular success. And there would have been no Gethsemane, no Calvary. But neither would there have been a Resurrection. Today, so far as history is concerned, he would have been as dead as the dodo.

We need vision. How may we get it? In order to discover the answer to that question I sometimes find it helpful to put to myself, Yankee fashion, another question, namely, "Who are the people who do not appear to have any vision?"

Some of them are cynics. Is it not a noteworthy fact that the cynics of this world have always been wrong? They have never been able to forecast the next move on the chess board of history. They said, for instance, that religious freedom was not to be thought of, that human beings were not wise enough to be entrusted with it. They poohpoohed the idea of a free public school. They declared that dueling was inevitable, that it could never be stopped, that human passions were too quick and violent ever to submit to the slow processes of the courts. They likewise declared that negro slavery was inevitable, that all abolitionists were fools. They said that business was business, that economic values and moral values like oil and water do not mix, that business need not be bound by moral considerations. But today we have religious freedom; and we have a free public school; and the vast majority of us no longer attempt to settle our individual disputes by drawing a sword or firing a pistol. We have liberated the slave; and we are discovering that when you attempt to divorce business from morality the result is a tragedy not only for morality but for business; that lack of morality produces loss of confidence, and loss of confidence produces loss of business.

The cynics of the world have always been wrong. They have been proved to be devoid of vision. Today they are saying that prohibition is a farce, that the Kellogg Pact is a farce, that the World Court is a farce, and that the League of Nations is a farce. What will history be saying tomorrow?

Another human group which seems to be lacking in vision is composed of persons who are predominantly selfish. Whenever you find an individual whose habitual question is, "What is there in it for me?" you may write it down in black and white without any fear of being contradicted that he is as blind as a mole. Sooner or later he is certain to overreach himself. Even when it comes to economic values he is liable to make costly mistakes; for even economic values are to a very large extent dependent upon human values. Any move that is prejudicial to the welfare of other people turns out to be a bad move even from a purely economic point of view.

How very significant that recent declaration of Lord Grey: "No people can in the future consider itself victorious if it has sought its own security and not at the same time the security of other peoples." And might not one venture to add that no people can in the future become or remain a prosperous people if it has sought its own prosperity and not at the same time the prosperity of other peoples? Today, the United States of America is far and away the richest country in the world. But in order to remain a prosperous people we must go on producing; and in order to go on producing we must find markets for what we produce. We must find them not only here in America but across the seas; for we ourselves can no longer consume all that we are producing. And in order to find necessary markets both at home and abroad we must concern ourselves with the prosperity of other peoples. The time has indeed come when no nation can long maintain its own prosperity unless it shows a decent and intelligent regard for the prosperity of other nations.

Always and everywhere, in the long run, selfishness is self-defeating. It is self-defeating because it is short-sighted. Any man who goes about asking, "What is there in it for me?" will presently discover that the answer to that question is, "Mighty little."

We have, then, at least two answers to our initial query as to how vision may be developed. One way to develop vision is to develop faith. Whether you are handling real estate or international affairs, you need to have vision, and in order to have vision you must have faith. No man has ever made money in a real estate transaction without exercising faith, without daring to believe in advance of proof that in certain directions business was destined to extend and that in certain localities population was destined to increase. And no man has ever made any significant contribution to human welfare without exercising faith. Abraham Lincoln, William Wilberforce, Walter Reed, Louis Pasteur—none of them was a cynic; everyone of them was a believer. They believed; therefore they discerned. They penetrated the future, saw the leading of God and the eventual liberation of mankind. And Jesus—why was he able to see so far into the future? Why was he able to say things that even yet, nineteen hundred years afterwards, appear to be not only true but tremendous? Was it not, for one reason, because of the faith that was in him? He believed in God. He believed in men. He believed in love. He believed in the possibility of a better world.

Another answer to our query seems to be that the way to develop vision is to become unselfishly interested in something that is beyond yourself and greater than yourself. Consider the men whose names have just been mentioned. We have said of them that they were men of vision because they were men of faith. Must it not also be said that their vision was born of their devotion to great causes? Lincoln labored to save democracy. Wilberforce labored to liberate slaves. Reed and Pasteur labored to rid the world of certain diseases. Jesus labored to build on earth the city of God. They all gave themselves to something that lifted them above themselves. They were able therefore to see more than selfish individuals whose eyes are glued upon their own little affairs ever do, will, or can see. They climbed above the smoke of sensuous desire; they climbed above the fog of selfish passion; they climbed above the mist of self-centered thinking, and stood at last upon a sun-lit peak of human vision.

Let us now return to our figure of the mountain and

permit the mountain to stand not only for vision but for idealism. The first successful ascent of the Matterhorn was made in 1865; from the Swiss side by an Englishman and almost simultaneously from the Italian side by an Italian. Among the hundreds of persons who have scaled the Matterhorn since then there has been one blind man. A blind man on the top of the Matterhorn! Why did he climb up there? For the sake of the view? The question is almost brutal. But if not for the view for what did he endure all that hardship and run all that risk? I hope that nobody will consider me irreverent when I venture to suggest that he did it for God's sake. What I mean is that he did it in order to experience certain values in which the eternal God abides. And that I venture to believe is one of the reasons why any man undertakes to climb a high mountain.

I can, I think, understand the point of view of the occasional tourist who thinks that mountain climbing is sheer lunacy, and who says concerning the view that you are supposed to get from the top, "Bah! In nine cases out of ten you don't get it, for the peak is enveloped in clouds and the valley is obscured by mist. And even though the sky and everything beneath it is as clear as a crystal, all the way up you must pay such close attention to the place where you are to put your feet that you have little opportunity to see the view. And when you get up, if you do get up, you are so dog-tired that all you can do is to lie down flat on your back or your stomach until the guide says it is time to go down." I can, I think, understand that point of view and I am constrained to acknowledge that there is a good deal of truth in it; but with all my soul I pity the man who has it. To see a mountain, a high mountain, whose head is blanketed eternally in snow, and not hear the call of it, not feel the challenge of it, have no desire to climb it, suffer no pain until you have climbed it or at least attempted to do so—that is pitiful. That is to fail to realize that the greatest of all the rewards of mountain climbing is not anything material, not even a marvelous material view, but something within the human spirit. A feeling that you are mastering your flesh, that you are conquering your fears, that in some deep and profound sense you are making a man of yourself, a feeling of elation, a sense of triumph, a kind of spiritual exultation—that is the reward of the mountaineer. The mountain, therefore, may stand for idealism.

What is idealism? Is it not, when all is said, just an enthusiastic appreciation of the greatest values of life? Writes William James in one of his essays, "As you sit reading the most moving romance you ever fell upon, what sort of judge is your fox terrier of your conduct? With all his goodwill toward you the nature of your conduct is absolutely beyond his comprehension. To sit there like a meaningless statue when you might be taking him to walk, throwing sticks for him! What queer disease is this that gets possession of you every day of holding things and staring at them for hours together?" There are, in human life, certain values of which a dog is entirely oblivious—no shame to the dog, for he is only a dog. But that there are in human life certain great values of which some men are unconscious, that is a shame to them. "To go into an unremunerative profession, teaching, or preaching, and turn your back upon the golden rewards of a successful business career! To use your business as a means of serving the community when you might use it as a means of piling up wealth for yourself! What queer disease is this which causes you to prefer the intangible to the tangible, spiritual values to economic values?" There are men who talk like that—men who are no more conscious of the great values of life than a dog is of the delights of reading.

Nor is this lack of appreciation confined to the illiterate. In an address which he delivered at a Harvard Commencement dinner, William James pointed out the fallacy of the popular notion that a college education is a panacea for social ills. He called attention to the fact that some of the staunchest supporters of Tammany Hall were Harvard men, that some of the most unscrupulous of American journalists were Harvard men, that there was indeed hardly any public abuse for which a Harvard advocate could not be found. And is there any other great American University against some of whose graduates a similar indictment could not be brought? It seems to be entirely possible for a man to go to and through college without ever climbing the mountain of vision or of idealism.

Now, the general opinion concerning idealism is that it is a kind of spiritual luxury, not any kind of human necessity. Like a Rolls-Royce, the average man may get along without it. But is that opinion true? Without any kind of spiritual mountaineering how flat, uninteresting, and ignoble a place this world of ours would be! One way to visualize the development of civilization is to imagine a mountain called Truth, and a Socrates climbing up it; another mountain called Beauty, and a Michael Angelo climbing up it; another mountain called Goodness, and a Jesus of Nazareth climbing up it. There is, one hopes, at least some recognition of the fact that idealism has social value. Even so, however, the average man feels that it is not for him. He sees no reason why he should do any kind of mountain climbing. He is perfectly content to leave that sort of thing to geniuses and cranks. He fails to see that in idealism lie the great values of life, values which no man can afford to go without.

It is written not only in sacred scriptures but in the very constitution of the human soul that a man simply cannot live by bread alone. Here is a man into whose life there has come a great sorrow. He has lost his wife, or it may be his child. Can he live on bread alone? Here is a woman who has discovered that the man to whom she has given herself is unworthy of her trust. Can she live on bread alone? Could even a million dollars worth of bread ease the ache of her spirit? Or consider a situation far less tragic than that—the loss of fortune, or of health. A man finds himself faced with the necessity of adjusting himself to an entirely different mode of living. Can he live on bread alone? No, when we are up against it, when we are hard hit, we know perfectly well that we cannot live on bread alone. We would go crazy if we could not find something other than bread to live on. We must find something that has enduring worth, something which is strong enough to hold us up in the midst of anything and great enough to lift us out of ourselves.

I venture to think that at least a few readers of this page will understand what is being said. They have known the meaning of sorrow, of cruel disappointment, of bitter disillusionment. They have worshipped a human idol and presently discovered that he or she had feet of clay. They have sat down at a table where there was plenty of bread and been unable to eat even so much as a mouthful of it. They have been surrounded with all the comforts and many of the luxuries of life and gotten no satisfaction from them, no release from their pain. Then in their awful need they have turned to the Ideal. They have lifted up their eyes unto the hills, and the hills have brought them the first peace they have known in months.

Yes, the hills bring us peace because they bring us God. Far up on the Matterhorn there is a little chapel where the guides stop to pray before they undertake the last steep ascent, and I am told that when climbing parties reach that little chapel even the sceptics among them uncover their heads and become thoughtful. Just so in the pursuit of the Ideal, you come presently to a little chapel within your own soul and there you find God.

XIX

IN THE GARDEN

ON first thought there may appear to be something inappropriate, not to say ungrateful, in the use of a garden as a symbol of suffering, and of suffering so intense as to produce on the body of the sufferer a kind of bloody sweat. Ought not a garden to be associated with ferns and flowers and friendliness and be regarded as "the veriest school of peace"? And yet, as a matter of fact, it was in a garden that Jesus faced his gravest crisis and experienced his greatest anguish. I, myself, can vividly recall times on the Western Front, during the War, when the cold beauty of a moon-lit night served only to intensify our feeling of littleness and loneliness, and nearly drove us mad with futile longing. Nature even at her best does not always soothe and comfort us. Sometimes her very beauty only adds to our pain. There is then, after all, a kind of justification not only historical but psychological for the use of a garden as a symbol of human anguish.

On the night when he was arrested, Jesus said to the three men who seemed to be closest to him in spirit, "My heart is sad, sad even to death." He took them with him into a garden called Gethsemane and said to them, "Stay here and watch." Then he himself went a little farther into the garden (a stone's throw, Luke says) and literally fell upon his face, as a man may do in utter anguish. And he prayed, "My father, thou canst do anything. Take this cup away from me."

Before this, Jesus had faced the possibility of crucifixion. He had tried to adjust himself to it. He thought he had adjusted himself to it. Even when his friends suggested that it was unthinkable, he had refused to be misled by their optimism. On Monday night of this very week—it was now Thursday night—when a grateful woman had taken one of her heirlooms, a box of ointment, very expensive, and had broken it and drenched his head and his feet with it and wiped his feet with the hairs of her head, he had justified her seemingly extravagant act by explaining that she was but anointing his body beforehand for the burying. The thought of a violent death was by no means new to Jesus. He had lived for many weeks in expectation of the very thing that was about to come to pass. But it is one thing to form an heroic resolve, another thing to go through with it. When crucifixion loomed before him as an immediate prospect he shrank from it, and would have been not more but less than human had he not.

We would, however, do Jesus an inexcusable injustice were we to suppose that it was merely the thought of crucifixion that caused him such agony of mind. If that had been true he would appear to have been somewhat less heroic than Socrates was under similar circumstances. Something else was clearly involved. Suppose he should go through with it. What would come of it? Would anything come of it? Would his sacrifice make even so much as a ripple upon the life of the world? And what would become of his disciples—his students—to whom he had devoted most of his time and given the very best of himself? Already one of them had betrayed him. And the rest? He got up and went back to the place where he had begged three of them to wait and watch, and found that they were asleep. In his soul he knew that when the teacher was arrested the students would flee. Would they ever come back? Would anybody carry on after his death? If there was anything to be gained by his crucifixion he could go through with it. He was not a coward. But suppose it should lead to nothing . . . He sweat, as it were, great drops of blood.

Recall also that significant statement which appears in the earliest of all the accounts of this Gethsemane experience. In Mark's Gospel, we are told that when Jesus entered into the garden he began to be greatly amazed. Professor Moffatt translates, "He began to feel appalled." Amazed, appalled; why? Perhaps in our own experience we may come upon an answer to that question. We build up a certain conception of God. It helps us, supports us. We do not live on bread alone; we cannot. To an extent that we ourselves hardly appreciate we live on this conception of God. It nourishes us, fortifies us, brings us peace. And then one day we enter into some experience that seems to contradict it. This conception of God on which we have been living, does it after all fit the facts of life? It certainly does not appear to fit all of them.

But if God is not what we thought he was, what is there on which we may depend? Is there anything beyond the human on which we may depend? Human beings, once and again, fail us. If they do not actually betray us, they manage to sleep while we suffer. ("The spirit is willing, but the flesh is weak.") Is there nothing beyond the human on which a man may depend in a time of need?

Jesus, you see, had staked literally everything on the belief that there was at the heart of the world a magnificent, unfailing love. That was the foundation of all his teaching: "How oft shall my brother sin against me and I forgive him? Until seven times? . . . I say unto thee, until seventy times seven"; "Love your enemies; do good to them that hate you"; "Ye therefore shall be perfect as your heavenly Father is perfect." Love at the heart of the world; on that foundation he had built his teaching, his very life. And it seemed to be crumbling! He who had done no wrong was about to be crucified. Did he feel appalled because his thought of God as a heavenly father seemed to be slipping away from him and he found himself face downward, wrestling with a great mystery?

Soon or late we all find ourselves in Gethsemane. We enter into experiences that amaze and appall us. Here is the way in which Dr. John Brown, famed author of "Rab and His Friends," describes a crisis in his own life: "My eldest sister and I were awakened by a cry of pain, sharp, insufferable, as though one had been stung. We knew whose voice it was and in our night clothes we ran out into the passage and on into the little parlor. There stood our father, his hands clenched in his black hair, his eyes full of misery and amazement, his face white. He frightened us. He saw this or else his intense will had mastered his agony for, taking his hands from his head, he said slowly and gently, 'Let us give thanks,' and turned to a sofa in the room. There lay our mother—dead." Gethsemane!

The last of Franklin K. Lane's "Letters" remains unfinished. It was started the day before he died but stops in the middle of a sentence; and at the bottom of the page on which this unfinished letter is printed, the editor or publisher has added two words, "The End." Was that the end? When you begin to ask that question concerning someone who has been dearer to you than your own life, you, too, are in Gethsemane.

Nor is it only a crashing bereavement that may take a man into the garden. An unrequited affection may do it, a cruel disappointment, a bitter disillusionment. Consciously or unconsciously we all make certain demands of life. We demand that life shall give us this, or if not this, that it shall at least give us that. And when we discover that life apparently will not give us what we have expected of it we begin to feel amazed. We make demands also of certain persons, and when they fail us or at least seem to fail us the effect sometimes is shattering. Some of us even make demands upon ourselves, high and hard demands—not too high, nor too hard—but we fail to measure up to them and begin to feel sick at heart. Then, too, a sensitive nature is apt to feel appalled at times by the amount of pain that there is in this world. It does sometimes seem as though there were too much pain, as though pain went beyond the point where it could render any beneficent service. That suspicion raises disturbing questions as to the meaning and value of life. And when in the midst of an earnest attempt to reduce the amount of the world's pain a man finds himself confronted with apparent defeat, then indeed is he in Gethsemane.

Now a crisis is always a dangerous thing. In the case of a serious illness, it is the point where it is being decided whether the patient will get well or die. In the case of a serious temptation or sorrow or affliction, it is the point where it is being decided whether the person involved will be made or broken.

Think of Jesus, kneeling in the garden in such utter anguish that his sweat becomes as it were great drops of blood falling down upon the ground. He is facing a crisis. Would it be too much to say that humanity in him is facing a crisis? For what if that amazement which fills his soul should turn to fear? And what if fear should cause him to falter? What if, in the awful confusion of that Gethsemane experience, he should utterly lose his faith in God, and his loss of faith should unnerve him? In that event all those beautiful, splendid things which he has spoken will become meaningless. Men will forget them, or recall them only to reflect that they were after all merely spoken, never acted. And for centuries, it may be, the world will go on unilluminated by a great faith, unaroused by a great challenge, and uninspired by a great sacrifice.

Today, it is an intolerable thought that Jesus might have weakened in Gethsemane, lost his vision, and therefore his courage, and therefore his claim to the gratitude and the adoration of mankind. But in the garden he does not weaken. He sweats blood, but he does not surrender. He cries out in instinctive protest, "My father, thou canst do anything. Take this cup away from me." But at last in utter trust and in utter devotion he says, "Not my will but thine be done." And when he leaves Gethsemane he is master of himself, and of the world.

Gethsemane is not only a danger point, it is an opportunity point. What we are choosing to call the garden may not break a man, it may make him. It may not drag him down to ruin, it may lift him to a higher level of life. Many a man has come out of a serious physical illness stronger than he was when he went into it. Many a man, too, has come out of a great sorrow bigger and better by reason of it. In a recent and enthusiastic appreciation of George Gershwin, who is perhaps the most brilliant of our younger American composers, Otto Kahn says that he cannot deliberately wish that some great tragedy may come into the life of America for the sake of chastening its soul, or into the life of George Gershwin for the sake of deepening his art, but he would like to quote to him a few lines by Thomas Hardy which are supposed to refer to America:

> I shrink to see a modern coast
>   Whose riper times have yet to be;
> Where the new regions claim them free

From that long drip of human tears
Which peoples old in tragedy
Have left upon the centuried years.

"The 'long drip of human tears,' my dear George! They have great and strange and beautiful power, those human tears. They fertilize the deepest roots of art, and from them flowers spring of a loveliness and perfume that no other moisture can produce."

Gethsemane always appears to be tragedy, but it may be opportunity. It all depends upon how you face it. What, then, must you do to be saved in a crisis?

I suggest that the first thing that a man needs to do when he finds himself in Gethsemane is to see his situation as it actually is. Nothing is ever gained by refusing to look facts squarely in the face. Facts are stubborn things which soon or late a man must face whether he wants to or not. And it is very much better to face them at once; for until you do face them, you cannot begin to adjust yourself to them, and until you do begin to adjust yourself to them you cannot hope to win out. Had Henry Ford refused to face the fact that his Model "T" was becoming unsalable, he would not have reorganized his factory, and if he had not reorganized his factory he would today be doing a losing business. Had Jesus refused to face the fact that his situation had become really desperate, he would hardly have been able to adjust himself to it, and had he not been able to adjust himself to it, there is no telling what would have happened. As it was, he was prepared for the arrival of Judas and the temple guards when they came with swords and staves to arrest him.

In order to meet a crisis in such fashion as to turn apparent defeat into actual victory, a man needs to see his situation as it actually is; and then he needs to accept it. By this, let me hasten to add, I do not mean that he needs to lie down and do nothing. All that I mean is that he must not waste precious time and energy in vain hopes that his situation will turn out to be something different from what it actually is. Henry Ford must not go on hoping that his Model "T" will sell; it won't. Jesus must not go on hoping against hope that crucifixion without compromise can be avoided; it cannot. So long as you allow yourself to hope that your situation may turn out to be something other than what it actually is, you will be full of fear.

When Jesus was hoping and praying that the cup would be taken away, he was amazed and appalled; but the moment he accepted the fact that it would not be taken away, he began to feel strangely calm and unafraid. When you find yourself confronted with something which you cannot but wish were otherwise, but which seems to be inevitable, you do yourself no good but rather harm by clinging to the hope that it may after all prove to be escapable. In case you do that you will find yourself alternating between hope and despair, feeling today somewhat encouraged, but tomorrow fearfully depressed. Meanwhile, your opportunity to adjust yourself to an untoward situation, and so to transform it from something that looks like tragedy into something that actually is triumph, will be slipping away. When a man has something unpleasant to face, the best thing for him to do is to face it.

Then what? Adjustment! How easy to speak the word; how difficult to do the thing which the word implies! Yet many human beings have done it, and done it gloriously. Robert Louis Stevenson adjusted himself to a fatal, lingering illness. He was made, he said, for contest and the powers had ordained that his battleground should be the dingy, inglorious one of the bed and the physic bottle. But on that inglorious battlefield he put up a glorious fight. George Matheson adjusted himself to total blindness and learned, without eyes, to see more than many a man with eyes has been able to see. Jesus adjusted himself to crucifixion and made his death serve and advance the cause to which he had given his life.

Think also of the people who, today, are making difficult adjustments. Here, a man who has lost his wife is bravely going the rest of the way without her. There, a man who lost his business is bravely beginning all over again at an age when it is extremely difficult to make a fresh start. Here, a woman who has been left penniless with two little children to support is undertaking not only to support but to educate them. There, a woman who has been denied motherhood is making a gallant attempt to sublimate a great and imperious instinct and to find at least a partial satisfaction for the hunger of her heart by mothering other people's children. Here, some young fellow who had intended to go to college has gone instead, without a word of complaint, and gotten a job in order to support his widowed mother and a younger brother and sister. There, some young woman has dropped out of college for a year or two in order to earn enough money to go back.

Adjustments—people are making them, all unaware of the fact that they are doing anything heroic. Not long ago I ran into a young friend of mine who for several years, since his father died, has been working during the day time and going to school at night. But when I suggested to him that he was entitled to a Carnegie Medal, or something of the sort, in recognition of supreme gallantry in action, he just laughed. "Why," he protested, "hundreds of fellows are doing the same thing." And so they are. And in their case, what might have been tragedy is being moulded into eventual triumph. Night after night finds thousands of human beings face downward in some Gethsemane earnestly praying that some cup of bitter disappointment may be taken away from them. But when they discover that it cannot, or at least will not, be taken away from them, some of them decide to drink it and make the most of it. And lo, what seemed to be a cup of gall turns out to be a cup of blessing.

Any one of us who has some difficult adjustment to make ought surely to be cheered and encouraged by the knowledge that other people are making adjustments no less difficult than his own. And yet, as I personally know only too well, that knowledge is not enough. When you are sweating blood in Gethsemane you can all too easily persuade yourself that your own situation is different, or that at least you yourself are different. You may say to yourself, "These others, no doubt, are adjusting themselves to situations no less desperate than mine, but they are made of heroic stuff and I am not." The bare knowledge that adjustments are being made by others is not enough. In Gethsemane a man needs to administer to himself a kind of shock. He needs to say to himself, "You have reached a turning point in your life. Before you lie two roads. One leads to certain defeat; the other leads to a possible victory. You may, on the one hand, give up and go down; or you may, on the other hand, get up and go on. Which are you going to do?"

But if a man is to get up and go on he must have help. What is the secret of adjustment? What does adjustment inwardly involve? It involves, does it not, the getting hold of something that will enable you under any circumstances to go on. A man enters Gethsemane the moment he is asked to give up something that he greatly values. The question is, Can he give it up and go on? The answer seems to be that he can if he finds something else to go on with. If one kind of support is taken away, some other kind must be found. No man can go on without anything to hold him up. Adjustment, then, means the discovery of some new kind of support, some new means of going on. In Gethsemane you are stripped of much that you held dear, and when you are stripped of old values you simply must find new values.

Must you not, indeed, find life's supreme and abiding values? In the autumn of his life, when he was just past sixty years of age, John Greenleaf Whittier wrote a memorable poem in which he said:

> The aster flower is failing,
>   The hazel's gold is paling,
> Yet overhead more near
>   The eternal stars appear.

This poem is not inappropriately entitled, "My Triumph." A man does triumph when he begins to see the eternal stars, the things that matter most and that last on. When he begins to live for and on life's supreme and abiding values, a man can get along without wealth, without health, and without many another satisfaction which he once craved and hoped for.

This, I suspect, is only another way of saying that in Gethsemane what a man needs is religion. After all, it is only in religion that the eternal stars appear. Not in nominal religion. I can understand perfectly well why some people say that they have never been able to get any comfort out of their religion. I can understand it because I myself have tried to get comfort out of nominal religion and have gotten none. How often have I talked about faith and then refused to exercise it! How often have I thought about trust, the absolute need of trust in something or somebody, and then refused to make the experiment! How often have I quoted the words, "Thou wilt keep him in perfect peace whose mind is stayed on thee," and then failed to stay my own mind on God. And of course nothing came of it. Nothing could come of it; no comfort, no peace, no sense of being supported by everlasting arms. It is easy to pronounce the great religious words and to repeat the great religious phrases, and make no attempt to get any first-hand experience of what they mean; but that does not get you anywhere. It certainly does not lift you up to a point where the eternal stars appear.

I may be wrong, but I do not think that I am, in the belief that a multitude of men today are hungry for religion, hungrier than they have been since the War. Men sometimes sit at a table full of bread and find that they cannot eat so much as a mouthful of it. They get up and go away, feeling nauseated and faint. Yet there is nothing physically wrong with them; their sickness is not of the body but of the soul. They might say, as Jesus did in Gethsemane, "My soul is exceeding sorrowful." What they need is religion. Not nominal religion, a mere recitation of religious language, but vital religion; and that may be achieved only by some such prayer as that which the Master offered in Gethsemane, a prayer which pours out all the pent-up anguish in a man's heart, but climaxes in a great act of self-surrender.

"Abba Father, thou canst do anything. Take this cup away from me. . . . My Father, if this cup cannot pass unless I drink it, thy will be done." That is not merely talking about faith, it is exercising faith. It is saying in effect, "I may not be able to prove that it is so, but in the name of the highest that I have seen and the noblest that I have felt, I am daring to believe that there is love at the heart of everything, and I am putting my trust in that love."

How significant the fact that once Jesus had definitely committed himself to that great venture of faith, the last shred
of uncertainty was stripped from his mind, the last tor-
ment of fear was taken from his heart, and he got hold of
something which brought him comfort and gave him
strength. He was then able to do what remained with a
calmness and a courage which were nothing short of
sublime.

XX

ON THE CROSS

HOW very astonishing the fact that one of the greatest of all our human symbols of Reality is a cross. The historic event which furnished the symbol represented the very worst that man may do to man. It was not an occasion for rejoicing; it wrung from the heart of an innocent victim an awful cry of despair. It was certainly not an occasion for self-congratulation on the part of those who brought it to pass; it secured for them a most unenviable place in the history of mankind. At the time, it seemed to be stark tragedy, the death knell of a great hope, the end of a cause that was lost. How strange, then, it is that humanity should have found in this event the most comforting and inspiring of all its symbols of Reality.

The cross has, to be sure, another aspect. If it stands for fears that led men to do a deed of infamy, it stands also for a faith that led one man to give up his life for an ideal. If it stands for a hate that stopped at nothing, it stands also for a love that did not fail. Even so, however, the cross remains a perpetual reminder of the awful odds which human faith is obliged to meet in this world, and of the awful price which human love is sometimes obliged to pay. That it has, nevertheless, become the most com-

forting and inspiring of all our symbols is surely a tribute
to the greatness of the human spirit.

> When I consider the heavens, the work of thy fingers,
>   The moon and the stars which thou hast ordained,
> What is man that thou art mindful of him?

One answer to that question is that man is a creature
who is great enough to see that the cross, which seems to
proclaim the defeat of all his highest hopes, is nevertheless
the victory which overcomes the world.

Now, the cross is no isolated fact in human experience.
Jesus lived in no world apart. He shared our common lot.
In the wilderness he was confused and tempted, even as
you and I. On the mountain he did, to be sure, see farther
into the heart of things than anyone before him had ever
seen; but even that mountain vision has proved to be
sharable. And in the garden he sweat blood as many another man has done. In every case which we have thus far
considered, Jesus' experience of life was by no means
unique.

Let us not make the mistake of supposing that his experience of the cross was anything unique. He himself,
apparently, did not so regard it. He associated it with the
fate of the prophets who had come before him and with
the fate which he foresaw of many a man who would
follow after him. To his first disciples he said, "Blessed
are ye when men shall persecute you . . . so persecuted
they the prophets that were before you." And he said to

them also this: "If any man would come after me, let him deny himself and take up a cross and follow me." On his way to Golgotha, as he passed some weeping women, he said to them, "Daughters of Jerusalem, weep not for me, but weep for yourselves and for your children . . . for if they have done these things in the green tree, what will they do in the dry?" Jesus did not regard his experience of the cross as anything unique in the life of mankind. He regarded it as something only too common in the path of progress. He himself was and remains a figure absolutely unique in human history. No one equal to him in spiritual splendor has ever appeared in our world. But there was and is nothing unique in the cross on which he died. In the wilderness, on the mountain, in the garden, his experience of life was such as other men have known. So also was his experience on the cross.

The cross, however, ought not to be associated with every kind of human suffering. You and I sometimes speak of the cross which we ourselves are obliged to bear. In so doing, consciously or unconsciously, we associate ourselves with one who stands before the eyes of history as the supreme moral hero of the race. The association compliments us and comforts us. But just what is the connection between the experience that we call our cross and the experience of Jesus when his enemies nailed him to a tree and made sport of him while he died? Must we not frankly acknowledge that any connection is a bit difficult to find? Life has hit us and hurt us, it has wounded us and bruised us; but not by reason of our devotion to any costly cause, not by reason of anything that we have undertaken to do to advance the coming of the kingdom of God.

I suggested a moment ago that the choice of the cross as a significant symbol of reality is a tribute to the greatness of the human spirit, and so it is; but let us not overlook the fact that we are constantly tempted to empty that symbol of all the meaning that has made it significant. When the cross is made a symbol of just any kind of pain or sorrow, it ceases to have any significance. A hot water bottle as the symbol of pain, a bit of crêpe as the symbol of sorrow, would serve as well. It is only when the cross is reserved as a symbol of pain and sorrow born of devotion to a costly cause that it proclaims the inextinguishable faith and glorious idealism of the human heart.

We are contending that the uniqueness of Calvary was in Christ, not in the cross. We are insisting that the cross is not only a common but a far too common fact in human history. It does not follow, however, that the cross is altogether devoid of mystery. There is always something mysterious in the rejection of truth and in the crucifixion of love. Truth would seem to be something that a man ought eagerly to embrace; love would seem to be something that ought to bring a man to his knees in gratitude and worship. Why, then, is it that once and again in human history truth has been rejected and love crucified? Why is it that the path of human progress is marked by crosses, that as Lowell puts it in an unforgettable line, "By the light of burning heretics Christ's bleeding feet I track?"

We may see in part but only in part by considering the

human passions that brought about the crucifixion of Jesus. One of them undoubtedly was fear. In Christian preaching during nineteen centuries the Pharisees of the New Testament have been treated with scorn. Even in the New Testament itself they are caused to appear in a very unfavorable light. But it is at least conceivable, and indeed probable, that the writers of the New Testament were too close to a great tragedy to be able to see with perfect clearness what it was that brought it about. Jewish scholars, and among them some who were very sympathetic toward Christianity, have always claimed that the Christian world has been unjust to the Pharisees of the New Testament; and one is compelled to admit that they have produced a good deal of evidence in support of their contention that many of the first opponents of Jesus, far from being brazen, brutal hypocrites, were sincere and earnest and honorable men. Let us grant for a moment the truth of this contention and then see whereunto it points. It points, does it not, to the fact that even perfectly sincere and very earnest men may conspire together to crucify a great prophetic spirit? Why? Through fear—fear that certain values which they hold to be infinitely precious are being endangered by the position which the prophetic spirit has dared to take.

Does not that appear to be a reasonable explanation of a good deal of the opposition that was encountered by Jesus, and by the prophets who came before him, and by those who came after him? How furiously in our own time evolution and evolutionists have been assailed by persons who were afraid that if the doctrine of evolution should be generally accepted, religious faith would be destroyed. How furiously at this present moment pacifism and pacifists are being assailed by persons who are afraid that if the principles of pacifism should be generally accepted, the very life of the nation would be imperiled. In order to account for history's recurrent Calvarys, it is not necessary to suppose that everybody who had a hand in them was a deeply dyed villain influenced only by sordid and sinister motives. In many cases all you need to do is to recognize the fact that a very sincere, earnest and honorable man may, through fear, stand in the way of progress.

We come, however, upon another fact the moment we begin to consider the part that Caiaphas played in the crucifixion of Christ. Here again one discovers the presence of fear, but of a very different kind of fear—fear not for the higher values of life, nor for the fate of a nation, but for one's own personal fortunes. Undeniably, the teaching of Jesus threatened the place and the power of a man like Caiaphas. The appearance of a prophet is always a threat to a profiteer. If a man like Jesus can get a hearing, a man like Caiaphas must step down and out; and a man like Caiaphas has no intention of stepping down and out if he can possibly avoid it. He will not resort to extreme measures if milder measures will serve his purpose; he will try flattery and bribery before he will resort to crucifixion. But the moment he discovers that he is backed against a wall, that his place and power are really threatened, he will stop at nothing. The lengths to which a man like Caiaphas will go when really threatened may be illustrated not only by the crucifixion of Jesus but by the burning of Savonarola, the hanging of Arnold of Brescia, the awful persecution of the Waldensians, the treatment accorded John Wycliffe, William Tyndale, and George Fox, and by the recent political bombings in Chicago. When a man who is selfish through and through finds that his position in society is being challenged and threatened, he will stop at nothing to save himself.

We are forced, then, to conclude that the crosses which mark the path of progress have been erected not only by the fears of men but by the cold and calculating selfishness of men. Prophetic spirits have been made to suffer, not only because many of their fellows failed to see the truth and beauty of what they pled for, but because some of their fellows saw only too clearly that what they pled for would, if granted, occasion the loss of their own place and power.

And to the fears of men and the selfishness of men, must one not add also the pathetic ignorance and stupidity of the crowd? On Palm Sunday Jesus rode into Jerusalem accompanied by a crowd of excited persons crying, "Hosanna! Hosanna!" (God bless him! God bless him!) Five days later an excited crowd cried, "Crucify him! Crucify him!" Perhaps it was not the same crowd; one hopes that it was not. But the crowd that did demand the crucifixion of Jesus—how did the members of it form their opinion of him? Had they made any attempt to discover what he really stood for? A hundred chances to one, they had listened only to vague rumors and considered only official pronouncements of his guilt. It was said that he was a heretic. It was rumored that he was planning to betray the nation. That was enough. Such a man deserved to die. And so, a multitude of excited persons turned against the very man who would have delivered them from burdens grievous to be borne.

So did the crowd in those days. So likewise does the crowd in these days—the crowd that reads newspapers and only the newspapers, that listens to hearsay and vague rumor and official pronouncements. Is it not exceedingly probable that in the event of another war of major importance, even though it were as sordid and unnecessary and ultimately futile as was the World War, the crowd in every country involved would turn against any man who would seek to save it from a great catastrophe? In generation after generation prophetic spirits have been obliged to contend, not only with the fears of men and the selfishness of men, but with the awful ignorance and stupidity of the mob which, when excited, always clamors for the release of Barabbas and the crucifixion of Christ.

Is the cross, then, inevitable? It would seem to be. Much, no doubt, may and should be done to avoid it. Dean Church has a memorable sermon on "The Imperfections of Religious Men" in which he says that even while we read with tears and a thrill of awe the acts of the martyrs, we sometimes wish there had been more self-restraint and less defiance. Personally I would not advise any young preacher to say to his congregation, as the prophet Amos said to his, "Listen to this, you cows of Bashan, you women in high Samaria." Many a man of prophetic quality has gotten into trouble, not so much by reason of what he said, as by reason of the way in which he said it. What he said was all right, but the way he said it was all wrong. When something unpleasant needs to be said, it ought to be said; but it ought not to be said in a needlessly irritating fashion. It is not necessary to be rude in order to be honest. It is not necessary to insult people in order to tell them the truth. If only the truth had always been spoken in love, there would probably have been fewer crosses on the path of progress. If only the prophets of mankind had, in some instances, been a little more patient with mankind, been willing to wait for the educational process to do its slow but certain work, the number of human Calvarys would doubtless have been reduced.

But all this being granted, the very significant fact remains that *Jesus was crucified*. It seems to be true that no matter how careful you are, no matter how considerate and patient you are, the moment you arouse fear or run counter to selfish ambition or cut across the grain of prejudice you are likely to get into trouble. Your technique may be ever so perfect and your spirit ever so commendable; neither the one nor the other will avail to ward off opposition. The cross is inevitable. In future generations, as in generations past, worshippers of light ancestral will make present light a crime. Worshippers of dead radicals —and, as someone has said, every living conservative is a worshipper of a dead radical—will make it awfully hard for living radicals. People who subscribe to the erection of monuments to prophets who have achieved immortality will go on despising and rejecting prophets who are destined to achieve immortality. Hitherto, the way of progress has been a Via Dolorosa. It has brought men into Gethsemane where they have sweat as it were great drops of blood. It has brought men to Calvary where they have wondered whether even God had not forsaken them. And so far as we can now see there is no less costly way of achieving progress.

I find, therefore, that I am personally confronted with a searching question: What price am I paying to secure progress, any kind of human progress? Am I making any sacrifice or running any risk? Walter Rauschenbusch once called attention to the fact that in some European countries Foreign Missionary service has been largely reserved for young men and women belonging to the artisan class, whereas in the United States it has been undertaken by college-bred men and women. Then he went on to call attention to the further fact that in the long struggle for human freedom European universities have played a far braver and more sacrificial part than American universities have ever taken. It is, I suspect, a fair and uncomfortable question whether the college-bred men and women of America have played anything like the sacrificial part that might reasonably have been expected of them in the great struggle for civil liberty and social justice.

Recently, however, on American campuses, there has been a marked change of attitude. In the colleges of today there is, no doubt, a sufficient amount of frivolity and thoughtlessness and irresponsibility and down-right selfishness; but there is also a most heartening amount of fine idealism, wedded to a calm and critical and astonishingly well-informed intelligence. After everything has been said that may truthfully be said about drinking and "petting" and all the rest of that sort of thing, the fact remains that college students today are interesting themselves in matters about which college students in preceding generations felt no concern. How many persons who were in college twenty-five years ago ever spent so much as an hour in intelligent concern about industrial relationships, international relationships, or inter-racial relationships? Yet in relationships such as these many students today are profoundly interested. They are asking, How may we secure justice in industry? How may we eliminate prejudice and cruelty from race relationships? How may we secure for our fellow students whose skins are black equality of opportunity? How may we secure peace for the world? On the present-day campus there is, undeniably, a growing number of young men and women who are not willing to acquiesce in things as they are, who sense the painful disparity between the pious professions and the selfish practices of a so-called Christian civilization, and who are attempting to regulate their own lives by standards for which society beyond the campus is not yet ready.

If they persevere in this attempt to live above the level and ahead of their time, soon or late they will get into trouble. But will they persevere? Or will they grow tired, or become discouraged by reason of repeated disappointments and prolonged delays? Will they go in for idealism only so long as it doesn't cost anything to be an idealist and then begin to back away from it the moment they discover that for them, also, idealism is likely to involve the cross?

In the year 1521, the year when Luther refused to recant, Erasmus wrote frankly to a friend: "All men have not the strength for martyrdom. If a tumult should arise, I very much fear that I should imitate Simon Peter." In a time of crisis, many of the rest of us would probably play a similarly unheroic part; but if we did, would it not be with a feeling of shame, a lingering sense of personal defeat, a haunting, tormenting realization of the fact that when our great hour came we were not brave enough to meet it?

Life appears to present this alternative: we may follow the line of least resistance, adjust ourselves to our social environment, acquiesce in things as they are, and endeavor to get out of them the very most possible of profit and pleasure for ourselves; or we may decide to sacrifice present advantages for the sake of ultimate values. We may decide to live not only for the present but for the future, to build our lives into a civilization that has as yet no existence save in the dreams of prophetic spirits and, as we hope and try to believe, in the mighty purpose of God. In the one case, life is very apt to prove easy for us. We shall probably make some money, live comfortably, even luxuriously. But we shall never live greatly. And when it is all over, this brief but important day which we call life, our names will be writ in water. We shall have made no contribution to the years that are to be. In the other case, life is not likely to be easy for us; on the contrary, it is likely to be hard. We may not live luxuriously or even comfortably, *but we shall live greatly*. Wealth, popularity, social position may be denied us. But the glorious company of the apostles, the goodly fellowship of the prophets, will be ours; and the satisfaction of knowing that we are building our lives into something that is destined to endure and have enduring worth; and the comforting hope that perhaps, by reason of something which we have said and done, those who come after us will be able to experience a little more of the joy and beauty of life.

When Jesus had been on the cross for six awful hours, he suddenly cried out, "My God, My God, why hast thou forsaken me?" Neither Luke nor John makes any mention of that cry; and in the apocryphal gospel of Peter, it is toned down to, "My strength, my strength, why hast thou forsaken me?" Evidently, the early Christians were afraid to acknowledge that Jesus ever knew despair; but in all probability some such cry as that which Mark reports was wrung from his soul. When a man has devoted everything that he has and is to a great cause, only to discover that his devotion has brought him to a cross, and that even his cause is about to be crucified, he cannot but wonder whether God really cares, whether indeed there is a God who could care. He is "in extremis" because he has sought to advance the kingdom of God; yet God stands by and does nothing. Why?

To this truly dreadful question there are, I believe, two

answers. One is that in a world that is morally conditioned you simply cannot secure the triumph of truth or of righteousness by the employment of violent methods. When a man is being tortured on a cross he cannot help wishing that God would physically intervene. I confess that sometimes when I myself am perfectly comfortable, but thinking of the awful injustices of life, I wish that for just five minutes I might be entrusted with the use of a few thunderbolts! But suppose that in Jesus' case God had intervened with a few thunderbolts. Suppose that God had struck down dead every would-be perpetrator of Calvary! What would have been accomplished? What single truth would have been made more clear by that kind of physical interference? What single victory for righteousness would have been won? Has human nature ever been changed radically and permanently by any demonstration of sheer physical force? *God did not, and indeed could not, intervene because of the very fact which seems so often to be in question, namely, the moral structure of the world.*

That, I believe, is one answer. Another is one that may be given only by faith, but by a faith for which there seems to be a vast deal of support in human history. God is not a passive spectator of human Calvarys. He is not indifferent to the fate of his suffering servants. He permits the cross to be erected, the tragedy to be consummated. Then he turns that tragedy into triumph. We reward people who make compromises. Perhaps we do so because we ourselves desire to be rewarded even when we make compromises. But in our heart of hearts, we never fully respect our compromisers. We crucify men who refuse to make compromises and then, in our heart of hearts, we worship them. They exercise a power over us such as successful worldlings never command. They rebuke us, they challenge us, and they redeem us.

Was Jesus forsaken by God? No, God saw to it that Jesus triumphed when he died. When the Master prayed, "Father, forgive them; for they know not what they do," he conquered in his own soul all hate and bitterness and self-concern. And when, having recovered the confidence which momentarily he had lost, he said, "Father, into thy hands I commit my spirit," and then with a loud inarticulate cry gave up the ghost, he made himself master of spiritual forces which slowly but surely are conquering the world.

XXI

THE FOOLISHNESS OF PREACHING

A FEW years ago, Mr. John Spargo published an article in which he said, chiefly, three things: first, as long as humanity endures religion will endure; second, as long as there is a future for man there will be a future for organized religion—the church; third, the weak spot in the church today, its Achilles' tendon, is the pulpit. It was, he thought, very doubtful whether all the preaching that would be done in America during the next twelve months would add as much to the well-being of America as the work of one honest, efficient farmer or of one humble school teacher in some little red schoolhouse. "Preaching," he went on to say, "is not a man-sized job. The pulpit is an anachronism in the modern world." It had its place in a day when the great multitude of folk could neither read the Bible nor understand it without the help of an interpreter. It has no place in a day when the average layman is quite as able to read and understand the Bible as the average clergyman. Too much, moreover, is expected of the modern preacher. He is expected Sunday after Sunday at a fixed hour to stand up and deliver a new message; and "given an intelligent congregation, there is no earthly reason for supposing that any man can possibly have anything of importance to say to it week after week. year in and year out"—et cetera. I shall make no attempt to recall the rest of the article, but I have recalled this much of it because Mr. Spargo is by no means alone in his conviction as to the foolishness of preaching. In a measure, at least, his conviction appears to be shared by many others.

It is probably true that the pulpit is the weak spot in the church of today. This, of course, is not true of the Roman Catholic Church; not because the average priest is any better sermonizer than the average preacher, but rather because the Roman Catholic Church is built, not around a pulpit, but around an altar. In Roman Catholicism preaching occupies but a subordinate place, on many occasions no place at all. The priest is chiefly an instrument for the administration of the sacraments, the efficacy of which is held to be unaffected by the character of the man who administers them. It cannot, therefore, be said that in the Roman Catholic Church today the weak spot is the pulpit, for in Roman Catholicism the pulpit is, in any case, relatively unimportant.

But the Protestant church is an incarnation of the prophetic type of religion. It *is* built around a pulpit. The medium on which Protestantism most depends for the conveyance of truth and grace is personality. In Protestant theory, the personality of the preacher is of supreme importance. It is through him, not merely through properly administered sacraments, that the eternal God must be enabled to speak. And if through him, whether by reason of any moral or any intellectual weakness, God is not able to speak, the Protestant church is badly handicapped.

Now, it is undeniable that many Protestant churches today are half empty: but not those in which there is a strong man in the pulpit. By a strong man I do not necessarily mean a great man, and certainly I do not mean an eloquent man. The number of great preachers, like the number of great artists, musicians, scientists, and statesmen, is small. It has always been small and doubtless it always will be. And as for the number of eloquent preachers, if it is growing less, let us all thank God and take courage. What the man on the street pronounces eloquence will kill any church in ten years. By a strong man I mean simply a man in whom to at least an average amount of intellectual ability is added a determination, at whatever cost, to have something to say that is worth saying Sunday after Sunday and who, moreover, is himself a living illustration of what he is attempting to preach. Whenever in a modern Protestant pulpit you find that kind of strong man, you do not find any considerable number of empty pews. The human heart today is as hungry for religion as ever it was. If the modern preacher has the bread of life to offer, people will come to get it. If he has anything vital to say about the great realities, the eternal values, people will come to hear it. That is not theory, but fact, as is proved by every church which, even under such social conditions as now prevail, is filled Sunday after Sunday with eager worshipers.

When some church, strategically located where numbers of people are, is found, Sunday after Sunday, with half its pews unoccupied, what is the conclusion that ought to be drawn? The man who stands in the pulpit of that church may cry out in bitter protest against what he considers his ill luck or the injustice that has been done him. He may damn human nature and modern civilization. He may tell himself, and especially his long-suffering wife, that the people in that community are too ignorant to get anything out of anybody's preaching, or that all they want is entertainment and pretty cheap and crude entertainment at that, or that they are hopelessly materialistic, money-mad, and given over to pleasure, or that for some other reason they are unresponsive to what the church has to offer. He may persuade himself that if only he were given an opportunity such as the favored few preachers have he would not be preaching very long to a lot of empty pews. But if only he were wise, would not the occupant of the pulpit of this strategically located church begin to wonder whether there was not something seriously wrong with himself; whether he was working hard enough and living dangerously enough; whether he was giving himself with that gay and reckless kind of abandon which is required of a minister of the gospel of Christ?

Too many preachers are lying down on the job. Oh, to be sure, they are keeping busy, busy as bees, but not in the study. There, they merely dabble and dawdle. The time which they do spend among their books, or, to speak more accurately, in the same room where their books are—what do they do with it? Mostly they kill it. Many a preacher has proudly boasted, "I spent four hours in my study this morning," when he ought to have confessed, "In my study

this morning I wasted four mortal hours. Two of them
I spent day-dreaming. The other two I spent scanning a
few unimportant magazine articles and leafing the pages of
some second-rate books." Such a man is lying down on the
job, notwithstanding the number of calls he may be making, or the amount of committee work he may be doing,
or even the number of speeches he may be delivering before
chambers of commerce and eating clubs. Neither calling
nor committee work nor luncheon club speaking is unimportant. Calling is essential, essential among other things
to preaching. No man can preach effectively unless he
knows the human heart, and no man can know the human
heart unless he keeps in close touch with human lives.
Nevertheless, a preacher who for any reason steps into his
pulpit on Sunday morning unprepared to discharge his
great prophetic function is lying down on the job. He is
not giving to his congregation a square deal. He is not
giving God a fair chance to speak to that congregation
through him. Except in communities that are obviously
and wickedly over-churched, and except also in those far
too numerous instances where churches are poorly located,
if the church is empty it is largely because the preacher is
empty.

Not long ago, a long-suffering layman said to me concerning his preacher, "He has been with us three years, and
he is a nice fellow and we all like him; but so far as his
pulpit ministry is concerned, the last two years have been
very unprofitable. He has brought no fresh insight to his
task. Before he even so much as opens his mouth, we

know in substance what he is going to say. He runs round and round in the little circle of ideas in which he was moving when he first came to us. And the congregation is beginning to dwindle." Of course it is beginning to dwindle; and unless there is a change in the pulpit, it will go on dwindling almost to the vanishing point. Here is a "nice fellow" whom everybody likes, and yet because of his pulpit inefficiency his church is rapidly disintegrating. Bye and bye he will be urging his ecclesiastical superiors to give him a better opportunity, and if he gets it, history will probably repeat itself.

Both the Roman Catholic and the Protestant systems have their weaknesses. One great weakness of the Roman Catholic system is that it does not make adequate provision for the saving truth which may come through a luminous and inspiring personality. One great weakness of the Protestant system is that it stakes so much upon the appearance of truth-revealing personalities that when they fail to appear it is left almost impotent. In a Roman Catholic church, even though you get nothing at all from the sermon, you have a fairly good chance of getting at least something from the service. In a Protestant church, if you get nothing at all from the sermon, you are "out of luck."

It is, I suppose, hardly to be wondered at that many Protestant churches are attempting to "enrich" their service of worship, not only or chiefly because they are beginning at long last to recognize the value of worship, but because they are beginning to despair of getting and maintaining an adequate pulpit. There are laymen today, belonging to non-liturgical churches, who frankly admit that their one hope of holding their young people lies in the erection of a beautiful church edifice and the development of a beautiful service of worship. Now, the religious value of Gothic architecture is, in my judgment, beyond dispute, as is also the religious value of a well-conducted service of worship. For both, even from the Protestant standpoint, there is a vast deal to be said; provided only that they are sought after as a supplement of prophetic preaching, not as a substitute for it. It will, I think, be nothing less than tragic if, because of an increasing dearth of prophets, the Protestant church begins more and more to subordinate the prophetic office and eventually to smother it with architecture and ritual. But when it comes to institutions, self-preservation is one of the recognized laws of life; and you can in any case hardly blame a group of earnest Protestants if, after years of listening to poor preaching and trying in vain to get their children to listen to it, they begin to hunger after the flesh pots of medievalism. The only way to keep prophetic religion and a prophetic church alive in the world is to go on producing prophets.

Let us look at some of Mr. Spargo's other statements. "Preaching," he says, "is not a man-sized job." At that statement we do not need to look very long; it is too palpably absurd, especially in view of his further statement that of the modern preacher entirely too much is being expected. The fact of the matter is that preaching today is so terrific a job that only the exceptional man ought ever to consider it, although once again let me hasten to say that by the exceptional man I mean not necessarily a man of brilliant intellectual gifts but rather a man who is willing to pay the full price of a prophetic ministry.

Mr. Spargo says that a preacher is expected at a given hour on a Sunday morning week after week, year in and year out, to stand up and say something worth listening to by intelligent people. And he says that even if the church drew to its ministry the ablest men of the country (which by inference it does not) that would be expecting entirely too much. Well, I too believe that to ask any preacher to produce two new sermons each week, sermons of such character that even intelligent persons would find it profitable to listen to them, is to ask too much. In most churches today a second preaching service on Sunday is not needed; and attempts to maintain one by introducing a kind of ecclesiastical vaudeville are ill-advised to say the least. In the relatively few churches where a second service on Sunday might really serve there ought to be two preachers, one for the morning service, another for the evening service; and if a second preacher for a truly needed second service is beyond the reach of any local church's purse, he should be financed out of some denominational fund.

But to ask any preacher to produce one helpful sermon each week, year in and year out, is not asking too much. It is undeniably asking a great deal, enough in fact to give any man pause, any man who is spiritually sensitive and not a conceited ass. But it is not asking too much. It is probably not asking more than is required of lawyers and editorial writers. What the preacher greatly needs to do is to stop pitying himself and get down to work. Let him resolve that never under any circumstances will he enter his pulpit unprepared, that at whatever cost of toil and tears he will be God's spokesman Sunday after Sunday. Even in that event he will not always be at his best. His sermons will not all be equally helpful. But after listening to him people will go away feeling that it has been worth while for them to come to church. By the vision and passion of the preacher they will have been lifted up into the presence of God and been enabled to see a bit more clearly life's great realities, its supreme and enduring values.

If this result is accomplished, people will go to church. They will go miles to church and in all kinds of weather. Spiritually helpful preaching is not passé, nor will it ever be. Nothing ever will or can take the place of it. For preaching is not only the presentation of truth, but the presentation of truth through personality. Truth may now be presented by means of print. It may be presented also by means of the radio. But never will it be presented with such uplifting power as when it comes through the lips of an inspiring and visible personality. Who could get as much from reading one of Phillips Brooks' sermons as from listening to Phillips Brooks preach? Who could get as much from listening to Harry Emerson Fosdick over the radio as from not only listening to him but seeing him in his own pulpit? As long as personality endures and remains, as it seems destined to do, the greatest power in the world, nothing will take the place of spiritually helpful preaching.

But can even great preaching accomplish enough to justify the price which the preacher must pay for it? Well, on any Sunday morning, in almost any congregation, there are at least a few persons who are in truly desperate need of personal help—men who are terribly tempted, women whose hearts ache, young people who are rather dreadfully confused, all sorts of people who feel baffled and beaten and ready to give up. And if all that even great preaching was able to accomplish were to give such persons a new grip on life, would it not abundantly justify the full price which the preacher is obliged to pay for it?

But that is not all that great preaching is able to do. Of the Evangelical movement, born in the soul of John Wesley and advanced by his preaching, John Richard Green says: "The great revival reformed our prisons, abolished the slave trade, brought clemency to our penal laws, and gave the first impulse to popular education." Nor is there any reason to suppose that the power of preaching to reform society is any whit less today than it once was. What was it that wrote an Eighteenth Amendment into the Constitution of the United States? Preaching. What was it that substituted an eight hour day for a twelve hour day in the steel industry? Preaching. What is it that even now is doing more than all else to open the world's eyes to the awful waste and wickedness of war? Would it be unfair to say that the answer to that question, likewise, is, Preaching? In this case, to be sure, not all the preaching is being done by professional preachers; nevertheless, it is preaching that is developing a new understanding and a new conscience with respect to war. The fact of the matter is that ideas govern the world. Not even war wages itself. It is waged by men who have certain ideas as to the efficiency of physical force. And this fact that the world is, in the final analysis, governed by ideas is the hope of mankind; for false ideas can be driven out of human minds, wrong ideals can be banished from human hearts, truth and right can be made to prevail.

What an opportunity, then, the preacher has, not only to minister to individuals, but to mold the life of the world. In "The Science of Power," Benjamin Kidd contends that by a consciously directed educational process almost any great social result may be achieved. "Give us the young," he says, "and in a single generation we will create a new mind and a new world." Well, it sounds a bit extravagant to say that it is humanly possible in a single generation to create a new mind and, therefore, a new world. Yet in Japan, in but little more than a single generation, the thing has actually been done. In the case of Japan, it is true, the educational process had back of it all the most powerful agencies of government. But here in America, without the support of any governmental agency, what is now known as the "social gospel" has in a time astonishingly short captured the attention of a nation. Such men as Washington Gladden, Walter Rauschenbusch, Father Ryan, Rabbi Wise, and Bishop McConnell have not been able in a single generation to create a new world, but they have been able in a single generation to create in thousands upon thousands of persons a new mind. And that new mind, if only it is properly nourished and directed, may eventually create a new world.

Preaching may change the very fabric of human society; and it may do something else that greatly needs to be done. It may give men some understanding of the meaning of life and, therefore, some guidance in facing the problem, What to do with life? Christianity maintains that the meaning of life has been discovered in Jesus. It holds that in him life has revealed the greatest of all its secrets. In support of that belief, Christianity may appeal with confidence to the judgment of history. For if history does not proclaim the essential rightness of Jesus, what under the shining sun does it proclaim? Insofar, then, as the preacher is able to interpret Jesus he has something to offer to the world without which all its labor and striving will be in vain, namely, an understanding of the meaning of life and so a solution of the problem, What to do with life?

If all the preaching that is done in America does not add as much to the well-being of America as the work of one honest, efficient farmer, it is not because the pulpit is an anachronism in the modern world. It is rather because the men who stand in pulpits are not qualified to preach; and surely the preacher does well to remind himself that the impotence of many a pulpit is due quite as much to moral failure as to intellectual failure. "Ideas," wrote George Eliot, "are often poor ghosts; our sun-filled eyes cannot discern them. . . . But sometimes they are made flesh. They breathe upon us with warm breath; they are clothed in a living human soul. . . . Then their presence is a power." Preaching becomes a power only when it is practiced. I wish I could believe that it were enough for the preacher to live Christianity; but that apparently is not enough. When the congregation goes home Sunday after Sunday saying, "He is a good man, but he cannot preach," the church must get another preacher or go out of business. But, considered from a thoroughly Christian standpoint, even a large and interested congregation is not enough. That may be found in the motion picture theatre. What is needed is a congregation becoming more and more persuaded that Jesus of Nazareth is the Way, the Truth, and the Life, and more and more eager to pattern their own lives after his. Can that result be achieved by able preaching alone? I very much doubt that it can. To the able exposition of Christian principles must be added the convincing demonstration of Christian practice. People must not only hear a man say that they ought to love their enemies, they must actually see this man loving *his* enemies. They must not only hear a man say that they ought, in their several fields, to seek first the Kingdom of Heaven; they must actually see this man in his *own* field seeking first, not public applause nor ecclesiastical preferment, but the triumph of truth and the redemption of society.

Nothing that is profoundly Christian is likely to be accomplished by a preacher who talks courage and acts cowardice, or who talks forgiveness and acts vindictiveness, or who talks spirituality and consecration and heroic unselfishness and then acts with an eye single to his own interests. Though I speak with the tongues of men and of angels and do not practice what I preach, I am become as sounding brass and a clanging cymbal, and this notwithstanding the fact that undiscerning persons may consider me a wonderful preacher. If all that was needed were to pack a church, it might be enough to preach Christianity in a brilliant fashion. But if what is needed is a new birth of faith and hope and love, Christianity will have to be lived by the preacher who proclaims it.